ADULT ASSESSMENT

A Source Book of Tests and Measures of Human Behavior

By

RICHARD S. ANDRULIS, Ph.D.

Associate Professor of Psychology
The American College
Bryn Mawr, Pennsylvania

With a Contribution by

John Bajtelsmit, M.S.

Assistant Professor of Psychology
The American College
Bryn Mawr, Pennsylvania

CHARLES C THOMAS • PUBLISHER
Springfield • Illinois • U.S.A.

Published and Distributed Throughout the World by

CHARLES C THOMAS • PUBLISHER
Bannerstone House
301-327 East Lawrence Avenue, Springfield, Illinois, U.S.A.

ISBN 0-398-03603-9

Library of Congress Catalog Card Number: 76-23465

With THOMAS BOOKS *careful attention is given to all details of manufacturing and design. It is the Publisher's desire to present books that are satisfactory as to their physical qualities and artistic possibilities and appropriate for their particular use.* THOMAS BOOKS *will be true to those laws of quality that assure a good name and good will.*

Printed in the United States of America
OO-2

Library of Congress Cataloging in Publication Data

Andrulis, Richard S
Adult assessment.

Includes indexes.
1. Psychological tests. I. Bajtelsmit, John.
II. Title.
BF431.A576 152.8 76-23465
ISBN 0-398-03603-9

to Linda

PREFACE

Purposes of Adult Assessment

INFORMATION and utility form the cornerstone of *Adult Assessment.* Expansion of knowledge coupled with a new focus on the development and growth of the adult's potential warrants, from this professional's viewpoint, a compilation of tests and measures for adults.

Adult Assessment can alternately be referred to as a source book — a compilation of data on tests and measures; the tests and measures are available from researchers and publishers and focus attention on appraisal of the wide variety of dimensions in adult human behavior. The nature of a source book demands that it be up-to-date, accurate, and easily utilized as a means to aid the practitioner in selecting and interpreting test information.

Adults have been selected for the focus of this book because of the expanding activity in industry and government on many, if not all, of the basic adult dimensions. Given the nature of assessment — as a mechanism to aid in decision making — this book provides detailed information on over 150 assessment devices for measuring human behavior across the wide spectrum of adult performance.

The background and basis for this book stemmed from the researcher's need to be aware of the wide diversity of devices available for use in research projects, as well as from the need for information on tests and measures beyond the researcher's perspective.

For instance, continuing adult education and training in both academic and business environments have fostered the growth of programs and materials which demand prior assessment of adult knowledge and skills as well as measurement of final outcomes.

Equally important are the continuing efforts of those in vocational, educational, and personnel guidance; whether performing in community service programs or in academic or business settings, these professionals must and should have access to assessment devices which will aid their clientele in proper counseling and planning.

Expansion and the Equal Employment Opportunity Commission's (EEOC) laws, and its regulations, has sparked a new interest in establishing valid instruments for adult selection into academia, government, and industrial settings. The successful evolution of laws demands that greater time and energy be spent on not only determining the validity of present selection devices, but also investigating viable alternative measures.

Finally, as increased emphasis is placed upon accountability of performance of adults as well as the training and educational programs they undergo, research in both the applied and basic social sciences requires the utilization of existing measures for determining changes in performance.

The *Adult Assessment* book quickly brings to the user a knowledge of the types of assessment devices that are currently available, whether recently evolved or dramatically adapted from previous editions.

Criteria Procedures

The criteria used in selecting the 155 instruments presented in *Adult Assessment* varied from objective to judgmental and are as follows.

The first criterion required that the test or measure be designed to assess adult behavior, that is, constructed for individuals at least sixteen years of age or older. (Sixteen was used because it is an acknowledged point signifying the transition of a child into early adulthood.)

The second criterion required that the device assess one of ten major dimensions of human behavior which were selected as representative of the diversity and complexity of adult behavior, including intelligence and aptitude, achievement, cognitive style, general measures of personality, specific measures of personality, personality adjustment, vocational and interest inventories, attitude devices, personal performance and history measures, and managerial and creativity devices.

The third criterion, requiring that the device be "representative" of one of the ten categories, posed a problem. One could neither justify the representativeness of one test over another at a specific assessment or content level, nor exhaust the universe of all measures due to fiscal and time restraints. This third criterion was used to select and allocate tests in one of the ten dimensions recognizing that the test may typify the dimension but may not be the only instrument available for that particular category. For example, there are many achievement tests of adult knowledge that assess reading comprehension, vocabulary, and grammar. Once these achievement domains are measured by one or two instruments, the need to identify additional tests becomes somewhat academic, realizing that three or four more instruments might be readily available.

The fourth criterion required that the device be available through a commercial or research organization. The commercial publisher typically has available resources for expediting delivery and scoring of tests, as well as for updating the norms, reliability, and validity.

The fifth criterion required that the device offer a certain amount of information. The instruments in this book attained the fifth criterion because each contained sufficient data describing the instrument's purpose and history, norms, reliability, validity, and interpretation of scores.

Unlike the first five criteria, the sixth was not an absolute for inclusion in this text. The sixth criterion established a preference for tests or measures which have been recently developed, which are available only in research form, or which are undergoing major modifications in design, norming, or standardization. These measures were chosen to reflect the constantly evolving instruments. For example, the Strong-Campbell Interest Inventory (SCII), with its combined male/female form (made available in 1973), and the Wonderlic Personnel Test, which recently published (1972) a reprint of annotated validity studies, are two devices which attained the sixth criterion.

Among all of the instruments in this text, several did not meet all the standards set forth; they were included because of their usefulness in clinical diagnosis, attitudinal assessment, or observation or interview situations. Placing a demand for these standards on all instruments would inhibit potential uses by practitioners who are both aware of the problems and capable (in many instances) of providing their own technical data on a local basis.

Intended Audiences

This book is aimed generally at four types of practitioners in the adult assessment field. Those who will constitute the readership most likely are individuals in the fields of personnel in industry, business, and education, as well as counselors in community or academic settings involved in vocational, rehabilitative, or therapeutic activities. Another group of practitioners includes researchers engaged in the development and implementation of investigations into training programs, selection procedures, and educational material. Finally, there are the evaluators who, in either an educational or industrial setting, must determine the effectiveness and efficiency with which a training or curriculum program has met its objectives. The common facet for these individuals is that they are practitioners concerned with real problems. Such problems are broad in dimensions but have one common element — the adult. The adult, with a diversity of capabilities and interpersonal traits, functions in the broad realms of business and education.

The practitioners who read and absorb the information in this book relate to the adult in a variety of settings but are usually dealing with a specific concern or issue. Therefore, readers will usually find only some sections and chapters directly pertinent to their level of activity.

It must be noted that each reader will bring a different level of knowledge and experience which may raise questions as to the most appropriate material in this book. It would be naive to expect all individuals using this information to have had a common background in education or in experience. Rather, it is to be expected that readers will be widely diverse, not only in the factors of education and experience, but in their application and tasks as well.

For this reason, the book is intended to reflect advanced as well as basic concepts regarding the assessment process; it can give the less sophisticated reader an opportunity to advance. And, even though this text is primarily a source book, it remains a supplement to the reader's knowledge, experience, and exposure to other sources of information and becomes a compendium for practical application.

Description of the Parts and Chapters

The initial three chapters of this book provide a focus on: (1) the various functions and styles of testing; (2) considerations in choosing tests and measures; and (3) validity and reliability concepts apropos to testing. In addition, they present a broad overview to provide the reader with information to expediate the selection and utilization of tests and inventories not reviewed within this book.

Chapters 1 through 3 are each self contained; they provide the reader with an overview, presented in a language and format which permits the appropriate selection and utilization of a device that will fit into the context of one's assessment objectives. Furthermore, the chapters are short; they do not represent all the innuendos and ramifications of each topic covered. Rather, they intend to refresh one's knowledge and to acquaint the novice with the terminology entailed in the review of assessment devices.

The key word for this part of the book is transference; the first three chapters provide a transference to the remaining chapters of the book.

After reading this preface, the reader should be able to decide whether or not a need exists to review the fundamentals of testing incorporated within Chapters 1 through 3.

Chapter 1 reviews the various functions of testing, defining the categories and characteristics of assessment devices, including specific information regarding the types of devices available. It also includes material on varied methods of testing relating to ways in which tests can be presented, as well as detailed information regarding the general purpose of assessment devices.

Chapter 2 elaborates on the consideration in choosing an instrument, including conditions related to the selection, administration, and environment under which a test is given. It also treats: principles to be considered in determining the cost of an instrument on either an individual or group basis; determining time requirements; the general issue of confidentiality of results; general information regarding norms as they impact upon both test selection and interpretation of information. Finally, Chapter 2 addresses interpretation of the assessment device by discussing the general information, available in a test manual or in other sources, which aids in the interpretation process. Issues such as how scores should be reported and how they should be transformed will also be raised.

Chapter 3 discusses validity and reliability, including identification of their characteristics and types and definitions of terms. It emphasizes the importance and value of both validity and reliability and what they mean in light of the two most typical problems encountered in the testing environment: selection of the proper assessment device and interpretation of results.

In addition to the general introduction to validity and reliability, Chapter 3 approaches a most important concept: the use of tests for the selection process in the industrial or business environments. The Equal Employment Opportunity Commission (EEOC) and the recent law requiring tests to meet certain validity criteria for use in the selection process has raised the concern and interest of persons in the field of assessment and personnel selection. This chapter briefly reviews the history of the EEOC, its current statutes and thinking, and summarizes information regarding the stand by the American Psychological Association on these validity criteria. Finally, Chapter 3 touches upon the basic characteristics of validity and reliability as they aid in the selection and interpretation processes.

Part Two, Tests and Measures, presents the assessment devices as they are grouped into their various areas of assessment permitting easy location of an instrument by category.

Chapter 4, Aptitude and Achievement Assessment, covers general Intelligence and Aptitude Measures, Achievement Measures, including the areas of language and number and other specific achievement devices, as well as various Cognitive Style Measures. Chapter 5, Personality Assessment, includes General Personality Measures, Specific Personality Measures, and Personality Adjustment Measures. In Chapter 6, Interest and Vocational Measures are presented. Chapter 7 details information regarding Attitude Measures. Chapter 8 includes Personal Performance and History Measures for both educational and industrial settings. Chapter 9, Other Assessment Devices, contains information regarding Creativity Measures and Managerial Measures.

Part Three, Resources for the Reader, provides various listings of organizations engaged in test research and publication. One list includes the Educational Resource Information Center (ERIC) which maintains over fifteen centers that compile studies appropriate to the educational process. Although not related to the business environment in a direct sense, it has many appropriate areas where information can be applied easily from an educational to a business environment. For example, one ERIC center, the Educational Testing Service, Princeton, New Jersey, is a source from which information may be obtained about different types of assessment devices used by researchers, evaluators, and other practitioners in education and business in investigating the wide variety of problems related to the adult assessment process.

ERIC publishes two monthly guides which list available resource material. *Current Index to Journals in Education* covers 700 publications on education and maintains abstracts of these articles by subject or author index. *Resources in Education* performs a similar function, however the content of material included reflects professional reports presented at conferences or in internal reports that are not currently published in any journal. Upon identification, one can request and obtain printed copies of an article selected from either one of these two ERIC resources.

Part Three also lists names and addresses of additional resources, such as Research and Development Centers and Regional Laboratories funded under the Education Act of 1964. As an aside, information can also be expanded within local communities; nearby universities, especially those with specialized social science libraries, are rich sources of information containing the latest data regarding assessment procedures and devices appropriate for the adult.

The listings in Part Three also include institutions that are actively involved in measurement and assessment. Two such organizations are the previously mentioned Educational Testing Service, Princeton, New Jersey, and The American College Testing Program, Iowa City, Iowa, both of whom are known for their development of aptitude and achievement materials for both college and graduate school students; both may be contacted for information about their ongoing research activities.

Finally, Part Three cites a special document of interest on the current status of testing and its uses.

The index system of *Adult Assessment* provides a guide for locating authors of measures, measures by title, publishers and sources of measures, and specific subject matter, including authors mentioned in the text of Chapters 1 through 3 and in the bibliographies of Chapters 4 through 9.

Format Used to Describe the Tests and Measures

The materials contained in Chapters 4 through 9 are presented in the following manner: title of the test or measure, Author(s), Variable, Type of Measure, and Source from Which Measure May Be Obtained. These areas describe the general purpose of the instrument and its characteristics. The "Variable" provides the reader with the specific domain or trait purportedly assessed by the test. Please note that while the categorical breakdown of some instruments is arbitrary in light of their titles or descriptions, further review of these tests, such as interpretation of scores or subscales, will reveal their suitability for application to areas other than the ones in which they have been grouped. "Type of Measure" indicates either individual or group administration, oral or written presentation, hand or machine scoring, and the time required for administration. "Source From Which Measure May Be Obtained" lists a distributor of the instrument and, in all cases, the address from which our materials were obtained.

Following these sections are materials classified into: Description, Norms, Validity and Reliability, and Bibliography. The "Description" elaborates on the nature of the test, including for example, the number of items, the scores obtained, and definitions of the traits or capabilities being measured, as well as statements regarding the use of the test, such as in the context of therapy, evaluation, selection, and counseling. The "Norms" section provides basic data on the sample from which interpretations of scores are to be made. The normative sample is described usually on the basis of the biographical and demographical characteristics of the subjects.

The "Validity and Reliability" section describes the empirical results of using the test in terms of determining both the consistency of score responses and their meaningfulness. This section is technical in that it demands an understanding of the nomenclature used in test development. The concepts of Norms and Validity and Reliability are addressed in Chapters 2 and 3. Finally, the "Bibliography" cites the test manual and its supplements, if any. It also includes, when applicable, a test number referring the reader to O.K. Buros' *The Seventh Mental Measurements Yearbook* (Gryphon Press, 1972), *Personality Tests and Reviews,* or *Reading Tests and Reviews,* (Gryphon Press, 1970 and 1968 respectively). References to the latter two books are preceeded by a P or R. In many ways, the tests incorporated within this source book are complementary to those contained in the *Mental Measurements Yearbook,* although there may be overlapping instruments.

In terms of effectively utilizing this book, a quick review of the instruments will determine whether or not the reader should write to the source indicated for additional information.

Carefully scrutinized review of the information in Chapters 4 through 9 permits one to choose a number of instruments for further inspection.

Typically, if more information about the device is required, one should request a "specimen set." Such a set normally includes a copy of the test, its manual, and answer and key sheets (used for responding and scoring the items). In addition, promotional materials may be included which further describe the assessment material.

It is most important to note that while the information provided in this book is not exhaustive, it is broad in scope and provides relevant information regarding the domains of each assessment device. The information is up to date but *does not* preclude information that is currently being processed, published, and otherwise available through a wide variety of other sources.

R.S.A.

ACKNOWLEDGMENTS

ADULT ASSESSMENT would not have been conceived without the environment of The American College, through its orientation and dedication to the education of persons in life and health insurance and the related financial sciences. In the Department of Research and Evaluation, the need to sort and review available adult assessment measures became evident. It was from this need that this work — a systematic and viable mechanism which conveys the collected data — was evolved.

... To Marjorie Fletcher and Lisa Ogletree, our research librarians, go out unending thanks. Their continuing efforts to search for and pursue information from a wide variety of sources stands as one fundamental reason for the scope of instruments presented in this book.

... To Susan Horne for her persistence and thoroughness without which the systematic review of instruments and the compilation and collation of the data presented in the inventory descriptions would not have been possible ... Also, to Sue for polishing the chapters, effecting the overall continuity of the text, and finally for typing the manuscript.

... To Phyllis Elberg for her standards of excellence in initially editing the chapters.

... To John Bajtelsmit for his comprehensive coverage of reliability and validity in Chapter 3.

... To Larry Starr and the many others connected with The American College who contributed to the initial conception of this book, our appreciation and affection will be with you long after this work is completed.

R.S.A.

CONTENTS

Part Three

RESOURCES FOR THE READER

ADULT ASSESSMENT

Part One
INTRODUCTION

Chapter 1

THE PURPOSES OF TESTS AND MEASURES

THE field of psychometrics, as the measurement of behavior, is not a part-time endeavor; it is a full-time occupation for not only individuals but corporations as well. Today, there are over a dozen well-known test publishing houses employing hundreds of professionals whose constant search is for the more refined instrument, the more objective measure. This is indeed an age of technology with rapid proliferation of new instruments and processing techniques, including scoring, analysis, and feedback of information to the consumer. Literally thousands of aptitude, achievement, personality, interest, and other special types of tests exist today; fifty or sixty years ago there were only a handful. The needs for them are obvious. As we discover the more complex characteristics of individuals, certain types of assessment devices must be evolved that are responsive to these characteristics and the situations in which they are found. It was in the present century that intelligence was thought of as a general factor with many associated factors; today it is conceived to have in excess of one hundred components.

The same is true for the area of personality. Once, only several components of a personality were assessed; now it is hundreds. Investigators are constantly revealing new areas of concern, such as learning problems in children, reactions of individuals in stressful environments, and others. These concerns reveal the need to search out that one instrument which is not bound by culture. The need to reflect the cultural heritage of each ethnic and racial group will not go neglected.

Different Assessment Measures

A common breakdown of assessment devices in terms of their

characteristics is their grouping into aptitude, achievement, personality, motivation, and interest inventories. The first two, aptitude and achievement tests, are typically considered on a single continuum from general skills measurement at the aptitude level to very specific knowledge measurement at the achievement level. The aptitude test's primary function is to assess broad intellectual factors and wide ranges of knowledge. The achievement test has as its objective the assessment of specific knowledge typically learned in a school or training program.

Personality and motivation inventories have their own classification under assessment devices. They refer to the broad assessment of an individual's characteristics as contrasted with capabilities or achievements. To some degree there is continuity among the most well-known personality inventories regarding the characteristics being assessed. However, this is not the case for all personality measures, because there are specific philosophies implied by each instrument. This may be exemplified in the Minnesota Multiphasic Personality Inventory (MMPI) which was originally developed on individuals with severe psychological and medical symptoms for the diagnosis of various types of psychopathology. The MMPI, which today is used on all types of subjects, can be contrasted with the Edwards Personal Preference Schedule (EPPS) and the Adjective Check List (ACL), both of which were founded on Murry's Need Theory to reflect basic and generic desires that are part of all men and women.

Interest inventories present another classification of assessment devices. Typically, these devices determine the theme and occupational orientation of an individual. Some instruments, such as the Strong Vocational Interest Blank/Strong Campbell Interest Inventory, go as far as identifying an individual's interest with regard to a wide variety of occupational areas. Others, such as the Kuder Preference Record, have forms which lend themselves only to determining the individual's interest in a wide arc of occupational orientations, while other forms are geared toward specific occupations.

Let us now move on to the specific categories contained

within this book. Aptitude and achievement measures presented in Chapter 4 are divided into three groups. The first group describes general intelligence and aptitude devices which provide a broad assessment of the individual's capability, usually in the verbal and quantitative areas. One can refer to many of these instruments as intelligence tests, as they yield the Intelligence Quotient (IQ) of the individual. In large part, intelligence measures provide a global measure of the inherent capabilities of an individual. Aptitude measures tend to focus on verbal and quantitative skills without necessarily yielding an IQ value. The practical difference between intelligence and aptitude measures is slight; both have a common goal of assessing the native capabilities of an individual.

The second group contains instruments which assess the individual's level of achievement. Achievement is a manifestation of the individual's knowledge, after having engaged in numerous educational and environmental experiences. Achievement measures are assessed by reading, mathematics, and a wide variety of skill tests. For example, there are assessment devices to measure reading comprehension, vocabulary, grammar, arithmetic problem solving, arithmetic computation, among others.

The third group describes cognitive style measures. These devices measure, much more precisely than intelligence or achievement tests, a skill or capability that the individual might possess. Assessment devices included in this section measure unique capabilities of the individual, such as spatial orientation, verbal associations or perceptual speed.

Personality measures in Chapter 5 are also divided into three groups. The first group, general personality measures, is so-called because all of the devices in it yield information regarding two or more personality dimensions. For example, the administration of one of these devices may yield as many as fourteen subscores in such areas as the individual's need to be with people, self-confidence, interpersonal relationships, need to achieve, and so on.

The second group is composed of measures, each of which focuses on one specific personality trait, such as neuroticism, interpersonal conflict, irrational fear.

The third group contains measures dealing with adjustment problems and/or potential. For example, these measures might assess such areas as an individual's environmental, familial, or job adjustment.

Interest and Vocational, Attitude, and Personal History and Performance (Chapter 6, 7, and 8, respectively) were selected as three meaningful categories by which tests and measures could be grouped. In studying the test descriptions, you will find that the chapter titles generally describe the inventories themselves.

The interest and vocational measures are generally broad based instruments which assess an individual in numerous occupational and/or skill areas. The attitude measures are useful in a variety of situations, especially in the evaluation of individuals' attitudes toward institutions, environments, or other individuals. Generally speaking, the attitude devices are so flexible that they are largely adaptable to the user who, in many cases, must specify the content in which the attitude measure is to be used.

Personal history and performance measures, like the attitude measures, are widely adaptable for specific use. It would be typical for a user reviewing these devices to make refinements and adaptations of them to fit the needs of a specific environment, such as for observing a group of individuals in a problem solving situation, for interviewing or reviewing past job performance of employees, or for observing students and teachers in a training class.

Chapter 9 is divided into two groups and has been included in this book in order to reflect a sampling of the variety of assessment devices available to practitioners. The first group presents creativity measures which identify and assess an individual's creative or divergent skills. These measures assess creativity in a wide range of areas, from artistic expression to engineering capabilities. The second group includes managerial measures which can either identify a subject's inherent managerial capability or assess the effectiveness of individuals who are already performing in that capacity.

Here again, as with the attitude and personal history and performance measures, the inventories in Chapter 9 are largely adaptable to the objectives of the user.

Different Methods of Testing

The most common type of assessment device is the paper and pencil test. Presented in a variety of forms, it remains the simplest and most economical of all devices. The paper and pencil device has evolved in the last fifty years, from the well-known essay examination to the sophisticated multiple choice test. Multiple choice items permit rapid and objective assessment of the subject's knowledge in a variety of areas and provide a mechanism for eliciting responses in not only personality and interest areas, but in special ability areas as well. Furthermore, paper and pencil devices are economical in that they do not use materials, such as form boards, cards, or other consumable objects. And, they lend themselves to easy scoring, especially with optical scanning systems and high speed computers. There is a common criticism of paper and pencil devices, and that is, although they reflect the individual's level of knowledge or attainment of skills, they are artificial — to the extent that they represent the individual's translation of knowledge from an environment or setting to paper.

This brings us to a second type of device — the situational test. This type of device presents the individual with a certain type of problem, whereupon the subject, either as an individual or in the context of a group, chooses a satisfying solution. In a way, the situational test detracts from the objectivity of the paper and pencil device, but in its place it adds realism. Typically situational tests are used to assess interrelatedness of individuals, group problem solving, group decision making, and individuals' handling and processing of information.

A third type of test is the manipulative or mechanical assessment device. These measures are used to assess manual skill ability, such as for the performance of a job requiring finger dexterity. Again, objective tests may be more reliable, but mechanical and manipulative devices are more representative of the real work world. Many of these instruments have been refined to a high degree of reliability in fields as diverse as carpentry, textiles, and engineering.

If we could point to an immediate need in the field of assessment, it would probably be to the further development of the situational instruments. For, as these instruments improve in their objectivity and reliability, they will reflect the functions that are to be performed by the individuals taking the tests. This in no way implies that paper and pencil tests will be slowly eliminated from the field of psychometric testing. Rather, it will not be surprising to find paper and pencil tests being used in conjunction with the other styles of devices in order to assess complementary traits.

Another factor to be considered when we discuss types of devices is the dichotomy of tests, such as speed versus power. Simply, speed tests are performed under a time limit with the expectation that most individuals will not complete all items. This is contrasted with the power test, in which all or most items are answered by all or most individuals because of the lack of stringent time constraints. Each of these methods has its own advantage. The speed test determines dexterity, finesse, or quickness of cognitive thought and is more typically seen in aptitude, achievement, or manipulative tests. Whereas, the need for time restraints in power tests, such as in the areas of personality and interest inventories, is less serious.

Another dichotomy that is made in the characteristics of assessment devices is the difference between individually and group administered tests. The group test has the distinct advantages of time and fiscal economy, although at times this advantage is fallacious. For example, individual tests tip the scales to increase costs but at the same time may yield observable clinical data, which is useful in decision making.

Different Purposes of Testing

Briefly mentioned in the last few pages is the need to focus upon the testing objectives, specifically, the purpose of an assessment device. The following pages present materials which reflect the typical testing objectives one has in mind. We will discuss the four basic dimensions of: (a) diagnosis, (b) prescription, (c) monitoring, and (d) evaluation. Collectively, this information provides an appropriate mechanism for determining which device should be used and how it may be interpreted.

Diagnosis

A diagnosis is used to search out and identify those characteristics which either inhibit or foster certain types of performance or behavior. In using the diagnostic approach we ask, what is the cause or reason for the subject's behavior? Implementing the diagnostic approach requires a sensitivity not only to the subject and his or her characteristics, but to the instrument being used as well. For example, a practitioner may use an interview strategy or may select items from only certain parts of an instrument and, in so doing, may choose from many subtests, administer them without specified time constraints, and administer them orally rather than in the prescribed written manner. Modifications of this nature can provide a practitioner with wide variations of information upon which to draw in order to help determine an appropriate prescription.

Prescription

A prescription allows one to make recommendations regarding the educational or remedial direction an individual should take, given the subject's measured "assets and liabilities." In recommending an appropriate prescription, we must ask, what is the current level of the individual's knowledge or skill. In asking this, we see that the relationship between diagnosis and prescription is very close. Let's use a medical analogy to point out this relationship.

An electrocardiogram (EKG) might be an appropriate device to *diagnose* the cause of chest pains, but given the results of the EKG, the physician is able to *prescribe* specific remedial actions which will be most beneficial to the patient.

A test which diagnoses a learning problem, such as a short attention span, can also be used to help define a remediation plan by determining the conditions in which the short attention span exists. In this latter case, the practitioner may diagnose the learning problem as being related to a short attention span with written material and then prescriptively use the test data to help determine the current level of the individual's capabilities and knowledge in order to plan accordingly. So, we can see that instruments being used in a diagnostic frame may, in many cases, be used to evolve a prescription as well.

Monitoring

Monitoring provides a measure of the ongoing development and change in the subject as he or she fulfills a prescribed course of action, such as a core of instruction, a therapy program, or a remedial process. Monitoring demands that selected tests be administered periodically (generally over short time periods) to determine if the goals set for the subject are being met in terms of expected level and frequency. In short, the question is whether or not the individual is proceeding according to schedule.

It is necessary to monitor the individual's progress through a course of prescribed activity, for deviations from the goals would indicate either a change in the prescription or a rediagnosis. On the other hand, a monitoring procedure should not be so cumbersome that it inhibits administration or cooperation from the subject participating in the program.

Unless a subject's performance is monitored, the outcome of the prescription will not be known until some final evaluative assessment.

Evaluation

Evaluative testing reveals whether or not the subject's goals and objectives have been attained. It answers broad-based questions appropriate for not only individual, but group evaluation as well. For example, did a therapy program work more effectively for one group than for another? Evaluation is the final step in testing, as it flows from the first three steps of diagnosis, prescription, and monitoring. It is not uncommon, however, for most tests to be used in an evaluative mode. Often we use test results in making a final judgment regarding selection, placement, orientation, and growth of individuals. If we analyze our testing purposes we find that the first three elements ask that evaluation be held in abeyance until specific direction is planned for the subject.

Modification of Devices for Specific Purposes

Most tests and inventories have applicability in each of the four dimensions, either as they presently exist or through adaptation. Furthermore, there is a wealth of information to be had by the practitioner who modifies an assessment device to a specific need or objective. But, the implications in implementing any of the four dimensions may have profound effects not only on the administration, scoring, and interpretation of results, but also on the meaningfulness and utility of data incorporated into the instrument in its unadjusted form.

Any modification, even a minor one, such as in the purpose of a test, will negate the interpretation of the results forthcoming from that instrument as provided by the publisher. Even a change in administration time or directions may result in misinterpretation of results. This type of adaptation is best performed by a practitioner who is accustomed to working within clinical assessment, whether in industry, education, or other areas in which the assessment purpose is typically combined with observation and introspection, and where the device used provides an added feature for a better understanding of the subject's capabilities.

Why Modify?

Let's take, for example, an industrial setting where assessment of an employee's promotion potential is desired. The personnel specialist knows that the subject has strong intellectual capabilities but also certain limitations expressing verbal material. In administering a company-required test battery which includes an aptitude test, the specialist finds that the subject has sufficient job content knowledge, as well as various socially desirable traits, all of which indicate the employee's suitability for promotion into a position of higher accountability. Knowing that verbal expression will be of moderate concern in the promoted position, the specialist does not require that this individual take an examination in which responses must be recorded on an answer sheet. Instead, the test is administered orally, and the answers are recorded by the examiner. Clearly, this practitioner has modified the assessment device from a diagnostic viewpoint, at the same time realizing that the publisher's intent has been greatly modified. Needless to say, interpretation of results from such an adapted test must be done very carefully in light of the fact that the practitioner has aberrated most of the rules regarding not only the test's development, but also the way in which the test was refined and standardized.

Another example of test modification can be seen in the use of a personality assessment device. Assume that an employee is having significant personality adjustment problems on the job, and the personnel specialist administers a personality assessment device in an individual oral manner; here again the items are read to the employee. This type of administration is not performed due to any lack of verbal facility on the part of the subject, but rather in light of the fact that responses can be interpreted and discussed at the time at which they are given. Even though the assessment device's standard methods of interpretation cannot be applied, modifying the device in this way might permit the specialist to isolate more relevant information concerning the employee's conflicts or fears and may even provide immediate insights into the problem. In justifying this type of modification — if an employee's absenteeism or tardiness can be discussed with a personnel specialist in a face to face situation, then it should follow that the same method can be used in the individual administration of a personality assessment device as well.

In summing then, we can see that once a diagnosis has been made, based upon the use of specific instrumentation, certain remedial actions can be planned based upon the results obtained from the administration of the instrument. Prescriptions are none other than a plan of action based upon the findings which indicate the current level of capability for an individual. In the case of the individual with poor skills in the expression of verbal material, one might recommend a prescription, such as courses in public speaking. For the individual who is having personality adjustment problems, prescriptions might vary from counseling therapy to a reduced workload or a changed work environment. The monitoring function flows from the prescription in that periodic checks must be made as to the changes occurring within the individual. Returning to our first example of the person with a lack of good expressive skills, periodic checks during a course of remediation, such as programs to increase expressive ability, might show that an aptitude test orally administered to this subject yields improved scores. Finally, evaluation speaks for itself. It is the culmination of the first three objectives one should have in testing.

As previously mentioned, most assessment devices lend themselves to adaptation when considered in light of a specific objective. This is not to suggest that all of the tests presented in this book, and others, lend themselves to the four specific elements of diagnosis, prescription, monitoring, and evaluation, or that a practitioner would use all four elements in testing every subject. The decision rests with the user.

As you become familiar with the various types of devices, adaptations to the four elements will be obvious. It is up to the practitioner, who feels sophisticated and assured in his or her own knowledge of how these tests may be used, to fit them within the context of the four dimensions. The uneasiness that might arise in adapting a test can be readily overcome by consulting with available resources, such as local universities or consultants presently on one's own staff. The concern is that the choice of objectives in test selection be clarified at the beginning of an assessment program. Because it is these objectives which will dictate one of the four elements for the user to follow, those methods of adapting and changing an instrument to fit within a certain context can be expediated through consultation with the resources available to both the examiner and program administrator.

One caution worth repeating is that any adjustment to an instrument, in terms of using it outside of the realm in which the publisher or author designed and produced it, must be cleared with the publisher first, before any use is actually undertaken. Restrictions and copyright laws must be determined before any adjustments are made in the formal use of an instrument. In addition, one should be aware of the fact that any significant changes in the stated form or procedures of a test will tend to negate not only the norms for interpretation of results, but, in many cases, the reliability and validity as well.

Chapter 2

CONSIDERATIONS IN CHOOSING TESTS AND MEASURES

ALTHOUGH Chapter 1 suggests that the selection of a particular assessment device is generally determined by the purpose one has in mind, it is by far not the only rationale for choosing a test. We can argue quite strongly that a test's purpose is of paramount importance. However, we must seek out and analyze the other characteristics of an instrument to assist in tailoring the selection process. One may find many instruments suited for a specific purpose, but it is the many other characteristics of instruments which determine that one to be selected and utilized.

Some characteristics which aid in the selection process entail the processes of obtaining, administering, and scoring the instrument, the conditions under which the instrument should be given, and its cost; we can refer to these as logistical considerations. A second area for consideration is test data — its confidentiality and the process by which it is disseminated. A third category concerns norms and test interpretation, determined from information available and provided by either the test publisher or other relevant sources that have utilized the instrument in previous situations. A final category of information which aids in the administration and selection of a test concerns the subject's characteristics, including age, test taking experience, and prior education, all of which influence the outcome behaviors on a performance device.

Logistical Considerations

The first consideration we will discuss regards the concern of obtaining the instrument. Assessment devices are classified by levels of security which designate the various instruments' availability either to a selected group of trained examiners or to a wider variety of individuals with minimal experience in the field of assessment. Although there appears to be no categorical system applying to all devices, most publishers have their own coding systems which advise the user of instruments available and to what levels of security they are available, based upon certain credentials and experiences. For instance, a publisher may specify requirements, such as a membership in the American Psychological Association, a terminal degree in psychology, or evidence of sufficient background and training in psychological instrumentation, in order for a potential user to qualify for purchase of those psychological measures considered to be a potent assessment of an individual's characteristics. However, there are devices which are available to individuals with only introductory backgrounds in the field of assessment or who are utilizing an instrument under the tutilage of other individuals who do meet the specified requirements.

The range of availability to the purchaser must be determined on the basis of the publisher's security system. The increased emphasis on ethical standards in the practice and utilization of data collection mechanisms has seen a corresponding increase in the security systems of publishers as they attempt to determine if the purchaser has not only the proper credentials, but also the proper intent for utilization of specific tests or inventories. This does not suggest that most instruments are so secure that individuals who practice in the fields of personnel selection, vocational guidance, rehabilitation counseling, and other related areas would be unable to select and obtain the proper instrument for the purpose and intent of their administration. It does mean, however, that one must first determine the credentials required and then, depending on the circumstances, either choose another instrument whose requirements are not as stringent, or secure the assistance and support of an individual who has the proper credentials to obtain the desired device.

A second logistical aspect is determining the length of time it takes to secure an instrument. Orders by telephone to a publisher usually expedite an instrument within a matter of days, and at the other extreme, requesting certain devices by letter may take several weeks for delivery. It is a fair assumption that the speed with which one wants an instrument is directly related to the cost of obtaining it.

A third logistical consideration deals with administrative responsibility for presentation of an instrument. A good administrator is one who carefully designs and follows the guidelines for the administration of the instrument. Well-designed assessment devices usually have comprehensive and detailed instructions regarding how to administer the test, including directions to the administrator and proctor(s) of the examination, as well as to the subjects. The directions can be very specific to the administrator detailing such information as seating arrangements and handling of emergency situations and often include instructions for returning the used and unused portions of the instrument to a scoring agency. Included in the administrative responsibility is the environment in which the test is to be given. Environmental considerations usually stem from where, in a building, a test will be administered and concern factors such as the heating, the lighting and the spacing of desks or tables in a room, all of which are important because of the detrimental effect that can arise from adverse climatic conditions or the crowding of individuals into a room. Adverse environmental effects, if they are strong enough, can depress the scores of all subjects taking a test. Therefore, it is most important to seek out a setting where the room is of reasonable size and free from noise distractions and adverse heating or cooling conditions.

Two final logistical considerations are cost and time. Cost may not be a deciding factor when ordering a small number of copies of an instrument or a specimen set; it does become important, however, when hundreds or even thousands of copies are required. The logistics of cost per individual must include not only those involved in securing the instrument, but also the administrator's time in setting up environmental conditions and scoring, handling, and processing the completed instruments.

Time is a consideration in that extended time periods are

common in test administration. A general rule is to avoid administrations that go beyond an hour and a half for an adult, after which a short break of five to ten minutes should be allowed. The upper limit, including time for rest periods, should not exceed three and one half hours. In this author's opinion, it is cruel to administer a three hour battery in the morning, allow a forty-five minute break for lunch, and then require the individual to participate in another three hour assessment session in the afternoon. One begins to wonder whether the responses on the test are, in fact, reflections of the individual's capabilities, personalities, and attitudes or merely a measure of fatigue level.

In considering the time element in testing, scoring can be a major concern. Tests given to one or two individuals can be hand scored by either the examiner or test administrator. Further, it makes sense to provide hand scoring when very few individuals are involved in an assessment approach or when the nature of the device dictates that it be hand scored. However, when testing a group of more than five or ten individuals, in addition to an increase in the complexity of the scoring itself, the time involved in hand scoring often demands a reasonable alternative. The alternatives to hand scoring are usually found in machine scoring systems available either from the test publisher or in referrals listed by the publisher in the test manual. With the availability of high speed scoring equipment, computers, and detailed analyses, the utilization of machine scoring is a decided asset. Even so, the criteria for selecting either hand or machine scoring must be determined by cost and time, as well as the speed with which one desires the information. Some scoring services have very quick return periods which provide detailed analyses as well as the final scores on an instrument. However, upper limits of several weeks may exist when using other scoring agencies, depending upon the complexity and number of instruments to be processed.

Confidentiality

Beyond logistics is the area concerning confidentiality of

results. A controversy stems, for the most part, from the rights of subjects to be aware of their responses to the various assessment mechanisms that may have been utilized in either an academic or an industrial setting. From an ethical viewpoint, it is difficult to justify the release of test results to counselors, parents, teachers, and other individuals, while withholding the results from the subject, especially when a subject evidences the proper maturity and knowledge to use the information properly. With the new federal government legislation (Public Law 93-380) requiring that schools and other organizations provide subjects with the knowledge of their responses to certain types of information within their files, under penalty of loosing federal funding, this question of confidentiality will arise again. Furthermore, the law has not been interpreted in the courts to limit accessability to parents or students over the age of eighteen, when no federal funding is provided. Public Law 93-380, Section 438, is included in Appendix I. Today, it appears that the direction is to provide as much information to individuals as can properly be used and justified in light of their capabilities and maturity.

Norms

Another consideration in the selection of assessment devices is norms and their availability on national, regional, and local levels. Norms purport to represent typical responses of individuals as categorized by demographical and biographical information. The criterion for ideal norms is the inclusion of information on the subjects' age, sex, geographical location, socioeconomic status, education, occupation, number of years of experience in a specific field, and, with the increasing acknowledgment of inherent bias in many tests, racial or ethnic background.

The more specific the norms, the more realistic and valuable the interpretation of results will be. However, it must be remembered that norms rise and fall in importance depending on the purpose for which an instrument is being used. For example, if the purpose of assessment is evaluative, the value of the norms is important because of the precision with which one will use the test results. Whereas, if one is monitoring a subject's behavior after a sufficiently thorough diagnosis has taken place, the need for well-developed and specific norms is less dramatic.

Generally, norms are seen in achievement tests at the elementary school level. But, even at the secondary, collegiate, and industrial and business levels, norms are sometimes available based on varied demographical and biographical information. National norms, which specify neither age nor sex, limit fine interpretations of results which could otherwise be made if norms were more specific. One usually finds normative data expressed by various divisions on the basis of sex, educational level, or geographical distribution, or some combination of these three factors. It is uncommon to see a norm table that breaks information into such a fine level of specificity to allow exact interpretations for a particular type of subject, such as for a thirty-three year old, black male, residing in the northeastern United States, with a high school education and eight years experience as a skilled craftsman. Just as, more often than not, if one were to inquire about the existence of norms for women, one might be told that such norms have not been evolved.

As one inspects the test reviews in Chapters 4 through 9, it will become evident that certain norms are specific and detailed regarding age, sex, geographical location, and racial composition, whereas others are not. But, lack of specificity does not mean that the device is inadequate in some way. Rather, it indicates that the necessary course of action to evolve such norms either has not been undertaken or has not been completed to permit their availability to the test user. The norm information provided with the tests in this book specifies the nature of the norm samples by geographical distribution, age, occupation, and sex, when this data is available in the publisher's manual. As you read the norm descriptions, realize that the data represented is as complete as possible, given the information in the publisher's manual for the various tests.

Often we find that the availability of well-developed norms depends largely on the scope of the instrument and its use. For example, the Wonderlic Personnel Test presently has norms available for both Caucasian and Negro races, divided by education, age, and occupational levels. One could determine the adequate level of performance on the Wonderlic for, say, a white, male, high school graduate, seeking entry into a middle level management position. However, in reviewing a personality instrument to be used to assess the general characteristics of an entering employee regarding a variety of motivational and personality traits, inspection of the norm tables might reveal nothing more than norms divided by sex, with a notation about the geographical distribution of the norm sample. In fact, some norms are identified so vaguely that we will find only a statement that indicates that they are based upon a wide assessment of individuals across the country. There are various reasons why such a difference exists in the detail of norms, and they warrant enumerating, especially in light of the federal government's current requirements regarding tests used for selection of employees.

One reason is that assessment devices are not used for selection purposes only, and many, therefore, do not require specification of detailed norms. Many instruments are used for placement, evaluation of programs, research, or counseling, and a need for very specific national norms has never been justified.

Another reason relates to the cost. The cost of evolving and providing norms, which would meet the criteria of age, sex, race, and so on, would be prohibitive in many cases. For example, it is common to see several reliability and validity studies on an instrument over a period of a few years, but new norms are not evolved at the same pace as these research studies. Evolving new norms demands carefully planned broad based testing of the instruments and the collection and collation of data; the cost implications are obvious.

Let us now turn to the problem of existing bias in instruments, especially in the context of instruments used on women and minority groups. Assessment measures by themselves are not infallible. Norms by themselves are not infallible either. Norms, when strictly interpreted, are examples of typical performance by individuals and are not necessarily indicative of how all subjects will respond on a particular instrument. How can we deal with the problem of inherent sex and racial bias in a norm table when using an instrument with a certain client group? One way is to recognize the limitations of the norms. They can be used as a guideline in arriving at a decision, but if interpreted too literally, they can inhibit proper interpretations regarding the performance of an individual.

The first course of action for a user who finds that norms are not appropriate for the client to be evaluated would be to contact the publisher to determine just how up to date the norms currently available are — especially in light of the sample being tested. If the desired norms are not available, the user can contact previous users of the instrument to determine whether they have developed appropriate norms. This approach can be expediated through the cooperation of the publisher of the instrument.

Another step for the user would be to conduct a literature search through the ERIC Centers (see Part Three — Resources for the Reader). This approach can determine if there have been other studies reporting on the instrument which have attempted to evolve norms on a sample similar to that being tested by the present user.

A third, more drastic, step is either to modify the current norms or to evolve a new set. The norms would necessarily be local to one's own environment and circumstances but might prove to be the most expedient and reasonable way of determining data for evaluation of a particular individual's performance. Consulting with individuals within one's own organization or at local universities could help the user to plan the necessary design to collect appropriate data for making decision and judgments in the context of the particular group being assessed, especially if the group has certain characteristics with regard to sex and racial composition.

However, it behooves the user to keep in mind that relevancy, or lack of it, in norms does not negate the impact of the instrument itself. One must consider the purpose for which the device is being used. If only limited norms exist, it does not necessarily require searching for a better instrument, but rather reconsidering the use of the instrument in light of the absence of appropriate norms or developing norms specific to one's needs.

Interpretation of Scores

There are two ways in which test scores are typically presented in a test manual or in a publisher's report: standard scores and percentiles. Standard score systems have an advantage of permitting comparisons among many instruments, providing that each has the same mean and the same standard deviation.

There are several standard score systems. One presents scores on the basis of a mean score of fifty and a standard deviation of ten points — as seen in the Minnesota Multiphasic Personality Inventory. Another is one in which results are reported with a mean of 500 and a standard deviation of 100 as is seen in the Educational Testing Service's Scholastic Aptitude Test. Still another is the "stanine" which refers to the standard nine, or nine levels of performance in which the mean is five and the standard deviation is two.

The interpretation of all standard score systems is identical. The mean or average score is the numerical middle of all scores; it is statistically derived and allows for comparison among all tests in which the same standard score system is used. The standard deviation refers to the number of cases that are dispersed from the mean. When considering plus or minus one standard deviation, we assume that approximately 34 percent of the cases are above the mean — up to one standard deviation, and approximately 34 percent of the cases are below the mean — to minus one standard deviation. This means that tests are built upon the normal bell shaped curve and that they are so predetermined. Beyond one standard deviation, the percentages of scores diminish. The number of cases between the first and second standard deviations are approximately 13 percent, where those above or below three standard deviations are approximately 2 1/2 percent. When considering the full range of potential scores from minus three standard deviations to plus three standard deviations, we assume that this incorporates 99 percent of all cases. It is academic, in most cases, to consider scores above and below the third standard deviation because of the scarcity with which these scores exist.

A second method for interpreting scores is in percentiles. Percentiles do not refer to the percentage of correct responses on an instrument but to the status that an individual holds in the distribution of all scores. When considering percentiles, which vary in range from the first to the ninety-ninth, we are referring to whether or not the score surpasses a percentage of individuals at each percentile level. Typically, at the ninety-ninth percentile, an individual score is higher than all scores on an instrument. Whereas, at the first percentile the individual score is below all scores in the distribution. No matter what the number of cases is, these scores can be translated into percentiles so that a subject's status in the distribution can be accurately represented.

The limitations of percentiles are easily understood; they are found in the nature of the percentiles themselves. Since percentiles reflect numbers of people, a small change in one score at either end of the distribution would produce little or no percentile change in comparison with a small change around the fiftieth percentile. Because most of the scores are grouped around the fiftieth percentile, a few points change in test performance around the mean will dramatically affect a subject's status in the distribution. But, because few cases are found at either extreme, a few points' change will not increase or decrease the percentile ranking of a subject. This presents the potential misinterpretation of percentiles, because performance in the center of the distribution — the fiftieth percentile — must be handled much more carefully in its interpretation since an individual's status could change so easily.

Age, Sex, and Prior Testing Experience

The final areas for consideration in test selection concern the age, sex, and prior testing experience of the subjects. In selecting a test, age is a concern mainly because of the effect it can have on a subject's performance. Take, for example, those at the elementary, secondary, and even collegiate levels who are constantly exposed to a variety of scholastic assessment sessions. These students greet the appearance of one more test with much less anxiety than does the individual who took his or her last test in high school, twenty or thirty years ago. Another consideration comes in choosing a speed test. Tests which impose stringent time limits will tend to lower the scores of older subjects, while having a positive influence on the younger ones. Also, instruments which emphasize performance and manipulation will probably result in higher scores for the younger individuals.

The sex of the subject also effects his or her performance on an assessment device. Close examination of many instruments, especially in the fields of interest and aptitude and achievement, denotes a specific direction with regard to sex typing of questions which are generally geared toward the male subject. Although one cannot pinpoint every instrument and classify its items, sex is a point for prime consideration when the subjects are either heavily mixed between male and female or are disproportionately higher in the number of women taking the instrument. A recently published article, "Guidelines for Assessing Sex Bias and Sex Fairness in Career Interest Inventories", speaks to the issue of inherent sex bias in interest measures.

The article, reproduced in Appendix II, summarizes the need to eliminate sex bias in career interest inventories and enumerates the ways to do so. Although these guidelines are not legally binding, they do reflect principles upon which developers and users of biased inventories can minimize decisions based upon the sex composition of the assessed group. The guidelines cover three areas: the inventory or assessment device, technical information, and interpretative information. They suggest such action as the elimination of the generic "he" or "she", the need for technical material from publishers indicating the extent to which these guidelines have been followed, as well as numerous interpretative rules for arriving at realistic judgments of subjects' responses, regardless of sex.

A subject's prior testing experience should also direct test selection because of its effect on test performance. Going back to the age factor, we will find that older subjects' last testing experiences were probably prior to the advent of sophisticated answer sheets, complex multiple choice items, and rigor with which tests are administered today. Subjects who are unfamiliar with multiple choice items, timed instruments, or tests which demand a complete understanding of a complex format may perform poorly because of their confusion with the instrument's format rather than its content.

In summary then, we can see that the purpose of a test is indeed a valuable and important guideline for the selection of any assessment device. But, we can also see that an instrument's availability, cost, time for administration, scoring methods, and intended subjects should all effect the selection decision.

Reliability and validity are also issues which must be considered when selecting an instrument. But, the nature of these concepts is such that Chapter 3 is devoted solely to them in order that the user may attain a thorough understanding of their implications.

Chapter 3

RELIABILITY AND VALIDITY OF PSYCHOMETRIC MEASURES

JOHN BAJTELSMIT

ANYONE who chooses tests, interprets scores, or makes decisions based on test scores should have a thorough understanding of the concepts of reliability and validity. Information describing test characteristics is typically provided by the test developer, but the effective use and accurate interpretation of tests depends upon the inferences made from these data by the test user. This requires a high level of expertise. In fact, the *Standards for Educational and Psychological Tests* (American Psychological Association, 1974, p. 1) suggests that meaningful interpretation of its reliability and validity sections requires, "... training approximately equivalent to a level between the master's degree and the doctorate in education or psychology." Not meeting these qualifications, however, does not let test users "off the hook." Instead, users should strive to increase their competence in order to more effectively use and interpret tests. The purpose of this chapter is to present the essential concepts of reliability and validity. Mastery of this material will not qualify one as a "test expert" but should increase the user's awareness of important testing considerations.

Reliability and validity are the two essential characteristics of a sound test. Reliability can be defined as consistency of measurement. This involves stability of performance as opposed to the effects of instrument defects and chance factors in influencing test scores. The basic concern of reliability is to assess the degree of "true" versus "error" components present in test scores. Validity, on the other hand, concerns itself with the degree to which a test measures what it purports to measure, and also how useful the test is in making inferences about other behavior.

The distinction between reliability and validity may be clarified in the following example. Suppose that a man wants to determine the length of a fence by using a tape measure. The first tape he uses is the kind used in tailoring or sewing and is constructed of a somewhat elastic material. To his dismay he finds that each time he measures the fence he gets a different result. The information provided by the tape is of little or no use since it is inconsistent and variable. Thus, because this measuring instrument is unreliable, it cannot be a valid indicator of the length of the fence. Concluding that the different results are due to the tape's stretchiness, the man borrows a friend's measuring tape, which is constructed of steel. He fails to notice, however, that this second tape has several feet broken from its end. Nevertheless, it provides identical results each time it is used, and because of its consistency of measurement, is a highly reliable instrument. However, in terms of measuring standard units of feet, the steel tape is clearly inaccurate, although consistently so. The measure of the fence's length provided by the steel tape is therefore not a valid indicator of what is meant by "length in feet." One would be mistaken to employ this data in determining for example, the lengths of lumber required to replace parts of the fence. Clearly, a reliable instrument (such as the steel tape) is not always valid. Even though reliability alone is not a sufficient condition for validity, however, it is necessary for validity.

Reliability

Every test should be accompanied by a statement of its reliability. This permits an assessment of the degree of consistency versus measurement error present in the test's scores. At the same time it is essential to note the characteristics of the sample, as well as the particular method, used in estimating reliability. Different sample characteristics and methods of reliability estimation deal with different sources of error and consequently result in different estimates. Their relevance to specific applications should be carefully considered by the test user.

Since reliability estimates deal with the degree of consistency or agreement between two sets of scores, they can be expressed in terms of a correlation coefficient. Applied to tests, this statistic is known as the reliability coefficient; it indicates the correspondence of test scores obtained on different occasions or with different sets of equivalent items. If each person had the same rank on each set of test scores, there would be a perfect correlation of +1.00. Since no test will achieve this degree of consistency, coefficients which fall in the .80's or .90's are usually considered adequate.

Methods of Estimating Reliability—Test Retest Reliability

This technique uses the results of the same test administered to the same group of individuals on two occasions. The correlation between the scores resulting from the two administrations is sometimes called the temporal stability coefficient. Advantages of this method include equivalent content on both tests, as well as the simpler task of developing only one form of the test. However, since there are two administrations involved, the time between the testings becomes a crucial factor to consider. If the interval is short, recall of previous items may inflate the reliability estimate; if it is too long, reliability coefficients may be lowered because of intervening factors, such as learning.

Parallel Forms Reliability

This method is test retest reliability using different but equivalent forms of the test. Thus, the same group of individuals completes two separate but parallel test forms on two occasions. The suggested time interval between the administration of two parallel forms is typically two to four weeks but can vary from minutes to weeks depending upon the nature of the test and the interpretation of the test scores. This method eliminates the effects of memory since the items in the two test versions are not identical. However, there is the cost and difficulty of constructing two different test forms which are truly equivalent. In addition, the interval between testings allows the interference of factors such as learning, skill improvement, attitude change, and so forth. Thus, persons are no longer the same in all respects on both test occasions. There is, however, a widely used method which eliminates the undesirable effects of learning, memory, and the impracticality of two test administrations.

Internal Consistency Reliability

Several techniques may be used to estimate reliability after only a single test administration. The split-halves procedure divides the items of a single test into halves, such as odd-even, which are separately scored. The correlation between the two sets of scores represents the degree of internal consistency or homogeneity of the scores. Since the two subdivisions are only half the length of the full test, a statistical formula (Spearman-Brown) is used to adjust the correlation to what it would have been for a full-length test.

Other methods of estimating test reliability based on a single administration were developed by Kuder and Richardson (1937). Their most commonly applied technique is known as Kuder-Richardson formula 20. The reliability coefficient obtained from K-R 20 is mathematically equivalent to the average of all split-half coefficients resulting from different splittings of a test. Unless the test items are highly homogeneous, however, the K-R 20 reliability will be lower than the split-half reliability. Another internal consistency method yields a reliability estimate known as Coefficient Alpha. This estimate is equivalent to K-R 20 when items are dichotomously scored (right or wrong) but can also be used to estimate the reliability of nondichotomously scored items. Similarly, Hoyt Reliability, which uses an analysis of variance approach, is another method of estimating reliability from a single administration. Like Coefficient Alpha, Hoyt's Anova Coefficient is equivalent to K-R 20 with dichotomously scored items but can also be used for nondichotomous data.

One important point to remember is that the test must be a "power" rather than a "speed" test for these internal consistency techniques to be applicable. On a speed test the number of items is usually so large that no one can complete the test within the given time limits. However, since the items are relatively easy, almost all attempted items are responded to correctly and the final test score is usually the number of items attempted. If the test is split, the number of correct items will usually be the same in both halves so that an internal consistency coefficient will be spuriously high. If the reliability of a speed test is required, or if an assessment of test reliability over time is desired, the appropriate procedure is the test retest method.

Scorer Reliability

If the examiner finds it necessary to judge the correctness or quality of responses, the test is not entirely objective. In this special case it is important to determine the consistency of scorers, or scorer reliability. A typical method might employ the same set of tests independently scored by two examiners. Each examinee would thus receive two scores which could then be correlated to determine a coefficient of scorer reliability. This coefficient of interscorer reliability should always be noted whenever creativity or projective personality tests are employed. In fact, all tests which depend to some extent on the judgment of a scorer require measures of scorer reliability, just as they do the usual reliability estimates.

Conditions Affecting Reliability

There are many factors affecting reliability estimates which should be considered when evaluating a test. For example, the following conditions may result in lowered reliability: a large amount of time between test administrations, restricted group variability (homogeneity), a small number of test items, items which are excessively simple or difficult, and poor interscorer consistency. The test user must assess the significance of each of these factors as related to the test's intended use. In order to do so intelligently, the user should be familiar with the effects of manipulating each of these variables on reliability estimates. Extensive treatment of these topics can be found in R. L. Thorndike's *Educational Measurement* (1971).

Standard Error of Measurement

Although reliability coefficients may be very helpful when comparing different tests, the standard error of measurement is essential when interpreting individual test scores. This type of reliability index also enables the construction of score boundaries which include the "true" score at a defined probability level. (A "true" score is the theoretical value that a person would obtain if he were tested an infinite number of times under the same conditions, and the results averaged.) The standard error of measurement is equal to the standard deviation of the test multiplied by the square root of 1-r, where r is the reliability coefficient. Thus, the standard error of measurement is dependent upon both the reliability coefficient and the variability of the distribution of sample scores. As an example of what the standard error of measurement tells the test user, consider the following. If a child's I.Q. score is found to be 85 on one occasion, his true I.Q. score may be surprisingly higher (such as 100) or lower (such as 70) than this obtained value. The practical significance of this is considerable since I.Q. scores of 100 and 70 give entirely different pictures of the child. It would be very important to determine what confidence we have in the obtained score of 85 by estimating the limits within which we are fairly certain the true I.Q. score falls. Assuming that the reliability coefficient (r) is .91, then 1-r = 1-.91, or .09. The square root of .09 is .3. Given a standard deviation of 16, we find that the standard error of measurement equals 16 times .3 equals 4.8 which, for didactic purposes only, will be rounded to 5 (the standard error of measurement is not normally rounded).

Now that we know the standard error of measurement, we can construct confidence limits around the observed score of 85. Assuming that the I.Q. scores are normally distributed (that is, they have a bell-shaped distribution) and that the errors of measurement are similarly distributed, the standard error can be interpreted in terms of the normal curve frequencies. Approximately 68 percent of the cases in a normal distribution fall between ± 1 standard error. We can thus conclude that the chances are about 2 to 1 (or 68:32) that the true I.Q. falls between ± 5 points of the observed I.Q. of 85. That is, we are 68 percent certain that the true I.Q. score is between 80 and 90. If we want to be 99.7 percent certain of the true I.Q. score, we must widen our confidence limits to three standard errors, so that the limits would extend from about 70 to 100 I.Q. points! The standard error of measurement is therefore quite useful in determining how much confidence should be placed in a score. Similar methods are available which first estimate a true score and then more appropriately construct a confidence interval around this estimate rather than the observed score. (Readers are encouraged to consult statistics textbooks for a more extensive treatment of these concepts.)

Test users are often interested in comparing the test scores of individuals or in interpreting differences in subscale profiles for a single individual. The standard error of measurement is especially useful for this purpose. It is used to calculate that difference which is meaningfully interpretable, that is, statistically significant at a given level of confidence. This information should be found in the test manual. Without it, it is not possible to determine whether an observed difference is due merely to chance or whether it is, in fact, a meaningful difference.

Information regarding a test's reliability coefficients and its standard error of measurement should be carefully scrutinized to determine whether scores are sufficiently dependable for the intended uses of the test. For example, samples and procedures used in the calculations of scores should be reviewed to determine their applicability for the intended use. The reliability of difference scores should be noted to determine whether differences can be reliably interpreted. If different forms of a test are used, their comparability must be investigated before equivalence can be assumed. Internal consistency measures should be avoided for speeded tests. For comparisons over time, the importance of the period between tests should be considered and the effects of varying this interval should be noted. These are just a few of the considerations to which the test user should be attuned. Such factors must certainly be considered if the user is to have any confidence in judgments and predictions based upon specific test findings, assuming, of course, that the instrument is sufficiently valid.

Validity

Test validity refers to the degree to which a test is capable of achieving its aims. Since different tests have different aims or purposes, they require different types of investigations in order to assess their validity. Thus, a test used for predicting performance requires a different kind of validity than a test used for describing individuals. The *Standards for Educational and Psychological Tests* (American Psychological Association, 1974) has distinguished four types of validity: content validity, construct validity, and criterion-related validities (predictive and concurrent). Each type of validity relates to a different aim of testing. Furthermore, each type of validation is conducted with, and sometimes restricted to, a certain validation group. Therefore, no test should be considered valid in the abstract. Instead, when assessing a test's validity, one should always ask, "valid for what?" and "valid for whom?"

Face Validity

This term is used to indicate whether a test, on the face of it, appears to measure what it claims to measure. It is basically a subjective judgment made by the subjects who take the test, administrative personnel who decide on its use, and other technically untrained observers. Although not technically rigorous, it is nevertheless important in determining the general acceptance of a test. A test will tend to be more acceptable to users when face validity is present along with the more rigorous types of validity. Face validity alone, however, can be dangerously misleading, just as its absence can lead to disbelief and resistence among potential users.

Content Validity

Content validation determines how well the test content samples the kinds of things about which conclusions are to be drawn. The primary concern is to determine the representativeness of the selected items. Explicit specification of the performance domain or universe becomes an important requisite. Hence, random sampling from within this universe then becomes the ideal method for assuring item representativeness. Sometimes, however, in practice, explicit definition of the universe and random sampling are not possible. Alternatively, a test outline or blueprint may be used to define the test parameters and to specify item content. In any event, a clear definition of the universe and a description of the procedures followed in sampling from it should always be available for evaluating the purported validity of the test's content.

Content validity is usually applied to achievement tests where "expert judgment" determines item appropriateness. The items are usually evaluated according to how adequately they constitute a definition of the achievement to be measured by the test. For example, in constructing an English literature test, specialists might examine textbooks, courses of study, relevant materials, and so forth to determine which topics and facts are most significant and what their relative weights should be. The final items are then expertly chosen so as to adequately represent the content universe of English literature.

A content-valid test is valid for persons of all types, because its purpose involves comparison with a type of absolute standard of performance.

Since these techniques are quite common, and on the surface rather simple, care must be taken to avoid their inappropriate use. Many achievement tests obviously require content validation. If they are also used for purposes of selection or placement, however, they must also be empirically validated as predictors of the future behavior.

Construct Validity

Constructs are theoretical entities, such as intelligence, anxiety, dogmatism, and so forth. If a test claims to measure such an ability, trait, or attitude, data relevant to its construct validation should be available.

A construct is accompanied by a theoretical elaboration from which predictions can be generated. Construct validation is the process whereby predictions derived from this theory are tested. A sample procedure might be as follows. First, the behavior of persons with high versus low scores is predicted on the basis of the theory. Data is then gathered to test the predictions. Finally, an inference is made as to whether the theory adequately explains the obtained data. The theory may be supported, rejected, or revised in light of the evidence. Alternatively, it may be concluded that the construct was poorly defined or that the test did not even measure the construct. Because of these several possible conclusions, a single study or a single coefficient of construct validity is never sufficient. A network of evidence from many investigations is needed to support or refute construct validity.

Many different techniques may be involved in the validation of theoretical constructs. Correlational studies alone take several forms. A new test may be correlated with other tests which are weak or indirect measures of similar constructs. Moderately high correlations are often supportive, but extremely high correlations might indicate needless duplication unless special advantages, such as shorter administration time, are present. Low correlations with other measures, although sometimes desirable, do not alone insure validity. In order to demonstrate construct validity, therefore, convergent validation (high correlations with variables which should theoretically be related) and discriminant validations (low correlations with irrelevant measures) are both required. One technique uses what is known as a "multitrait-multimethod matrix." This matrix presents intercorrelations between two or more traits as measured by two or more methods (Campbell & Fiske, 1959).

Satisfactory construct validity requires that the correlations among similar traits measured by different methods be higher than the correlations among different traits measured by the same method.

Factor analysis is another correlational technique relevant to construct validation (Thorndike, 1971). This statistical procedure can analyze tests into their common elements. Thus, a factor analysis might indicate that the subscales of some tests may be further analyzed into additional scales, whereas other scales could be combined to form new sets of related items. More pertinent to construct validation, however, factor analyses may show that different tests which theoretically should indicate a single factor, are in fact, related, that is, "load highly" on the same factor. Interpretation of these rather sophisticated techniques obviously demands considerable knowledge which is beyond the introductory content in this chapter.

Experimental procedures which alter test performance may also relate to construct validation by either confirming or challenging the theoretical interpretation of the instrument. Similarly, a logical analysis of test content or scoring may lead to counterinterpretations of test results which can then be empirically tested. For example, measuring a construct by means of a speed test might lead to questionable results if the construct is theoretically unrelated to speed. Empirical evidence concerning the effect of speed on test scores should then be required. Thus, construct validation involves judgments based upon an accumulation of research studies conducted by several methodological techniques.

Predictive Validity

As a form of criterion-related validity, predictive validity involves the effectiveness of a test in predicting a criterion. In fact, a commonly noted difference between reliability and validity is that reliability always reflects the correlation of a test with itself (or with a parallel form of itself), whereas validity typically requires a correlation with some external criterion. The correlations relating test scores and criteria are commonly referred to as validity coefficients. Predictive validity is relevant to tests which are used to forecast academic achievement, predict vocational success, prognosticate reaction to therapy, and so forth. The criterion in the case of predictive validity is some future measure which is unavailable at the time of predictor measurement.

Concurrent Validity

Statements of concurrent validity indicate an individual's existing status on a criterion rather than a prediction of future outcome. Typically, test results are correlated with a criterion that is immediately available. For example, individual results from a group intelligence test can be compared with those obtained on the Stanford-Binet. Although this type of validation is often convenient, it should only be used when the primary interest is present behavior. Concurrent validity should not be used as a substitute for predictive validity, although under appropriate conditions it can estimate the upper limits for predictive validity coefficients.

Tests used for selection and placement decisions require appropriate criterion-related validation. For example, a test used for employee selection would have job performance as a criterion. Predictive validity would be the ideal model for such an employment test. Applicants selected by the test would be expected to become better employees than some randomly selected group of applicants. Similarly, allocating students to classes according to test scores should result in improved performance if validity for placement is assumed.

Recent legal developments in the area of civil rights and fair employment have underscored the importance of validity when tests are used for employee selection, placement, and promotion. The Equal Employment Opportunity Commission, pursuant to the Civil Rights Act of 1964, Title VII, has issued its *Guidelines on Employment Testing Procedures* (1966, 1970). These guidelines clearly establish the requirement of using properly validated tests for selection decisions. The term "test" is defined quite broadly to cover even scored interviews and application forms. The guidelines also define unfair test discrimination and outline the minimum standards and evidence required for demonstrating the validity of selection instruments. The *Standards for Educational and Psychological Tests and Manuals* (American Psychological Association, 1966) is noted as the reference source for generally accepted test validation procedures. In addition, the American Psychological Association has submitted to the courts an *Amicus Curiae* brief (1972) as an independent discussion of the complex technical and legal regulations regarding the validation of employee selection procedures (see Part Three of this book, Resources for the Reader). Basic considerations involved in using employment tests and subjecting them to validation are discussed in this document. These various references are required reading for anyone involved in employment testing. Test users should certainly maintain an awareness of new developments in this area.

Evidence concerning criterion-related validity must be obtained, presented, and interpreted in considerable detail. The test manual should accurately describe the criteria as well as comment on their adequacy. For example, job titles by themselves are sometimes inconsistent and should therefore be accompanied by a description of duties based on sufficiently detailed job analyses. In many cases the criteria themselves should be studied for validity. Their relevance and reasons for their selection should be justified. A serious validation error to avoid is criterion contamination. This occurs when the test scores themselves influence an individual's criterion status. For example, a rater's knowledge of a person's aptitude score might affect his or her subsequent ratings. This lack of independence between test scores and the criterion will artificially raise the validity coefficient and should obviously be avoided.

Since test validity is often restricted to a specific validation situation, limits on generalizability should always be noted. Because of the considerable risk in generalizing to other situations, local validity studies are often more useful than published data. In any case, the validation sample must be comparable in all relevant respects to the group about which inferences will be drawn. Sample variables which often affect validity include: age, sex, socioeconomic status, ethnic origin, residential region, educational level, and other demographic and psychological characteristics. Small sample sizes will obviously yield less reliable statistics. Validation procedures should parallel eventual test uses and purposes; time intervals, for example, should be comparable. Dates of validation studies should be fairly recent, and the difficulties involved in long-term predictions must be considered. Data should be regularly updated to assure continual validity, and test users should consult the latest available information.

Test users should be especially aware of possible bias in their test applications. Because subgroups often have differential validity (differences in criterion-related validity), results presented in the test manual should be reviewed for each of the separate subsamples. For example, blacks and whites, men and women, and so on may have differential validity coefficients or different slopes or intercepts on the regression lines relating their test and criterion scores. Thus, a test may be predictive for one subgroup and not predictive for another or consistently over or underpredictive of one group's performance. In the interest of fairness, it should be determined whether persons with similar criterion performance (such as, equal job success) may be discriminated against by different criterion predictions (such as, unequal probabilities of being hired).

Evidence for validity may be presented by correlation coefficients, descriptions, expectancy tables, graphs, and charts. Blind confidence in test statistics must be avoided by the test user. Statistics can be misleading and their availability alone does not merit confidence in the test. For example, corrections for attenuation (that is, lessened correlations) may be misinterpreted when they are based on obtained correlation coefficients that are very low or from a small or inappropriate sample. Statistical corrections for factors, such as restricted range, must be accompanied by enough information to permit a proper assessment of their appropriateness.

How does one interpret the reliability and validity figures for a particular test? Unfortunately, there is no simple answer to this question. As noted previously, a reliability coefficient in the .80's or .90's is typically considered adequate for most purposes. It is difficult to recommend a minimum value for a validity coefficient, however, without considering the particular use of the test. As an example, when correlating a single employment test, such as, the Wonderlic Personnel Test (see Chapter 4), with a measure of job performance, a rough rule of thumb would suggest that a validity coefficient of approximately .20 is often high enough to be useful. In fact, such correlations rarely exceed .50. Ordinarily, a validity coefficient of .40 is considered very good, and a correlation of .30 will usually satisfy most personnel research workers. It should be emphasized, however, that the many additional considerations which should be taken into account have only been introduced in this chapter. The test user's expertise must further seek out and evaluate those validity data which are relevant to a specific occupation, environment, and so on.

As a further example, consider the Remote Associates Test (see Chapter 9). The general reliability estimates seem within the acceptable range. However, determining whether this test is sufficiently valid demands that we revert to the previously mentioned validity questions. In considering "valid for what?" we note that the validity of the Remote Associates Test would differ according to its use, that is, basic theoretical research versus applied employee selection. Although an industrial study may be cited in the test review, its relevance to a specific hiring circumstance must be carefully assessed.

When considering "valid for whom?" note that this test's criterion of verbal ability in concatenating remotely associated words effectively denies creativity in less literate persons and may, therefore, be of questionable validity with this particular subgroup. Although this type of information is not specifically pointed out in a test review's validity section, its importance is obvious. Note also that a low relationship cited without comment under the validity section does not automatically suggest low validity. Awareness of the distinction between convergent and divergent validity should be maintained. In some cases a low correlation of an emotional measure, for example, with tests of general intelligence may be theoretically desirable (divergent and construct validity). It would be impossible, however, to list all such reliability and validity considerations for all possible uses of each test in Part Two. The test user's expertise becomes an obvious necessity.

The test user should also be aware of the special considerations involved when using test batteries. Relevant statistical techniques, such as multiple regression and discriminant analysis, require considerable competence for appropriate use. Discussions concerning the use of these techniques in selection and placement, among others, can be found in several chapters of the Thorndike text (1971).

Additional reliability and validity information can be found in journals such as *Educational and Psychological Measurement*, the *Journal of Educational Measurement*, as well as in other documents, monographs, and textbooks.

BIBLIOGRAPHY

American Psychological Association: *Standards for Educational and Psychological Tests*. Washington, D. C., Author, 1974.

American Psychological Association: *Standards for Educational and Psychological Tests and Manuals*. Washington, D. C., Author, 1966.

Campbell, D. T., and Fiske, D. W.: Convergent and Discriminant Validation by the Multitrait — Multimethod Matrix. *Psychological Bulletin*, *56*:81-105, 1959.

Equal Employment Opportunity Commission (EEOC): Guidelines on Employee Selection Procedures. *Federal Register 35*(149):12333-12336, 1970.

Equal Employment Opportunity Commission (EEOC): *Guidelines on Employment Testing Procedures*. Washington, D. C., Author, 1966.

Kuder, G. F., and Richardson, M. W.: The Theory of Estimation of Test Reliability. *Psychometrika*, *2*:151-160, 1937.

Thorndike, R. L. (Ed.): *Educational Measurement* (2nd Ed.), American Council on Education, Washington, D. C., 1971.

Part Two
TESTS AND MEASURES

Chapter 4

APTITUDE AND ACHIEVEMENT ASSESSMENT

GROUP 1 — INTELLIGENCE AND APTITUDE MEASURES

Analysis of Relationships

Author: Edwin E. Ghiselli

Variable: The Analysis of Relationships assesses general intellectual abilities.

Type of Measure: The analysis is a paper and pencil test, suitable for administration to either individuals or groups. It is untimed and typically takes thirty minutes to complete. Scoring is done by hand.

Source from which Measure may be Obtained: Consulting Psychologists Press, Inc., 577 College Avenue, Palo Alto, California 94306.

Description: The Analysis of Relationships test includes forty multiple choice items. The purpose is to measure abilities typically assessed by intelligence tests, with slightly more emphasis on verbal facility, reasoning, and problem solving. The test is also designed to provide a finer discrimination at higher levels of capabilities without concern for a speed factor. Scoring is done by simply adding the number of correct answers. Application of the analysis has proven successful with high school, college, and university students and with clerical, managerial, and sales personnel, as well as with industrial employees, especially where verbal facility and problem solving are integral to job success.

Norms: Normative data is provided in percentiles on the following groups: general populations, university students, management personnel (mostly middle management), salesmen (excluding retail sales), line supervisors, clerical workers, and skilled workers (trades and crafts with over half having some college work). The ages range from twenty to sixty-five for many of the norm groups.

Validity and Reliability: Significant correlations of the Analysis of Relationships scores with grade point averages for groups of high school, university, and graduate students yielded values ranging from .32 to .65. Additional studies yielded significant coefficients ranging from .35 to .78 when the Analysis of Relationships was correlated with the California Test of Mental Maturity and Vocabulary, as well as, Otis Self-Administering, Arithmetic, and Mechanical Principles Tests based on working subjects. Also, correlations of the Analysis of Relationships scores with a variety of occupational criteria including superiors' ratings, yielded values ranging from .22 to .76 on groups of twenty to forty persons.

Odd-even reliabilities yielded coefficients ranging from .70 to .90 for varied occupational groups with groups varying in number from 30 to 402. Test retest data is presently being gathered.

Bibliography:

Ghiselli, E. E.: *Preliminary Manual for Analysis of Relationships.* Palo Alto, Consulting Psychologists Press, Inc., 1960.

Appraisal of Occupational Aptitudes

Author: Aurelius A. Abbatiello

Variable: The Appraisal of Occupational Aptitudes (AOA) series provides an assessment of aptitudes and developmental skills in office tasks of both business and industry.

Type of Measure: The AOA is a battery of eight paper and pencil subtests, suitable for administration to either individuals or groups. Each subtest is timed and the entire series takes approximately ninety minutes to complete. Scoring is done by hand using a key.

Source from which Measure may be Obtained: Houghton Mifflin Company, 53 West 43rd Street, New York, New York 10036.

Description: The AOA consists of eight subtests, however, it is not necessary to administer the entire battery at one time. Each of the subtests can be used individually to assess a particular skill. Aptitudes measured by the battery include: checking letters, checking numbers, filing names, filing numbers, posting names, posting numbers, arithmetical computation — reasoning, and desk calculator. Each test has two distinct purposes: counseling of students for business careers and the selection and placement of office personnel. Raw scores may be converted to percentile ranks by using the tables provided in the manual.

Norms: Individuals from government, industry, business, and educational institutions, representing varied geographical areas, make up the normative sample. These include subjects representing clerical employees, job applicants for positions in industrial and business organizations, and students enrolled in school business training programs. The total number of persons included in the present sample is approximately one thousand. Norms are available for men and women, separately, for each subtest.

Validity and Reliability: Validity studies include correlation of students' grades in clerical skills programs with subtest scores on the AOA. The values, all significant, range from .24 to .57. Also reported are significant relationships between AOA subtest scores and a "hire" versus a "no-hire" criterion, as well as with a supervisor rating criterion. Generally, correlation values in the range of from .30 to .50 and above were obtained for these two criteria.

Split-half reliability coefficients ranged from .80 to .99 for the eight subtests. Test retest reliabilities, obtained for each of the subtests, ranged from .65 to .75 over an approximate six month interval. The number of subjects was not indicated.

Bibliography:

Abbatiello, A. A.: *Instruction Manual for Administration and Scoring: Appraisal of Occupational Aptitudes.* Boston, Houghton Mifflin Company, 1971.

Aptitudes Associates Test of Sales Aptitude

Author: Martin M. Bruce

Variable: The Aptitudes Associates Test of Sales Aptitude is an aid in measuring an individual's sales aptitude.

Type of Measure: The test of sales aptitude is a paper and pencil inventory, suitable for administration to either individuals or groups. It is untimed and typically takes twenty to thirty minutes to complete. Scoring is done by hand and takes about three minutes.

Source from which Measure may be Obtained: Western Psychological Services, 12031 Wilshire Boulevard, Los Angeles, California 90025.

Description: The function of this test — as an aid in assessing sales aptitude — makes it a valuable tool both in the selection of sales personnel when coupled with the screening and testing of applicants and in vocational counseling. It has fifty multiple choice items which yield a specific measure of the subject's knowledge and comprehension of basic selling principles. The sales market referred to here includes retailers, wholesalers, and consumers, covering the sales of products varying from heavy capital industrial goods to door-to-door type household items. The user is cautioned that this test is intended only for use as an aid and that considerations, such as interest, intelligence, motivation, appearance, and health, among others, should be taken into account before making a final decision. It is also well to note that no average has been set down regarding "satisfactory score" for the simple reason that those attributes akin to or desired in one type of salesman, such as door-to-door, are not necessarily those which satisfy the qualifications of a sales engineer.

Norms: There are three basic sets of norms: salesmen; sales applicants; and high school, college, and special groups which include nonsalesmen. Norms for women are composed of females without sales experience, and the norms for men are composed of men in nonsales positions. Norms for "salesmen in general" and other groups listed in the manual should be used only as a guide.

Validity and Reliability: Critical ratio showed significance beyond the .01 probability level when scores on this test were compared for groups of salesmen with groups of non-salesmen. No relationships were shown between the test of sales aptitude and the Otis Self-Administering Test of Mental Ability or the Kuder Preference Record Scale of persuasive interest. Further validity studies are also reported.

The test has an estimated test retest reliability of .74, when administered to a group of 658 men, women, and salesmen over a three month interval.

Bibliography:

Bruce, M. M.: *Examiner's Manual Revised: Aptitudes Associates Test of Sales Aptitude*. New Rochelle, Martin M. Bruce, 1960.

Aptitude Tests for Occupations — Adult Form A

Author: Wesley S. Roeder

Variable: The Aptitude Tests for Occupations are designed to provide vocational counseling information.

Type of Measure: The aptitude tests are a battery of six paper and pencil subtests, suitable for administration for either individuals or groups. Each subtest is timed and the entire series takes 107 minutes to complete. Scoring may be done manually or by machine.

Source from which Measure may be Obtained: CTB/McGraw-Hill, Del Monte Research Park, Monterey, California 93940

Description: The aptitude tests are available in separate booklets for each subtest. A subject may take the tests singly or in any combination, but the value of this battery lies in administering the entire series for this will yield a total profile. The uses of the test extend to vocational counseling of high school and college students and adults, as well as selection and placement of personnel. The subtests are: personal-social with forty-five items timed for twenty minutes; mechanical with sixty items timed for twenty minutes; general sales with forty-five items timed for twenty minutes; clerical routine with sixty items timed for twelve minutes; computational with forty-five items timed for fifteen minutes; and scientific with forty-five items timed for twenty minutes. It is well to note that the aptitude tests are most valuable when used in conjunction with a vocational interest inventory. Raw scores may be converted to percentile rank by using the tables provided in the manual.

Norms: Norms are based on over seven thousand students in grades 9 through 13, geographically spread throughout the United States; 85 percent of the sample was Caucasion, the remainder was Mexican, Negro, and other. The norms are divided by sex and grade level for each of the six subtests.

Validity and Reliability: Numerous tests were in the validity studies, including the Differential Aptitude Tests (DAT) — verbal reasoning scale — which yielded a correlation value of .61 for fifty females and of .61 for thirty-nine males. Also reported is the relationship of the Aptitude Tests for Occupations with the Science Research Associates Mechanical Knowledge subtests of spatial relations and mechanical aptitude, as well as with the DAT abstract reasoning, clerical, and numerical ability subtests. Correlation values generally ranged from .40 to .80 for groups varying in size from thirty to fifty students. The majority of the studies indicate a high degree of relationship exists for the Aptitude Tests for Occupations with the well-known aptitude and achievement tests used as a criterion.

Reliability coefficients for five subtests, computed by Kuder-Richardson formula on a sample of 1,847 male subjects in grades 9 to 13, ranged from .79 for mechanical sales to .91 for computational. The only subtest not computed by K-R was clerical routine, which yielded a test retest reliability of .88 on one hundred males in each grade level. On a sample of 1,721 female subjects in grades 9 to 13, reliability coefficients for five subtests computed by K-R were found to range from .72 for mechanical to .85 for general sales. Test retest, on five hundred females in grades 9 to 13, yielded a total reliability of .92 on the clerical routine subtest. The time interval for test retest reliability was not specified for the male and female samples.

BIBLIOGRAPHY:

Roeder, W. S.: *Manual: Aptitude Tests for Occupations*. Monterey, CTB/McGraw-Hill, 1951.

Brown-Carlsen Listening Comprehension Test

AUTHORS: James I. Brown and G. Robert Carlsen

VARIABLE: The Brown-Carlsen Listening Comprehension test was developed to assess the capability of individuals to understand spoken language.

TYPE OF MEASURE: The listening test is administered orally to either individuals or groups. It is untimed and typically takes fifty minutes to complete. Scoring may be done manually with the use of a key or by machine.

SOURCE FROM WHICH MEASURE MAY BE OBTAINED: Harcourt Brace Jovanovich, 757 Third Avenue, New York, New York 10017

DESCRIPTION: The listening comprehension test provides an assessment of the subject's ability to assimilate spoken symbols in a face-to-face speaker situation, based on the fact that oral and visual cues, as well as aural information, are available. The test is available in two parallel forms, Am and Bm. Each includes seventy-six test items, grouped into five subtests: immediate recall which measures one's ability to remember information long enough to answer subsequent questions about it; following directions which assesses one's ability to follow oral instructions; recognizing transitions which measures one's knowledge of the purpose of transitional words or phrases included within sentences; recognizing word meanings which is a vocabulary measure of words in context; and lecture comprehension which measures one's capability to abstract details, ideas, and inferences from spoken words. The unusual method of administration demands that the examiner be in complete control of the class, therefore size might be limited. Any subject with a hearing problem should be seated in order to maximize his or her hearing. Application of the listening comprehension test extends to its use as a diagnostic tool in identifying those subject's, at both high school and college levels, whose grades reflect specific difficulty other than lack of either study skills or aptitude, but rather in this case listening comprehension.

Norms: The Listening Comprehension Test — Form Am was standardized on a sample of 800 students in high schools with a wide geographical base, and on 300 college freshmen. The samples were drawn and tested in 1952. Norms are available for the high school into college ages, in both standard scores and percentiles, for the total test score.

Validity and Reliability: Extensive validity data is reported. High correlation values for the Listening Comprehension Test with the California Test of Mental Maturity — Advanced Form, ranged from .67 to .78; with the ACE Psychological Exam, ranged from .29 to .43; and with the Termen McNemer Test of Mental Ability, ranged from .70 to .74, all on varied samples ranging from 52 to 150 high school and college students. Also, validity evidence is reported with the Nelson-Denny Reading Test and other reading comprehension measures. In addition, correlation of high school rank in class with the Listening Comprehension Test scores yielded values ranging from .21 to .29, for two different groups of 138 subjects each.

Split half reliability methods yielded correlations ranging from .85 to .86 for three groups of tenth graders. Six studies of test retest reliability with alternate forms yielded a median correlation estimate of .78; time period not specified.

Bibliography:

Brown, J. I. and Carlsen, G. R.: *Brown-Carlsen Listening Comprehension Test. Manual of Directions: Forms Am and Bm.* New York, Harcourt Brace Jovanovich, 1955.

California Short-Form Test of Mental Maturity — Level 5

Authors: Elizabeth T. Sullivan, Willis W. Clark, and Ernest W. Tiegs

Variable: The California Short Form Test of Mental Maturity provides a measure of those capabilities basic to the learning process.

Type of Measure: The test of mental maturity is a battery of seven paper and pencil subtests. Each subtest is individually timed, and the entire series takes fifty-one minutes to complete. Scoring may be done manually or by machine.

Source from which Measure may be Obtained: CTB/McGraw-Hill, Del Monte Research Park, Monterey, California 93940.

Description: The Test of Mental Maturity includes seven subtests, each with a different assessment goal. Subtests numbered one through four comprise the non-language section of the series in which minimal verbal skills are needed to deal with the material presented. The items ask the subject to respond on a visual level to material dealing with logical analysis of abstract relationships. Subtests five through seven comprise the language section. These subtests measure the capacity of the subject to understand verbal and numerical concepts. Sixty items are contained in each of the sections, both the non-language and language. The seven subtests are structured over four factors, including logical reasoning in which inductive or deductive reasoning is used, numerical reasoning which requires the subject to use reasoning in determining quantitative relationships, verbal concepts in which the subject's capacity of verbal comprehension is assessed, and memory in which the subject's capacity to remember, based on presented material, is assessed. The profile yielded by the test of mental maturity is useful as an aid to the counselor or teacher in assessing a subject's mental capabilities. Its application also extends to prescriptions of appropriate instructional or training programs, as well as the selection and placement of employees.

Norms: Subjects numbering 38,793 from high schools and colleges across seven geographical regions were used to derive the scaling and norms for the 1963 revision of this test, including division by chronological age; the norms are based on deviation units.

Validity and Reliability: Extensive validity studies have been carried out correlating the Test of Mental Maturity with the Otis Gamma, Henmon-Nelson, School and College Ability Test, and California Analogies and Reasoning Test, at grade 12 level. Significant correlation values range from .70 for the Henmon-Nelson to .86 for the Otis Gamma. Extensive data is also provided establishing a significant relationship between the Test of Mental Maturity and the Stanford-Binet Intelligence Scale — Form L-M, 1960 revision.

Reliability coefficients for level 5 of the Test of Mental Maturity, computed by Kuder-Richardson formula 21, were .93 for the total score and between .56 and .87 for five subtest variables. The language and non-language reliability values reported were .91 and .86, respectively. Also reported are test retest reliability coefficients.

Bibliography:

Buros, O. K.: Test Number 337.

California Test Bureau, A Division of McGraw-Hill Book Company: *Technical Report on the California Test of Mental Maturity Series, 1963 Revision.* Monterey, Author, 1965.

Sullivan, E. T., Clark, W. W., and Tiegs, E. W.: *Examiner's Manual: California Short-Form Test of Mental Maturity.* Monterey, CTB/McGraw-Hill, 1963.

Cooperative Academic Ability Test

Author: Cooperative Test Division, Education Testing Service

Variable: The Cooperative Academic Ability Test (AAT) obtains estimates of verbal and mathematical capabilities for advanced secondary school students.

Type of Measure: The AAT is a paper and pencil test, suitable for administration to either individuals or groups. It is timed at exactly forty minutes. Scoring may be done manually or by machine.

Source from which Measure may be Obtained: Educational Testing Service, Cooperative Test Division, Princeton, New Jersey 08540.

Description: The AAT measures skills in dealing with specific kinds of verbal and mathematical material and is implicitly related to school achievement, rather than to assessment of native intelligence. Although the test is timed, it is considered one of power rather than speed. The tasks in the AAT do not generally overlap activities found in a school program, and thus responses are not likely to be based primarily on rote memory. The AAT is divided into two parts, verbal and mathematical. There are fifty items in each part. Verbal items are presented as analogies to which the subject responds by indicating a like analogy from a choice of four alternatives. The mathematical items are quite different from those in any other major published test. Each item presents two possibilities, one in Column A and one in Column B, to which the subject responds by indicating one of four alternatives. The AAT may be used effectively as a predictive tool in assessing a subject's success at the college level. Raw scores may be converted to percentile ranks or standard scores.

Norms: Normative data is based on the mid-year performance of a representative group of high school seniors with two common characteristics: they all intended to go to college, and they were all enrolled in high schools which normally send 75 percent or more of their graduates to college. More specific norm information has been developed by varied educational organizations, such as the Educational Records Bureau.

Validity and Reliability: Validity coefficients of .52, .51, and .56 were obtained for AAT verbal, mathematical, and total scores, respectively, when correlated with class rank for 518 students in the norm sample. These may be compared to correlations of .28 to .64, reported by Traxler (1964), for AAT verbal and mathematical scores with grades obtained in ninth and tenth grade English and mathematics. Verbal and mathematical scores on the Scholastic Aptitude Test of the College Entrance Examination Board were available for 244 of the 568 students in the norm sample, and correlation values of these with the verbal and mathematical scores of the AAT were found to be .83 and .86, respectively. For small samples of twelfth grade pupils in two independent schools, Traxler found somewhat lower correlations, ranging from

.52 to .81, based on scores of the SAT taken in the junior year.

Internal consistency reliability coefficients, using Kuder-Richardson formula 20, yielded a correlation value of .94 taken from the norm group. Likewise, reliability for the verbal and mathematical subtests was found to be .88 and .92, respectively.

Bibliography:

Buros, O. K.: Test Number 346.

Cooperative Test Division, Educational Testing Service: *Cooperative Academic Ability Test Handbook.* Princeton, New Jersey and Berkeley, California, Author, 1964.

Traxler, A. E.: *The new Cooperative Academic Aptitude Test compared with the American Council Psychological Examination.* Educ. Rec. Bull. No. 85, 1964, 62.

Traxler, A. E.: *The new Cooperative Academic Aptitude Test compared with the American Council Psychological Examination.* Educ. Rec. Bull. No. 85, 1964, 63.

Cooperative School and College Ability Tests — Level U

Author: Cooperative Test Division, Educational Testing Service

Variable: The School and College Ability Tests (SCAT) assess the capabilities of a subject in the verbal and quantitative areas.

Type of Measure: The SCAT is a paper and pencil test, suitable for administration to either individuals or groups. An administrator who is totally familiar with the test booklet and answer sheet should give the test, and additional proctors are desirable if the number of examinees is large. The SCAT is timed at seventy minutes. Scoring may be done manually with the use of a key or by IBM machine.

Source from which Measure may be Obtained: Educational Testing Service, Cooperative Test Division, Princeton, New Jersey 08540

Description: The SCAT — Level U is designed primarily for subjects at the college sophomore level or above. It provides the "top" to the SCAT series, which extends down into high school and the lower grades. The levels of the SCAT provide useful information to indicate the potential of academic success. Level U was evolved to aid counselors in the decision-making process for students in the last two years of college, to aid admissions offices in determining the potential of junior-college students applying for upper level positions in colleges and universities, and to help guide students toward vocational and academic goals. The format of SCAT — Level U includes Part I, sentence understanding, which contains thirty items timed for fifteen minutes; Part II, insightful computation, which contains twenty-five items timed for twenty minutes; Part III, word understanding, which contains thirty items timed for ten minutes; and Part IV, mathematical reasoning, which contains twenty-five items timed for twenty-five minutes. Three scores may be obtained, including verbal which is equal to Part I plus Part III; quantitative, which is equal to Part II plus Part IV; and a total score. The manual provides tables which will convert raw scores into a corresponding SCAT score; this makes possible direct comparisons of scores obtained on different forms and levels of the SCAT.

Norms: National samples of college students at the freshmen, sophomore, junior, and senior levels are available separately by grade level. Junior-senior groups ranged in size from 1,378 to 1,419 students in more than sixty colleges. Freshmen and sophomore norms are available from the *Cooperative School and College Ability Tests Manual for Interpreting Scores* (1957).

Validity and Reliability: Correlation studies reported estimated values of from .75 to .89 for SCAT forms 1C and 2A (earlier forms of the SCAT) with the American Council on Education Psychological Examination. Also, correlations of the SCAT with the Scholastic Aptitude Test of the Educational Testing Service, verbal and mathematical scores, yielded significant values ranging from .78 to .86. The latter study was carried out on over five hundred students. Conversion tables are also provided between the U forms of the SCAT and the Graduate Record Examinations (a test widely used at the same level as the SCAT).

The reliability coefficients, computed by Kuder-Richardson formula 20, were found to be .95 for form UA and .95 for form UB for the total score; .92 and .92 for forms UA and UB verbal scores; and .92 and .94 for forms UA and UB, respectively, quantitative scores. These were computed on a norm sample.

Bibliography:

Buros, O. K.: Test Number 347.

Cooperative Test Division, Educational Testing Service: *Cooperative School and College Ability Tests Handbook-Level U*. Princeton, Author, 1963.

______ : *Cooperative School and College Ability Tests, Manual for Interpreting Scores*. Princeton, Author, 1957.

______ : *SCAT Technical Report*. Princeton, Author, 1957.

Differential Aptitude Tests — Forms S and T

Authors: George K. Bennett, Harold G. Seashore, and Alexander G. Wesman

Variable: The Differential Aptitude Tests (DAT) measure abilities important in school and job success.

Type of Measure: The DAT is a battery of eight paper and pencil subtests, suitable for administration to either individuals or groups. Each subtest is individually timed and the entire series takes two hours to complete. Scoring may be done manually or by machine.

Source from which Measure may be Obtained: The Psychological Corporation, 304 E. 45th Street, New York, New York 10017.

Description: The DAT is useful both in assisting students in the selection of courses for high school or college and in the selection of occupations to explore as career possibilities. The subtests include verbal reasoning, numerical ability, abstract reasoning, clerical speed and accuracy, mechanical reasoning, space relations, spelling, and language usage. Time limits range from six to thirty minutes per subtest. The total of the verbal reasoning and numerical ability subtests provides an indication of the subject's general scholastic aptitude; therefore, the DAT yields a total of nine scores. It is well to note here that revisions have been made in some of the subtests to reduce "culture" loadings, to which minority groups might object, such as in the verbal reasoning subtest. Another asset of the DAT is that in addition to the one-booklet edition which includes all of the subtests, there is an edition of Form T which is printed in eight separate booklets, for those who prefer to administer only selected tests.

Norms: Forms S and T of the DAT were standardized in the fall of 1972 on a sample of over sixty thousand students in grades 8 through 12, in schools over a wide geographic spread. Schools included public and parochial systems with varying enrollments and socioeconomic status. Minority students are appropriately represented in the sample. Spring and fall norms are provided for students in grades 8 through 11; fall norms are provided for grade 12. Norms are presented in percentiles as well as stanines and separately for men and women in order to reflect changes and differences in capabilities. Finally, percentile ranges are provided for all subtests and combinations of subtests.

Validity and Reliability: Extensive validity studies have been carried out on the earlier forms of the DAT (L and M). These studies included the prediction of course grades for English and science, based on the subtests of the DAT, by sex. These results indicate correlation values ranging from .30 to .70, depending on subtest and sex and school curriculum of the subjects. Very extensive correlation tables are provided for widely varying school samples, showing the relationship between English, mathematics, and other school grades and subtests of the DAT. Many of these correlation values are significant.

Reliability values are reported between Forms S and T, by grade and sex of student. Correlations between the two forms vary from .79 to .93 over ten groups tested. Also reported are subtest reliabilities, determined by odd-even methods, for each sex and grade levels from 8 to 12.

Bibliography:

Bennett, G. K., Seashore, H. G., and Wesman, A. G.: *Fourth Edition Manual for the Differential Aptitude Tests — Forms L and M.* New York, The

Psychological Corporation, 1963.
———, ———, ———: *Forms S and T — Differential Aptitude Tests, Administrator's Handbook*. New York, The Psychological Corporation, 1973.
Buros, O. K.: Test number 673.

Full Range Picture Vocabulary

Author: Robert B. Ammons

Variable: The Full-Range Picture Vocabulary (FRPV) attempts to assess an individual's intelligence.

Type of Measure: The FRPV is an oral-visual test, most suitably administered in an individual situation. The test is untimed. Scoring is done by hand at the time of administration.

Source from which Measure may be Obtained: Psychological Test Specialists, Box 1441, Missoula, Montana 59801.

Description: The FRPV is available in two forms, A and B. It consists of sixteen plates, each with four pictures on it. The subject is given a stimulus word to which he or she responds by indicating one picture on the plate. Originally designed to yield an estimate of general intelligence, the FRPV has proven useful in the clinical screening of rehabilitative patients having either physical and/or psychiatric handicaps, especially in circumstances where the subject has limited comprehension or communication. It is interesting to note that this test might also be a useful tool in assessing personality and vocational abilities, as it serves as a guide toward more selective I.Q. measures. Raw scores are converted into I.Q. equivalents.

Norms: Norms tables are based on a general white population, at various age levels from sixteen and one-half years through the adult range. The total sample consisted of 589 subjects. No other descriptive information is provided.

Validity and Reliability: Several studies have been carried out. One involved the correlation of the FRVP with the total score from the Wechsler Adult Intelligence Scale for forty male and female psychiatric patients and yielded significant values of .84 and .88 for forms A and B, respectively. A second study yielded similar correlation values between the same instruments for clients in a vocational rehabilitation center of a county hospital.

The only reliability data provided is a correlation value of .95 between Forms A and B. No other descriptive data is indicated.

Bibliography:

Ammons, R. B.: *Provisional Manual for the Full-Range Picture Vocabulary Test. Missoula, Psychological Test Specialists, 1949-1950.*

______ , and Huth, R. W.: The Full-Range Picture Vocabulary Test: I. Preliminary scale. *J. Psychol., 28*:51-64, 1949.

______ , and Rachiele, L. D.: The Full-Range Picture Vocabulary Test: II. Selection of items for final scales. *Educ. Psychol. Measmt, 10*:307-319, 1950.

______ , and Holmes, J. C.: The Full-Range Picture Vocabulary Test: III. Results for a preschool-age population. *Child Develpm., 20*:5-14, 1949.

______ , Arnold, P. R., and Herrman, R. S.: The Full-Range Picture Vocabulary Test: IV. Results for a white school population. *J. Clin, Psychol., 6*:164-169, 1950.

______ , Larson, W. L., and Shearn, C. R.: The Full-Range Picture Vocabulary Test: V. Results for an adult population. *J. Consult. Psychol., 14*:150-155, 1950.

______ , and Manahan, N.: The Full-Range Picture Vocabulary Test: VI. Results for a rural population. *J. Educ. Res., 44*:14-21, 1950.

______ , and Aguero, A.: The Full-Range Picture Vocabulary Test: VII. Results for a Spanish-American school-age population. *J. Soc. Psychol., 32*:3-10, 1950.

Coppinger, N. W. and Ammons, R. B.: The Full-Range Picture Vocabulary Test: VIII. A normative study of Negro children. *J. Clin. Psychol., 8*:136-140, 1952.

The user can either obtain these through his or her own library, or order a set from Psychological Test Specialists, Box 1441, Missoula, Montana 59801, remitting $2.75.

International Primary Factors Test Battery

Author: Wolfgang O. Horn

Variable: The International Primary Factors Test Battery (IPF) is a wide-ranging instrument designed to assess mental capabilities.

Type of Measure: The IPF is a battery of sixteen paper and pencil subtests, suitable for administration to either individuals or groups. Each subtest is individually timed, and the entire series takes about forty-five minutes to complete. Scoring may be done manually or by machine.

Source from which Measure may be Obtained: International Tests, Inc., Box 634, Stevens Point, Wisconsin 54481.

Description: The use of the IPF is found in the guiding principals enumerated by the author in the development of the battery. The results of administering these instruments will allow assessment of specific mental abilities, while being sensitive to the effects of neurological impairments, age, and other clinical symptoms. The IPF consists of sixteen subtests, including vocabulary, word fluency, memory — words, memory — numbers, memory — designs, mazes, reasoning — designs, reasoning — letters and numbers, hidden designs, space, mutilated pictures, mutilated words, spelling, addition, comparison — words, and comparison — numbers. These subtests were evolved over many years of concentrated effort to adhere to basic and fundamental principles of test development. A model entitled *The Structure of Abilities Model* provides a theoretical and practical focus for the IPF.

Norms: Norms are based on recent studies in the midwest. The sample consisted of students in various high schools and colleges; most were white (Mexican and black equalled less than 1 percent). The norms tables include 100 occupational groups in professions and services, such as mathematicians, engineers, architects, programmers, physicians, dentists, among others; and in business, such as accounting majors, business majors, underwriters, marketing majors, managers (industry), accountants and auditors, claims adjusters, among others; and in industry and crafts, such as electronic technicians, chemical and metallurgical technologists, air traffic control specialists, illustrators, draftsmen, clothes designers, among others. Norms are presented in a standard score system, and with a mean of fifty and a standard deviation of ten.

Validity and Reliability: A value of .71 was found in correlating the weighted IPF result with gradepoint averages for 129 college students. Correlations of the IPF total or subtest scores with the School and College Ability Test yielded significant values ranging from .51 to .77 on the aptitude section of the SCAT and from .42 to .79 on the achievement sections of the STEP. Construct validity studies used factor analysis to yield twelve major factors, corresponding closely to the sixteen subtests.

The split-half method yielded reliability values ranging from .70 to .94 for the sixteen subtests, based on administration to 800 students in elementary and high schools.

Bibliography:

Horn, W. O.: *Manual A: International Primary Factors Test Battery*. Stevens Point, International Tests, Inc., 1973.

______: *Manual B: International Primary Factors Test Battery*. Stevens Point, International Tests, Inc., 1973.

Multiple Aptitude Tests

Authors: David Segel and Evelyn Raskin

Variable: The Multiple Aptitude Tests (MAT) provide a battery of broad-based assessment devices to measure aptitude patterns of individuals.

Type of Measure: The MAT is a battery of nine paper and pencil subtests, suitable for administration to either individuals or groups. Each subtest is individually timed, and the entire series takes about three hours to complete. Scoring may be done manually or by machine.

Source from which Measure may be Obtained: CTB/McGraw-Hill, Del Monte Research Park, Monterey, California 93940.

Description: The MAT is designed to yield specific information regarding an individual's strengths and weaknesses in the aptitudes measured by any of the subtests. The subtests are structured over four factors, including Factor I, verbal comprehension, which is assessed through the word meaning and paragraph meaning subtests; Factor II, perceptual speed, which is assessed through the language usage and routine clerical facility subtests; Factor III, numerical reasoning, which is assessed by the arithmetic reasoning and arithmetic computation subtests; and Factor IV, spatial visualization, which is assessed through applied science and mechanics, spatial relations — two dimensions, and spatial relations — three dimensions subtests. The four factors incorporated in the subtests provide a profile intended to help subjects understand their aptitudes in order that decisions relative to furthering education or choosing a suitable occupation can be properly directed in light of strengths and weaknesses in certain areas.

Norms: The normative group consisted of 11,004 males and females, representing the major geographic areas in the United States. Each examinee took all nine subtests. Norms tables are reported in percentiles and standard scores for males and females separately, from grades 7 to 13, for subtest scores and factor scores.

Validity and Reliability: Validity data is extensive at the construct, concurrent, and predictive levels. Included are the average scores on each subtest and standard deviations for forty-two occupational groups, including engineers, salesmen, skilled and unskilled workers, office and maintenance supervisors, among others. Extensive studies for different grade levels evidence relationship between the MAT test scores and the following tests: Minnesota Clerical Test — Numbers One and Two; Differential Aptitude Tests of clerical speed and accuracy, numerical ability, spelling, and sentences; California Achievement Test — Language; among others, correlation values ranged from .60 to .80 for groups varying in size from twenty-five to fifty, for correlations of the MAT subtests with the various criterion tests.

Reliability coefficients, generally computed by Kuder-Richardson formula 21, on a sample of male students in grade 13 yielded values ranging from .79 for paragraph meaning to .92 for arithmetic computation. Similar information is reported for females, as well as for other grade levels. The number of cases generally exceeds five hundred subjects.

Bibliography:

California Test Bureau: *Technical Report on the Multiple Aptitude Tests.* Monterey, CTB/McGraw-Hill, 1959.

Segel, D. and Raskin, E.: *Manual: Multiple Aptitude Tests.* Monterey, CTB/McGraw-Hill, 1959.

Ohio Classification Test

Authors: Dewitt E. Sell, Robert W. Scollay, and Leroy N. Vernon

Variable: The OCT is a general measure of intellectual abilities.

Type of Measure: The Ohio Classification Test (OCT) is a paper and pencil device, suitable for administration to either individuals or groups. There are four subtests, each of which is timed; the entire series takes fourteen and one-half minutes to complete. Scoring is done by hand with the use of a key.

Source from which Measure may be Obtained: Psychometric Affiliates, P.O. Box 3167, Munster, Indiana 46321.

Description: The OCT is a test of general intelligence with its emphasis on power. It is broken down into four subtests including: block counting which assesses both spatial perception and reasoning capacity; digit-symbol which measures perception and associative learning speed; number series which assesses number facility and reasoning; and memory span which measures apperception and memory. Collectively, the subtests tap at least five of the seven primary mental abilities as analyzed by Thurstone (1938). The OCT provides an estimate of the subject's mental capabilities and is suitable for use with general adult populations, such as in industry, as well as with prison inmates.

Norms: Experimental work utilized 550 prison case subjects for the normative sample. The demographic characteristics of the group are male and female, black and white, with age ranges from seventeen to thirty years and a mean age of twenty-three. Additional norms are available for male and female factory workers, sales and management applicants, middle management men, graduate engineers, and advanced science students.

Validity and Reliability: Validity studies established the following correlations: .79 with the Wechsler-Bellevue Tests (an earlier form of the Wechsler Adult Intelligence Scale), for 155 penal inmates; .73 with the Revised Beta, for 90 penal inmates; .64 with the Revised Army Alpha, for 160 industrial job applicants; among others. Additional validity evidence is presented showing the relationship of years of school completed to the mean OCT scores, for over one hundred subjects. Finally, merit ranking by supervisors and hourly earnings of sales and management personnel and machine operators is provided, showing the validity of the OCT.

Test retest yielded a reliability coefficient of .87, based on 138 subjects selected at random from the standardization sample. The time interval was not specified. A second reliability value is reported to be .93; however, descriptive information, about the nature of the reliability procedure and sample upon which it was based, is not stated in the manual.

Bibliography:

Sell, D. E., Scollay, R. W. and Vernon, L. N.: *Manual: Ohio Classification Test.* Munster, Psychometric Affiliates, 1957.

Thurstone, L. L.: *Primary Mental Abilities.* Chicago, University of Chicago Press, 1938.

Otis Quick-Scoring Mental Ability Tests — Gamma Test

Author: Arthur S. Otis

Variable: The Otis Quick-Scoring Mental Ability Tests assess an individual's mental capability.

Type of Measure: The Otis is a paper and pencil test, suitable for administration to either individuals or groups. It is timed for thirty minutes. Scoring may be done manually with the use of an overlay stencil or by IBM machine.

Source from which Measure may be Obtained: Harcourt Brace Jovanovich, 757 Third Avenue, New York, New York 10017.

Description: The Otis is designed to assess the effect that an individual's mental capability has had in assisting him or her to gain knowledge and mental skill. The Gamma test is designed for use with subjects at the high school and college levels and is available in six parallel forms, C and D (for manual scoring only) and Am, Bm, Em, and Fm (for manual or machine scoring). Although the test items present an appearance of being measures of school achievement, they were selected to reflect thinking capability rather than the effect of school knowledge.

Norms: Normative data for Gamma forms Am and Bm were determined through an equating process for students taking the Otis-Gamma and the Otis Higher Examination; for students taking the Otis-Gamma and the Otis-Beta; and for students taking the Otis-Gamma and the Pintner Advanced General Ability Test. The norms for forms Em and Fm are derived from comparing total score on forms Em and Fm with that of form Am. Norms are presented for combined sex and age from eleven to eighteen and over and are representative of the country as a whole.

Validity and Reliability: The validity of each item of the Otis Higher Examination, from which the items on forms Am and Bm of the Gamma were taken, was determined through biserial correlation of each item, with the total test score. The scores of 100 adults of each sex were used in the experiment; the coefficients for the items were, without exception, positive for both sexes, having a median value of .61.

> "This experiment indicates that all the items of the Higher Examination have real validity in a mental ability test." (p. 96, manual)

Split-half reliability coefficients for form Am were found to be .90, .91, and .85 for grades 10, 11, and 12 respectively. Split-half coefficients for form Em were found to be .92, .91, and .92 for grades 10, 11, and 12 respectively. Finally, a corrected split-half reliability coefficient of .88 for form Em was found on a sample of 489 college freshmen.

Bibliography:

Buros, O. K.: Test number 370 (Reference Only)

Otis, A. S.: *Otis Quick-Scoring Mental Ability Tests, Manual of Directions for Gamma Test.* New York, Harcourt Brace Jovanovich, Inc., 1954.

Proverbs Test

Author: Donald R. Gorham

Variable: The Proverbs Test measures abstract verbal reasoning and qualitative intellectual functioning.

Type of Measure: This is a paper and pencil test, suitable for administration to either individuals or groups. It is untimed and, depending on whether it is individually or group administered, may take anywhere from ten to forty minutes to complete. Scoring may be done manually with either a scoring card, in the case of individuals, or a stencil, in the case of groups.

Source from which Measure may be Obtained: Psychological Test Specialists, Box 1441, Missoula, Montana 59801.

Description: The Proverbs Test is based on the natural appeal of proverbs to normal, as well as mentally disturbed, subjects in a wide age range. It measures verbal comprehension, specifically in the area of abstraction. Uses of the test include individual clinical assessments, research, and screening and survey. It has also found a value in the counseling of subjects with high level intelligence. There are two different methods of administration of the Proverbs Test. Method A includes forms I, II, and III which consist of twelve items to which the subject responds by writing in, under a given proverb, what he or she thinks that saying means; these three forms are used for individual administrations only. Method B includes the Best Answer Form (multiple choice) which is used for group administrations and consists of forty multiple choice items, all scaled for difficulty.

Norms: The standardization samples included 1,345 children and adults. Adult norms are based on Air Force basic airmen, high school and college students (all levels), plus clinical groups of schizophrenics and organic patients, for both the individual and group forms of the test.

Validity and Reliability: Correlation values were found to be .61 with the Wechsler Adult Intelligence Scale similarities subtest and .56 with the full Wechsler scale, for the clinical form I on eighty-six subjects. Also, a correlation value of .54 was found for the combined clinical forms of the Proverbs Test with the Otis I.Q., based on 149 high school students. Correlating form I with the Wechsler Adult Intelligence Scale, based on forty-eight high school students, yielded values of .62 for comprehension, .60 for the total verbal scale, .59 for information, .58 for total scale, .56 for digits span, and .53 for similarities.

Intercorrelations between forms I, II, and III, based on 181 subjects including students in grades 10, 11, and 12 and Air Force enlistees, yielded reliability coefficients of .79 when one form was used, .88 when two forms were used, and .92 when all three forms were combined. The split-half method yielded a reliability coefficient of .88, based on 366 Air Force enlistees. Test retest reliabilities over a one-week interval for thirty-three chronic schizophrenic patients were found to be .94 for the group form and .93 for the individual form.

Bibliography:

Benjamin, J. D.: A method for distinguishing and evaluating formal thinking disorders in schizophrenia. In J. S. Kasanin (Ed.): *Language and Thought in Schizophrenia*. Berkeley, University of California Press, 1944.

French, J. W.: The description of aptitude and achievement tests in terms of rotated factors. *Psychometric Monographs*, No. 5, 1951.

Fruchter, B.: The factorial content of the Airman Classification Battery. Research Bulletin, 49-1, 1949. San Antonio, Lackland Air Force Base.

Gorham, D. R.: *Clinical manual for the Proverbs Test*. Louisville, Psychological Test Specialists, 1956.

______ : A progress report on the Proverbs Test. Paper read at Southwest Psychological Association, Dallas, 1956.

______ : A proverbs test for clinical and experimental use. *Psychological Reports*, Monograph Supplement 1, 1956.

Pounders, C. J.: A study of the Proverbs Test as a measure of the abstract level of concept formation. Unpublished M. A. thesis, Baylor University, 1956.

Purdue Non-Language Personnel Test

Author: Joseph Tiffin

Variable: The Purdue Non-Language Personnel Test is designed to measure mental ability.

Type of Measure: The non-language test is a paper and pencil device, suitable for administration to either individuals or groups. It is timed for ten minutes. Scoring is done by hand with the use of a stencil.

Source from which Measure may be Obtained: University Book Store, 360 State Street, West Lafayette, Indiana 47906.

Description: The non-language test is available in two parallel forms, A-S and B-S, each consisting of twenty-four items. Each item includes five geometric figures; the subject responds by crossing out that figure which appears different from the other four. It is interesting to note that since the test is non-language in construction, its application extends to subjects of most any cultural or educational background. The test is useful in measuring the level of an individual's mental ability and can be utilized in the assessment of present employees or in the selection of potential employees without discrimination towards position to be held, such as supervisory ability versus clerical ability.

Norms: Tentative norms are based on three groups: 67 supervisory personnel at four midwestern manufacturing companies, 182 die-setter applicants at a midwestern company, and 110 candidates for foreman or supervisor job at a midwestern company. It is advisable for users to establish their own sets of norms.

Validity and Reliability: Correlation values ranging from .64 to .72, for 150 job applicants, were found for the Purdue Non-Language Personnel Test forms A-S and B-S with the Purdue Clerical Adaptability Test. This latter instrument is a standard mental abilities device requiring reading skills. Also reported are non-language test scores for white and Negro male and female samples who were rated as most or least effective in clerical stenographic positions. Differences in scores on the non-language test correlated significantly with most and least effective ratings and are reported for white females alone, white and Negro females, white and Negro males, and other groups.

A test with immediate retest reliability procedures, using

both forms A-S and B-S, yielded correlation values in the .80's for three groups of subjects; varing in size from 40 to 74.

Bibliography:

Buros, O. K.: Test number 377.

Tiffin, J.: *Purdue Non-Language Personnel Test, Preliminary Manual.* West Lafayette, University Book Store, 1969.

Shipley-Institute of Living Scale

Author: Walter C. Shipley

Variable: The Shipley-Institute of Living Scale (SILS) is designed to assess intellectual impairment.

Type of Measure: The SILS is a paper and pencil inventory, suitable for administration to either individuals or groups. There are two subtests, and each is timed for ten minutes. Scoring is done by hand.

Source from which Measure may be Obtained: Western Psychological Services, 12031 Wilshire Boulevard, Los Angeles, California 90025.

Description: The SILS is based on the clinical and experimental observation that mental deterioration is accompanied by discrepancies in measures of vocabulary and the capacity for abstract (conceptual) thinking. The scale consists of a vocabulary test and an abstract thinking test. Impairment is assessed by the discrepancy between the individual's subtest scores. Originally designed to assess mild degrees of intellectual impairment in normal individuals, it is not intended for use with persons who are obviously mentally disturbed or intellectually subnormal or who have language handicaps. Raw scores are converted to the Conceptual Quotient (C.Q.), which is the index of impairment, by using the table provided in the manual.

Norms: The SILS was standardized on 1,046 individuals which includes students ranging from the fourth grade through college level.

Validity and Reliability: No formal studies of validity are reported in the manual. Evidence reported shows differences in percentile scores of patients in private hospitals versus those in state hospitals, on the C.Q. scale.

Reliability coefficients, based on 322 army recruits, were found to be .87 for the vocabulary subtest, .89 for the abstraction subtest, and .92 for the two combined. A study by Shaw (1966) yielded test retest reliability values of .54 for vocabulary, .47 for abstraction, and .62 for the two combined; tests were administered over a three month interval for forty-three female subjects.

Bibliography:

Buros, O. K.: Test number 138.

Shaw, D. J.: The Reliability of the Shipley-Institute of Living Scale. *Journal of Clinical Psychology, 22*:441, 1966.

Shipley, W. C.: *Shipley-Institute of Living Scale for Measuring Intellectual Impairment, Manual of Directions, and Scoring Key.* Los Angeles, Western Psychological Services, 1946.

SRA Primary Mental Abilities — Adult

Authors: L. L. Thurstone and Thelma G. Thurstone

Variable: The SRA Primary Mental Abilities (PMA) tests are designed to provide both multifactored and general measures of intelligence.

Type of Measure: The PMA is a battery of four paper and pencil subtests, suitable for administration to either individuals or groups. Each subtest is individually timed, and the entire series takes thirty-four minutes.

Source from which Measure may be Obtained: Science Research Associates, 259 East Erie Street, Chicago, Illinois 60611.

Description: The PMA battery is directed at assessing five primary mental abilities: verbal meaning, number facility, reasoning, perceptual speed, and spatial relations. These abilities are constructed within four subtests: verbal meaning, number facility, spatial relations, and reasoning which includes subsections on letter series, word grouping, and number series. The profile yielded by the PMA is a useful tool which aids counselors and teachers in the assessment and evaluation of the individual differences in behavior and performance among subjects who appear to be of comparable intelligence. Use extends to academic assessment of potential students and/or applicants in a wide variety of occupational areas. Its relatively short administration time allows for a quick aptitude measurement.

Norms: The standardization sample was comprised of 32,393 students, ranging in levels from kindergarten through grade 12, representing thirty-nine school systems in five major regions of the United States. In grades 10 through 12, over seven thousand students were included in the norm group. Students were from schools which were selected at random from the United States Health, Education, and Welfare document, *Directory of Public and Secondary Day Schools, 1958-59.*

Validity and Reliability: One validity study, based on a sample from one school including 200 subjects at each grade level, correlating PMA total scores with overall grade point averages, yielded values of .33 for grade 9, .32 for grade 10, .47 for grade 11, and .30 for grade 12. Other validity studies based on course grades found, for example, a correlation value of .39 for the verbal meaning subscore with English grades in school for 821 students in grades 9 through 12. Correlations of the PMA with the Kuhlman Anderson and the Iowa Test of Basic Skills are also reported.

Test retest reliability values, over a one week interval for groups ranging in size from twenty-seven to thirty-three subjects in grades 9 through 12, ranged from .84 to .94 for the total scores. Test retest, for the same groups over a four-week interval, yielded reliabilities ranging from .85 to .94 for the total score.

Bibliography:

Buros, O. K.: Test number 680.

Science Research Associates, Inc.: *SRA Primary Mental Abilities Technical Report.* Revised 1962. Chicago, Author, 1962.

Thurstone, L. L. and Thurstone, T. G.: *Examiner's Manual — IBM 805 Edition: Primary Mental Abilities for Grades 9-12.* Chicago, Science Research Associates, 1963.

Stanford-Ohwaki-Kohs Block Design Intelligence Test for the Blind

Authors: Richard M. Suinn and William L. Dauterman

Variable: The Stanford-Ohwaki-Kohs Block Design Intelligence Test for the Blind is a non-verbal performance measure for the blind.

Type of Measure: The block design test is a tactual device, most suitably administered in an individual situation. Time limits for each of the seventeen designs of the test vary with administration to functionally blind or partially sighted subjects. Scoring is done by hand at the time of administration.

Source from which Measure may be Obtained: Western Psychological Services, 12031 Wilshire Boulevard, Los Angeles, California 90025.

Description: This test was evolved from the Ohwaki-Kohs Tactile Block Design Intelligence Test for the Blind and should be administered only by a trained clinician. The block design test requires the subject to redo a design by assembling blocks. The stimulus designs are combinations of four different fabrics: flannel, silk, flax, and cotton with raised projection. Although eighteen blocks of fabric are provided in the test, the maximum number used for completion of any stimulus design is sixteen. The stimulus design is presented along with the blocks. Surfaces are covered with the differing fabrics so that designs can be duplicated by placing up to sixteen blocks in correct positions. In addition to a quantitative score, the observant administrator can obtain much valuable clinical data, including the subject's approach to solving the problems, desire to seek assistance, expressions relating to self regard, and emotional responses to the test. Raw scores may be converted to percentile ranks and I.Q. equivalents by using the tables provided in the manual.

Norms: The normative sample was comprised of 202 persons who met a criterion of being legally blind. All subjects had been blind for a minimum of one year. The subjects varied in distributions over wide geographical locations, age, employment status, educational achievement, visual characteristics, travel aid used, and cause of blindness.

Validity and Reliability: Significant correlation values for test scores with ratings of school achievement were found to range from .24 to .55. The relationship between intelligence and age is evidenced through a decrease in performance in the block design test with advancing age. This tends to confirm the construct of intelligence in this test, because it follows a generally expected pattern of performance in relation to age. Correlation values (eta's) were obtained for test scores with criterion of occupation, salary, and number of years employed, for four classes of blind subjects. However, none of the eta coefficients were significant although the values were in the expected direction. Significant relationships were established for test performance with braille reading ability, for partially sighted subjects.

Two test retest studies were carried out in Japan; one, conducted over a seventy-five day interval, resulted in a reliability coefficient of .85 (N = 33), and the other, conducted over a sixty day interval, resulted in a reliability coefficient of .71 (N = 46). Additional test retest studies yielded reliability coefficients of .90, .86, and .90, for an adult sample, (N = 51), a functionally blind sample (N = 32), and a partially blind sample (N = 19), respectively; these studies were done over a thirty-three day interval.

Bibliography:

Buros, O. K.: Test number 427.

Suinn, R. M. and Dauterman, W. L.: *Stanford-Ohwaki-Kohs Block Design Intelligence Test for the Blind — American Revision of the Ohwaki-Kohs Test, Manual.* Los Angeles, Western Psychological Services, 1966.

Thurstone Test of Mental Alertness

Authors: L. L. Thurstone and Thelma G. Thurstone

Variable: The Thurstone Test of Mental Alertness (TMA) is a test of general mental ability.

Type of Measure: The TMA is a paper and pencil test, suitable for administration to either individuals or groups. It is timed for twenty minutes. Scoring is done by hand with the use of a key.

Source from which Measure may be Obtained: Science Research Associates, 259 East Erie Street, Chicago, Illinois 60611.

Description: The TMA was developed to assess the ability of a person to obtain new knowledge and skills and apply them in solving problems, thereby measuring the subject's capability to answer those problems quickly as well as accurately. It has a wide range of uses, including counseling at the high school and college levels and selection and placement of personnel in all levels up to, and including, management positions. The test consists of 126 items covering four areas: arithmetic reasoning which involves solving word problems; number series which involves determining progressions of numbers in a series; same-opposite which involves finding a word with the same or the opposite meaning as the stimulus word; and definition which involves reading and understanding a definition well enough to indicate the letter of the word, rather than the word, that fits the definition. The TMA yields three scores: one of problem solving or quantitative ability, called the "Q" score; one of linguistic or verbal ability, called the "L" score; and the total score which is the total of Q and L. The TMA is available in two parallel forms, A and B.

Norms: Normative data collected in 1967 is available for both male and female, junior and senior high school students; college students; business personnel, including sales and insurance supervisors, retail store salespersons, managers of small retail stores, bank tellers, clerical workers, managers, and salaried office employees; sales representatives; accountants; typists; secretaries; unskilled labor; and others. The number of cases for each occupational and educational level varied from twenty to 900.

Validity and Reliability: Validity data using educational and industrial criteria is provided. Generally, correlations of TMA total test scores with school grades are high, ranging from .40 to .77, for varying groups of from 90 to 200 twelfth grade students. Industrial validity studies are extensive, having been performed on sales managers, bank tellers, and others. Significant correlations were found for ratings of individuals by their supervisors as good or poor workers with L, Q, and total scores on the TMA.

Test retest reliabilities, based on 140 twelfth grade students, range from .91 to .95 for the L and Q subscores of form A; the time interval was thirty days. Test retest reliabilities, based on 150 twelfth grade students, range from .84 to .96 for the L and Q subscores of form B; the time interval was one month.

BIBLIOGRAPHY:

Buros, O. K.: Test number 392.

Thurstone, L. L. and Thurstone, T. G.: *Thurstone Test of Mental Alertness, Examiner Manual.* Chicago, Science Research Associates, Inc., 1968.

The Verbal Power Test of Concept Equivalence

AUTHOR: E. Francesco

VARIABLE: The Verbal Power Test of Concept Equivalence (VPT) measures verbal ability or intelligence.

TYPE OF MEASURE: The VPT is a paper and pencil test, suitable for administration to either individuals or groups. It is untimed and typically takes eight minutes to complete. Scoring is done by hand with the use of a key.

SOURCE FROM WHICH MEASURE MAY BE OBTAINED: Western Psychological Services, Box 775, Beverly Hills, California 90213.

DESCRIPTION: The VPT is a brief measure of general verbal intelligence. It is available in two parallel forms, A and B, each consisting of seventy-five paired word items. The subject responds by indicating whether the two words in each set have similar or dissimilar meanings. The VPT is suitable for use with subjects of age fourteen through adulthood. It has a wide range of uses, including rapid assessment of general intelligence and verbal ability in schools, clinical situations, and industrial, business, and governmental settings.

NORMS: Norms are based on 1,096 subjects in five groups as follows: 320 Ivy League university sophomores, 142 Ivy League university seniors, 173 southwestern school of education freshmen, 261 eastern high school seniors, 200 east central unselected prisoners (sex not specified).

VALIDITY AND RELIABILITY: Correlating forms A and B of the

VPT with the Stanford Achievement Test yielded a value of .75. Correlating 200 male adult prisoners' scores on form A with total scores on the Wechsler Adult Intelligence Scale yielded a value of .62; for the same group of prisoners, correlation of the VPT with the Wide Range Achievement Test yielded a value of .69.

One reliability study, using a slightly longer test form, yielded a product-moment coefficient of .86 with forms A and B.

Bibliography:

Buros, O. K.: Test number 394.

Francesco, E.: *The Verbal Power Test of Concept Equivalence (VPT) Manual.* Beverly Hills, Western Psychological Services, 1963.

Watson-Glaser Critical Thinking Appraisal

Authors: Goodwin Watson and Edward M. Glaser

Variable: The Watson-Glaser Critical Thinking Appraisal assesses individuals' aptitude and knowledge, in addition to their capability in employing and applying these skills.

Type of Measure: The appraisal is a battery of five paper and pencil subtests, suitable for administration to either individuals or groups. It is untimed and typically takes fifty minutes to complete. Scoring may be done manually or by machine.

Source from which Measure may be Obtained: Harcourt Brace Jovanovich, 757 Third Avenue, New York, New York 10017.

Description: The appraisal is currently available in two parallel forms, Ym and Zm, each consisting of five subtests designed to measure different, though interdependent, aspects of critical thinking. The one hundred items of the test are distributed as follows: test 1, inference, consists of twenty items and samples one's ability to discriminate among degrees of truth or falsity of inferences drawn from given data; test 2, recognition of assumptions, consists of sixteen items and samples one's ability to recognize unstated assumptions taken for granted in given statements; test 3, deductions, consists of twenty-five items and samples one's ability to reason deductively from given statements, recognize relationships between propositions, and determine whether that which seems to be an implication is indeed such; test 4, interpretation, consists of twenty-four items and samples one's ability to weigh evidence and to distinguish between generalizations from data not warranted beyond a reasonable doubt and generalizations seemingly warranted beyond a reasonable doubt; test 5, evaluation of arguments, consists of fifteen items and samples one's ability to distinguish between arguments which are strong and relevant and those which are weak or irrelevant. The appraisal may be used as a measure of critical thinking achievement at the secondary school or college levels or in industrial and executive programs, where an attempt is made to develop critical thinking abilities; as a predictive instrument in certain occupations or instructional programs; as a diagnostic instrument in psychometric and clinical situations; or as a research tool to determine relationships between critical thinking abilities and other abilities.

Norms: Separate conversion tables are provided by form for each high school grade individually, for grades 9 through 12 combined, for liberal arts college freshmen, and for college senior women. Selected percentile ranks are based on results from 5,297 freshmen at fifteen liberal arts colleges in thirteen states and from a sample of 554 first semester senior women at ten Catholic liberal arts colleges for women in seven states. Additional norm group data is provided for various samples of manufacturing and service personnel at management and executive levels for an earlier edition, form Am, of the test. Percentile ranks and stanines are also provided, based on a sample of 20,312 high school students in grades 9, 10, 11, and 12 at fourteen school systems in thirteen states.

Validity and Reliability: Significant values were obtained when the critical thinking appraisal raw scores were correlated with the raw scores of the Otis Mental Ability Test — Gamma for groups of high school and college students varying in size from 500 to 20,000. Additional studies yielded correlation values of .68 with the California Test of Mental Maturity for 169 high school students and of .65 with the

Quick-Word Test — Level L — Form Am for 20,000 high school students. Finally, a correlation value of .55 for forty-nine managers and executives was obtained with the Miller Analogies — Form H, and a value of .41 for the total score of the Wechsler Adult Intelligence Scale was obtained.

Split-half reliability coefficients, for the tenth grade norm group, ranged from .40 to .74 for the subtests on both forms of the critical thinking appraisal. Split-half reliabilities, for six normative samples, on form Ym ranged from .85 to .87 for the total test score.

Bibliography:

Buros, O. K.: Test number 783.

Watson, G. and Glaser, E. M.: *Manual for Forms Ym and Zm: Watson-Glaser Critical Thinking Appraisal.* New York, Harcourt Brace Jovanovich, 1964.

Wechsler Adult Intelligence Scale

Author: David Wechsler

Variable: The Wechsler Adult Intelligence Scale (WAIS) assesses the intellectual ability of an adult.

Type of Measure: The WAIS is an oral test, most suitably administered in an individual situation by a trained clinician or psychologist. The subtests of the WAIS are individually timed, and the entire scale takes about two hours to complete. Scoring is done by hand at the time of administration.

Source from which Measure may be Obtained: The Psychological Corporation, 304 East Forty-fifth Street, New York, New York 10017.

Description: The WAIS consists of eleven subtests. Six of the subtests comprise the verbal scale; they are information, comprehension, arithmetic, similarities, digit span, and vocabulary. The remaining five subtests comprise the performance scale; they are digit symbol, picture completion, block design, picture arrangement, and object assembly. In addition to its use as a test of adult intelligence, the WAIS can be applied as a basic diagnostic instrument. Raw scores are converted to scaled scores and I.Q.'s by using the tables provided in the manual. I.Q.'s are developed separately for each age group.

Norms: Normative data was evolved, based on the 1950 census, for seven age groups ranging from sixteen to sixty-four. Other norm studies have extended the age range to seventy-five and over. Equal numbers of men and women were included in each age group. The norms are distributed over a wide geographical spread. Cases were also distributed over an urban rural proportion for each age group. The sample includes both white and nonwhite subjects of varied educational levels and occupational categories based on the census groupings.

Validity and Reliability: Extensive studies have been carried out using the WAIS as both a diagnostic and an evaluative device. The reader is directed to the bibliography for reference material. One study comparing the WAIS and the Stanford-Binet yielded a correlation value of .86 for verbal, .69 for performance, and .85 for the total scale score of the WAIS; this test was conducted with a group of 100 subjects ranging in age from sixteen to twenty-six.

Reliability coefficients were found to be .97 for total scale I.Q. for three age groups: eighteen to nineteen, twenty-five to thirty-four, and forty-five to fifty-four; there were 200 subjects in each group. Verbal I.Q. reliability for the same three groups is .96, while for performance I.Q., the reliabilities are .93, .93, and .94, respectively.

Bibliography:

Buros, O. K.: Test number 429.

Matarazzo, J. E.: *Wechsler's Measurement and Appraisal of Adult Intelligence*. 5th ed. Baltimore, The Williams and Wilkins Company, 1972.

Wechsler, D.: *Wechsler Adult Intelligence Scale*. New York, The Psychological Corporation, 1955.

Wesman Personnel Classification Test

Author: Alexander G. Wesman

Variable: The Wesman Personality Classification Test (PCT) measures verbal reasoning and numerical ability.

Type of Measure: The PCT is a paper and pencil test, suitable for administration to either individuals or groups. It is timed at twenty-eight minutes. Scoring is done by hand with the use of a key.

Source from which Measure may be Obtained: The Psychological Corporation, 304 E. Forty-fifth Street, New York, New York 10017.

Description: The PCT consists of two parts: part I, verbal, which contains forty items, timed for eighteen minutes; and part II, numerical, which contains twenty items, timed for ten minutes. The PCT is available in three parallel forms, A, B, and C. The two parts of the test not only yield information on two ability levels of the subject, but also provide separate scores for use in the selection of personnel and in individual counseling. The score for each part is determined by the number of correct answers; raw scores may be converted to percentile ranks by using the tables provided in the manual.

Norms: Normative data is based on a number of industrial and business groups, including chain store clerks, production workers, production and inspection supervisors, male office supervisors, female clerical workers, salaried workers, male shop supervisors, United States Air Force captains, manufacturing company personnel, job analysts, sales trainees, applicants for mechanical apprentice jobs, female applicants at a utility company, applicants for foreman or mechanic, applicants for pre-supervisory training, merchandising trainees, applicants for job of hearing aid salesman, male applicants for salaried field sales positions, applicants for job of life insurance salesman, executive trainee applicants for white collar jobs, applicants for high level positions, students in evening high school, tenth grade students, high school seniors, nursing school applicants, male college freshmen, and college sophomores. The manual provides information regarding the characteristics of each group. Norm tables are available for each of these groups, which report percentile scores for the verbal, numerical and total scores.

Validity and Reliability: Correlation of the PCT total score with general mental ability measures, including the Wonderlic Personnel Test, the Otis Self Administering Test, the Terman Concept Mastery Test, the Oral Directions Test, and the ACE Psychological Examination, among others, yielded values ranging from .33 to .80 for samples ranging in size from 77 to 343. Other studies have shown that for industrial and educational groups, as the complexity of a job increases the mean PCT scores attained by incumbents in those positions also increase. Predictive validity studies yielded correlation values of .62 and .48 for parts I and II of the PCT, respectively, with rating by supervisors. Correlations of part I with part II ranged from .21 to .61, with a median between .48 and .49. This shows that verbal and numerical ability are reasonably independent measures.

Correlations among the alternate forms of the PCT for several norm groups yielded reliability coefficients ranging from .84 to .91 for the total score of the PCT.

Bibliography:

Buros, O. K.: Test number 400.

Wesman, A. G.: *Wesman Personnel Classification Test, Manual.* New York, The Psychological Corporation, 1965.

Wide Range Intelligence and Personality Test (formerly The Jastak Test)

Author: Joseph F. Jastak

Variable: The Wide Range Intelligence and Personality Test (WRIPT) assesses abilities as well as behavior of an individual.

Type of Measure: The WRIPT is a battery of ten pencil and paper subtests, suitable for administration to either individuals or groups. Each subtest is timed individually, and the entire series takes about fifty minutes to complete. Scoring is done by hand with the use of an overlay stencil.

Source from which Measure may be Obtained: Guidance Associates, 1526 Gilpin Avenue, Wilmington, Delaware 19806.

Description: The WRIPT consists of ten psychometric subtests, useful in both wide-scale assessment of subjects and in personal counseling. The subtests are separate and discrete psychological dimensions, including vocabulary, number series, coding, picture reasoning, space series, verbal reasoning, social concept, arithmetic, space completion, and spelling; they may be administered in two or more sessions on different days; however, they should be given in their order of appearance in the test booklet. Raw scores may be converted to standard scores which, in turn, are converted to "range" scores. Tables are provided in the manual for these conversions.

Norms: Normative data is based on a wide range of individuals, ages nine and one-half to fifty-four years. Norms are derived separately for males and females. The norms are based on samples typically used for both the Wechsler Intelligence Scale for Children (WISC) and the Wechsler Adult Intelligence Scale (WAIS). The standardization samples include approximately three thousand males and over twenty-five hundred females.

Validity and Reliability: Validity data is not stated.

Reliability estimates were reported prior to the extension of the WRIPT to the adult level. The reliability coefficients, computed by the Rulon formula using split-half methods, ranged from .82 for space completion and social concept to .89 for verbal reasoning, for a group of 200 males and females, age thirteen and one-half.

Bibliography:

Jastak, J. F.: *WRIPT: The Jastak Test of Potential Ability and Behavior Stability, Manual.* Circle Pines, Educational Test Bureau, 1959.

____: *WRIPT: Wide Range Intelligence and Personality Test, Supplement to Manual.* Wilmington, Guidance Associates of Delaware, Inc., 1971.

Wonderlic Personnel Test

Author: E. F. Wonderlic

Variable: The Wonderlic Personnel Test assesses the mental capabilities of adults in business and industrial settings.

Type of Measure: The Wonderlic is a paper and pencil test, suitable for administration to either individuals or groups. It is timed for twelve minutes. Scoring is done by hand with the use of a key.

Source from which Measure may be Obtained: Western Psychological Services, 12031 Wilshire Boulevard, Los Angeles, California 90025.

Description: The Wonderlic is useful in examining employees' as well as applicants' mental ability levels. The test includes fifty items, covering the areas of analogies, analysis of geometric figures, arithmetic problems, disarranged sentences, sentence parallelism with proverbs, similarities, logic, definitions, judgment, direction following using clerical items, spatial relations, among others. There are fourteen comparable and similar forms of the Wonderlic currently available. Each form assesses the same set of abilities and yields similar results; and each form measures the subject's ability to learn, regardless of job position or educational level. Raw scores may be converted to percentile rank by using the tables provided in the manual. Also indicated are score adjustments for the age of the applicant; no correction is necessary for sex.

Norms: The Wonderlic, including each of the fourteen forms, has been extensively standardized in business situations for adults. The age range of the norm samples is from sixteen to sixty-five. Three standardization studies including 36,864 applicants in 1950, 53,864 applicants in 1960, and 251,253 applicants in 1970 have been used to illustrate the consistency of results over time. Norms are available by education level, such as high school and college, by sex, and age combinations. The manual provides descriptive data, such as means and quartile ranges for over seventy-five occupational groups. The groups cover the occupational areas of professional and executive; office, plant and sales management; office staff, including clerical, sales force, and staff; plant staff and line personnel; and others, such as day laborers, and so forth. Also available are norms for both Caucasian and Negro applicants separately; and, each of these is further subdivided by education, age, and sex.

VALIDITY AND RELIABILITY: Validity coefficients ranging from .95 to .996, correlating Wonderlic tests scores with years of education, are reported. It is also indicated that over one hundred and fifty separate and independent research studies have yielded data on the validity of the Wonderlic. The reader is advised to seek out those studies which treat a particular occupation, as well as other environmental characteristics pertaining to the validity of this instrument. Through E. F. Wonderlic and Associates, Inc., an annotated listing of validation studies is available.

Test retest reliabilities with different forms of the Wonderlic yielded correlations ranging from .82 to .94, when the tests were given sequentially. Odd-even reliability yielded values ranging from .88 to .94.

BIBLIOGRAPHY:

Buros, O. K.: Test number 401.

Wonderlic, E. F.: *Wonderlic Personnel Test Manual.* Northfield, E. F. Wonderlic and Associates, Inc., 1970.

Wonderlic, E. F. and Associates: *Validation Reprint Service: Wonderlic Personnel Test.* Northfield, Author, 1972.

GROUP 2 — ACHIEVEMENT MEASURES

Adult Basic Learning Examination — Level III

AUTHORS: Bjorn Karlsen, Richard Madden, and Eric F. Gardner

VARIABLE: The Adult Basic Learning Examination (ABLE) assesses achievement levels of adults.

TYPE OF MEASURE: The ABLE is a battery of four subtests, three of which are paper and pencil and the fourth, vocabulary, is dictated. The ABLE is suitable for administration to either individuals or groups. The three paper and pencil subtests are timed individually; the vocabulary subtest is not. The entire series takes about three and one-half hours to complete. Scoring may be done manually or by machine.

SOURCE FROM WHICH MEASURE MAY BE OBTAINED: Harcourt Brace Jovanovich, 757 Third Avenue, New York, New York 10017.

Description: The ABLE — Level III was originally developed to provide a battery of tests which would assess general educational level of adults without a formal high school diploma, that is, up to the twelfth grade. It also serves as a device with which to plan educational programs for adults. The four subtests include: vocabulary which contains sixty multiple choice items, permitting subjects' oral vocabulary to be measured independently of reading ability; reading, comprised of sixty items, which determines the subject's comprehension of paragraphs and new material; spelling, measured in fifty items; and arithmetic, further divided into the subsections of part A, computation, which is comprised of forty-two items to test numerical competence, and part B, problem solving, which is comprised of forty-two items to test practical application of computations. All of the ABLE subtests are available in two parallel forms, A and B. Raw scores may be converted to stanines or percentile ranks with the use of the tables provided in the manual.

Norms: The normative sample is well designed and includes a distribution across the dimensions of sex, age (from under twenty to over fifty), race, last school grade completed, and median score on the Stanford Achievement Test, as well as wide geographical spread, including students in Newfoundland and Canada. Data for interpretation is provided by subtest, in percentiles, stanines, and standard scores for grades 9 to 12, by each form. Means and standard deviations are also reported by each standardization sample which comprise different proportions of sex, race, and school attainment level, so that individual group interpretation could be made depending on the nature of the group tested.

Validity and Reliability: Correlation of the four ABLE subtests and total arithmetic score of the Stanford Achievement series were found to vary with grade level (10 to 12), from .44 to .85. For example, a significant correlation value of .75 was obtained for one standardization sample on the reading subtest of the SAT and that of the ABLE, for grade 10 students. Also, intercorrelation of the ABLE subtests is moderately high.

Kuder-Richardson formula 21 reliability estimates ranged from .82 to .96. These values varied with the standardization sample which usually exceeded one hundred subjects.

BIBLIOGRAPHY:

Buros, O. K.: Test number 3.

Karlsen, B., Madden, R., and Gardner, E. F.: *Level III ABLE Handbook.* New York, Harcourt Brace Jovanovich, 1971.

California Achievement Tests — Level 5 — Form A

AUTHORS: Ernest W. Tiegs and Willis W. Clark

VARIABLE: The California Achievement Tests (CAT) assess school achievement with emphasis upon the basic curricular areas of reading, mathematics, and language.

TYPE OF MEASURE: The CAT is a battery of nine paper and pencil subtests, suitable for administration to either individuals or groups. Each subtest is timed individually, and the entire series takes three hours and eleven minutes to complete. Scoring may be done manually or by machine.

SOURCE FROM WHICH MEASURE MAY BE OBTAINED: CTB/McGraw-Hill, Del Monte Research Park, Monterey, California 93940.

DESCRIPTION: The CAT was designed to span grades 9 through 12 by assessing the three basic skill areas of reading, mathematics, and language. Reading is assessed by two subtests, vocabulary and comprehension. Mathematics is divided into three subtests, computation, concepts, and problems. Language is assessed in four subtests, mechanics — capitalization, mechanics — punctuation, usage and structure, and spelling. The CAT battery measures the skill with which the student performs in curricular tasks which are basic to learning progress as well as to all further academic endeavors. Skills measured include the ability to understand the meaning of content material, application of rules, facts, concepts, conventions, and principles in problem solving situations, and the student's capabilities in using the tools of reading, mathematics, and language in progressively difficult situations. Use of the CAT extends to the selection of students for academic remediation, vocational planning at the secondary and post secondary school levels, and for identifying strengths in perspective employees in order to facilitate training. In addition, administration of the CAT in conjunction with the Short Form Test of Academic Aptitude (SFTAA) yields Anticipated Achievement Grade Equivalents (AAGE) or Anticipated Achievement Scale Scores (AASS). Also, in addition to being able to hand score the CAT, the user may take advantage of the CompuScan scoring service, provided by CTB/McGraw-Hill (for the CAT — 1970 edition, only).

Norms: The standardization design and testing was accomplished in late February and March, 1970, on a carefully selected nationwide sample of 203,684 students. The CAT was standardized jointly with the Short Form Test of Academic Aptitude, SFTAA. Norm tables are provided by grade levels 9 to 12 in percentiles and stanines, for subtests and total.

Validity and Reliability: Validity data reported was based on the subtests of the CAT and the SFTAA. Significant correlations reported indicate a value of .84 for the total battery score of the CAT with the total score of the SFTAA. Other significant values in the .70's are reported for the language and nonlanguage scores of the SFTAA and the total battery score of the CAT.

Reliability computed by Kuder-Richardson formula yielded values ranging from .84 for language usage and structure to .95 for language mechanics; these values are based on grade level 12.6 for the CAT — 1970 edition. Other significant reliabilities are reported for grade levels, including 11.6, 10.6, and so on.

Bibliography:

Buros, O. K.: Test number 5.

Tiegs, E. W. and Clark, W. W.: *Examiner's Manual: California Achievement Tests — 1970 Edition*. Monterey, CTB/McGraw-Hill, 1970.

_____ and _____ : *Bulletin of Technical Data Number 1: California Achievement Tests*. Monterey, CTB/McGraw-Hill, 1970.

Tiegs, E. W. and Clark, W. W.: *Bulletin of Technical Data Number 2: California Achievement Tests*. Monterey, CTB/McGraw-Hill, 1972.

Educational Skills Test — College Edition

Author: California Test Bureau, a Division of McGraw-Hill Book Company

Variable: The Educational Skills Test — College Edition (EST/CE) measures English and mathematics skills at the college level.

Type of Measure: The EST/CE consists of two paper and pencil subtests, suitable for administration to either individuals or groups. The subtests are further divided into subsections, and each of these is individually timed; the entire series takes two hours and thirty minutes. Scoring may be done manually or by machine.

Source from which Measure may be Obtained: CTB/McGraw-Hill, Del Monte Research Park, Monterey, California 93940.

Description: The EST/CE consists of two subtests. English, which is comprised of 171 items, yields data in five areas, including phonetic information, syntactic information, semantic information, knowledge of writing conventions, and knowledge of organizational schema. Mathematics, which is comprised of 236 items, yields data in three areas, including background information, algorithmic information, and problem-solving information. The English subtest is divided into five subsections: sounds, comprehension I, comprehension II, mechanics of writing, and organization of ideas; and the mathematics subtest is divided into three subsections: basic information, computation, and problem analysis. The EST/CE yields a total of eleven scores, and its usefulness lies in the evaluation of a student's strengths and weaknesses in basic skill areas for the purpose of deciding on an effective course of remediation. Raw scores can be converted to standard scores or percentile ranks.

Norms: Samples from two year community colleges with wide ranges in geographical location, tuition charges, and freshmen enrollment were used for the norm base. An excess of eleven thousand students was included in the standardization sample. Norms are available for three reference groups: transferring English or mathematics college majors; students in developmental English/mathematics courses or communication courses; and students in remedial or review English /mathematics courses.

Validity and Reliability: One source of validity presented is the low intercorrelation of the subtests with each other. This could provide valuable differentiating and predictive criteria for community college use. Correlation with the School and College Ability Test (SCAT) and Cooperative English Tests (CET) was also investigated. The size of the relationship varied from .42 to .70 for the five subsections of the EST/CE English subtest with the SCAT verbal scale, based on over one hundred thirty students. These values and other correlations that are reported appear to support the contention that these tests are generally related, but provide differential information.

The English and mathematics subsections and total test score reliabilities, computed by Kuder-Richardson formula 20, yield correlation values ranging from .65 to .94 for the subsections and .97 for the English and mathematics total test score.

Bibliography:

California Test Bureau, A Division of McGraw-Hill Book Company: *Educational Skills Test — College Edition, Examiner's Manual.* Monterey, Author, 1971.

Gates-MacGinitie Reading Tests — Survey F

Authors: Arthur I. Gates and Walter H. MacGinitie

Variable: The Gates-MacGinitie Reading Tests measure an individual's reading capabilities in the areas of speed, vocabulary, and comprehension.

Type of Measure: The reading tests are a battery of three paper and pencil subtests, suitable for administration to either individuals or group. Each subtest is individually timed, and the entire series takes thirty-five minutes. Scoring may be done manually or by machine.

SOURCE FROM WHICH MEASURE MAY BE OBTAINED: Teachers College Press, Columbia University, New York, New York 10027.

DESCRIPTION: The reading tests are available in two parallel forms, 1 and 2, for grades 10 to 12. They can be utilized in assessing a subject's reading capabilities for the purpose of vocational planning or as a diagnostic tool by revealing significant insights into the strengths of reading skills for diverse groups of subjects. There are three subtests: speed and accuracy assesses the rapidity with which a subject can read with comprehension and includes thirty-six short paragraphs. The vocabulary subtest assesses a subject's reading vocabulary through the use of fifty items. The comprehension subtests assesses the subject's capability to read prose passages with comprehension and includes twenty-one passages. Raw scores may be converted to standard scores or percentiles.

NORMS: Norms for Survey F of the reading tests were developed on a nationwide sample of 5,000 students in grades 9 to 12, in thirty-four communities. The communities were balanced on the basis of size, geographical location, average educational level, and average family income. Norms are reported in standard scores, with a mean of fifty, and percentiles, by grade level.

VALIDITY AND RELIABILITY: Correlations of the reading subtests with the Lorge-Thorndike Verbal I.Q. Test are reported. Significant correlation values by subtests and by grade levels 10 to 12 range from .41 to .80. Highest correlations were obtained for vocabulary and comprehension and lowest for number of items attempted (speed) and number correct (accuracy), with verbal I.Q.

Alternate form reliabilities for each of the subtests ranged from .64 to .92 for tenth, eleventh, and twelfth grade students. Split-half reliability, based on samples of students ranging in size from 184 to 205 in grades 10, 11, and 12, yielded values varying from .92 to .95.

BIBLIOGRAPHY:

Buros, O. K.: Test number 690.

Gates, A. I. and MacGinitie, W. H.: *Teacher's Manual: Gates-MacGinitie Reading Tests — Survey F.* New York, Teachers College Press, 1969.
Teachers College Press: *Technical Supplement: Gates-MacGinitie Reading Tests — Survey F.* New York, Author, 1970.

Iowa Tests of Educational Development — Forms X-5 and Y-5

Author: prepared under the direction of E. F. Lindquist and Leonard S. Feldt

Variable: The Iowa Tests of Educational Development (ITED) assess levels of achievement in the areas of reading, language arts, mathematics, social studies, natural science, and use of sources.

Type of Measure: The ITED is a battery of eight paper and pencil subtests, suitable for administration to either individuals or groups. Each subtest is individually timed, and the entire series takes about four and one-half hours to administer. Scoring may be done manually or by machine.

Source from which Measure may be Obtained: Science Research Associates, 259 East Erie Street, Chicago, Illinois 60611.

Description: The ITED is a battery of subtests which attempts to determine the degree to which a student is able to understand and critically analyze materials found in adult and real world situations which, although not yet presented in the classroom, require the student to draw upon knowledge already accumulated. This exercise yields an assessment of the skills presumably already possessed by the student in the light of how he or she will apply them as a productive adult. The eight subtests are: reading which is subdivided into comprehension, consisting of fifty-four items timed for forty minutes and vocabulary, consisting of forty items timed for fifteen minutes; language arts which is subdivided into usage, consisting of fifty-four items and spelling, consisting of forty items, timed together for forty minutes; mathematics, consisting of thirty-six items timed for forty minutes; social studies, consisting of thirty items timed for twenty minutes; science, consisting of thirty items timed for twenty minutes; and use of sources, consisting of forty-six items timed for twenty minutes. Raw scores may be converted to standard scores and percentile ranks.

Norms: Normative data is based on 5,000 students in grades 9 to 12, from many schools in diverse locations throughout the United States, who took the ITED during late April and early May of 1970. Standard scores and percentiles are reported for part scores of the battery.

Validity and Reliability: Content validity is provided through a breakdown of the item exercises in each subtest by content and skill. This allows for individual judgment on the pertinence of the items and the tests. Correlational studies of varied subtests of the ITED, with either cumulative or subject matter grades, yielded significant values ranging from .50 to .70, for grades 9 to 12. Finally, correlation of the ITED — forms X-4 and Y-4 (earlier forms) with the American College Testing Program yielded significant values generally in the .50 to over .60 range, for subtests of the ITED and composite ITED score. Additional validity studies are reported.

Reliability coefficients, computed by Kuder-Richardson formula 20, ranged from .95 to .97 for the composite score on form X-5 and from .95 to .99 on form Y-5. Test retest reliability, based on administration of forms X-5 and Y-5 and previous editions of the ITED over a more than one year interval, yielded coefficients ranging from .85 to .91 for the composite score; coefficients for part scores are also reported. The number of cases for each sample generally exceeded 350.

Bibliography:

Lindquist, E. F. and Feldt, L. S.: (directors) at the University of Iowa. *SRA Assessment Survey, Test Coordinator's Handbook: Iowa Tests of Educational Development — Forms X-5 and Y-5*. Chicago, Science Research Associates, 1970.

Science Research Associates: *SRA Assessment Survey, Handbook for Teachers and Examiners: Iowa Tests of Educational Development — Forms X-5 and Y-5*. Chicago, Author, 1970.

Science Research Associates: *SRA Assessment Survey, Technical Report: Iowa Tests of Educational Development — Forms X-5 and Y-5*. Chicago, Author, 1972.

——— : *Technical Report: SRA Assessment Survey*. Chicago, Author, 1974.

Iowa Silent Reading Tests — Advanced Test

Authors: H. A. Greene, A. Jorgensen, and V. H. Kelley

Variable: The Iowa Silent Reading Tests — Advanced Test measures the level of achievement of students at the high school and junior college levels in doing silent reading of the work-study variety.

Type of Measure: The reading tests are a battery of seven paper and pencil subtests, suitable for administration to either individuals or groups. Each subtest is individually timed, and the entire series takes forty minutes to complete. Scoring may be done manually or by machine.

Source from which Measure may be Obtained: Harcourt Brace Jovanovich, 757 Third Avenue, New York, New York 10017.

Description: The reading tests are available in four parallel forms, Am (revised), Bm (revised), Cm, and Dm. The reading tests are divided into seven subtests, including rate and comprehension, directed reading, poetry comprehension, word meaning, sentence meaning, paragraph comprehension, and location of information, which use eleven types of materials. The tests yield a total of nine significantly different subscores. One of the most valuable aspects of the tests exists in their use by a teacher in areas in which silent reading abilities are critical for school performance. Raw scores may be converted to standard scores and percentile ranks with the use of the tables provided in the manual.

Norms: Norms for the Advanced Test were developed on over ten thousand cases and checked against an additional population of over eighteen thousand. This data represents a wide sampling of the high school population in the United States. Norms are available for grades 9 to 13 for each subtest and total standard score; age and grade equivalents are also reported.

Validity and Reliability: Content validity, as judged by experts in their respective fields, was used to determine the meaningfulness of the reading tests.

Reliabilities, based on the odd-even method, ranged from .68 to .87 depending on the subtest; a value of .91 was found for the total median score.

Bibliography:

Greene, H. A., Jorgensen, A. N., and Kelley, V. H.: *Iowa Silent Reading Tests — New Edition — Advanced Test, Manual of Directions*. New York, Harcourt Brace Jovanovich, 1943.

McGraw-Hill Basic Skills System

Author: Alton L. Raygor, Consulting Editor

Variable: The McGraw-Hill Basic Skills System (MHBSS) is a flexible, interrelated series of tests, designed to provide an accurate assessment of basic academic skills for both college and college-bound students.

Type of Measure: The MHBSS is a battery of six paper and pencil tests, suitable for administration to either individuals or groups. Each test is individually timed, and the entire series takes approximately three and one-half hours to complete. Scoring may be done manually or by machine.

Source from which Measure may be Obtained: CTB/McGraw-Hill Book Company, Del Monte Research Park, Monterey, California 93940. (Please note that specimen sets of the MHBSS must be ordered by the individual name of the test, such as MHBSS Specimen Set for Mathematics.)

Description: The MHBSS is comprised of six tests: reading, writing, spelling, vocabulary, study skills, and mathematics. Each of these is available in two parallel forms, A and B. The difficulty level of the tests is related to grades 10 through 13, while the material is based on college academic disciplines. The materials are most valuable in assessing remedial needs in counseling and study skills centers, as well as providing essential instruction for improvement of English and mathematical skills. Application of the MHBSS extends to its use by counselors and teachers, providing them with information in order to plan an organized and systematic way of dealing with the improvement of students' basic academic skills. The six tests may be used separately or in any combination, although it is unlikely that they will all be used together by one instructor or for one student. The flexibility of this open-ended system permits diagnosis and evaluation of all those areas covered by it.

Norms: Normative data is based on school samples over a wide geographical spread in the United States, including approximately equal numbers of freshmen (and a few sophomores) in four year colleges and universities, two-year college students, and college-bound high school juniors and seniors. The publisher's manual advises that the user establish local norms in order to acquire a more meaningful interpretation at any one school, since percentile ranks for a defined group of students at a given school will probably have more meaning for examinees as well as counselors than would derived scores based on the publisher's reference groups.

Validity and Reliability: Since the amount of information available is extensive, only two tests will be treated in this section.

Based on sixty-four first year students at a two-year college, correlating the vocabulary and reading tests with the Nelson-Denny Reading Test yielded values of .74 for vocabulary and .67 for reading. These relationships were between total score of each instrument (subscore correlations are also available). No criteria validity has been performed on the study skills test, although content validity has been satisfied regarding the purpose of the items in the test.

Reliability coefficients, computed by Kuder-Richardson formula 20, were found to be .88 on both forms A and B of the vocabulary test, .89 on both forms A and B of the reading test, and .78 and .80 for forms A and B, respectively, of the study skills test.

Bibliography:

Buros, O. K.: Test numbers, 477, 704, 230, 781, 236, and 214.

Raygor, A. L., (consulting editor): *McGraw-Hill Basic Skills System.* Monterey, CTB/McGraw-Hill, 1970.

Metropolitan Achievement Tests — High School Battery

Author: Walter N. Durost, Editor

Variable: The Metropolitan Achievement Tests (MAT) assess an individual's learning progress.

Type of Measure: The MAT is a battery of eleven paper and pencil subtests, suitable for administration to either individuals or groups. Each subtest is individually timed, and the entire series takes five hours and fifteen minutes to administer. Scoring may be done manually or by machine.

Source from which Measure may be Obtained: Harcourt Brace Jovanovich, 757 Third Avenue, New York, New York 10017. (Please note that specimen sets of the MAT must be ordered by skill area, such as MAT Specimen Set for Language Arts.)

Description: The MAT measures four basic skill areas in eleven subtests: language arts are measured in the reading, language, language study skills, and spelling subtests; mathematics skills are assessed in the computation and concepts and analysis and problem-solving subtests; science is assessed in information and concepts subtests; and social studies are assessed in the information, vocabulary, and skills subtests. In addition to assessing the subject's levels of achievement, the MAT may also be used in vocational evaluation and guidance or in the evaluation of instructional programs.

Norms: Norms are presented for grades 9 to 12 by two classifications: age-controlled norms, such as middle of the academic year students, selected from the total populations; and college preparatory norms for high school students pursuing college preparatory courses. Data is reported in percentiles for each subtest, as well as in stanines for each grade level and norm sample.

Validity and Reliability: Validity studies on over two hundred subjects, correlating the eleven subtests of the MAT with the Otis Intelligence Test, yielded values of .70 for reading, .57 for spelling at grade 9, .64 for social studies information, and .73 for mathematic computation at grade 12. Data is provided establishing the interrelationship of the Otis with mathematics scores for grade levels 9 to 13 and eleven subtests. Also, separate studies are available on the validity of the subtests, such as spelling, as well as additional technical data on the content of the tests, by level and form, in order to arrive at judgments regarding content validity.

Reliability, determined by the split-half method, yielded values ranging from. 83 to .91 on a sample of at least one hundred students, on form Am for the two mathematics subtests. Alternative form reliability values, for over five hundred subjects in grades 10 and 11, were found to be in the .80 to .90 range for form Am versus form Bm on the two mathematics subtests.

Bibliography:

Buros, O. K.: Test number 15.

Durost, W. N. (general editor): *Manual of Directions: Metropolitan Achievement Tests.* New York, Harcourt Brace Jovanovich, 1964.

Test Department, Harcourt Brace Jovanovich: *Metropolitan Achievement Tests; Special Report, 1970 Edition.* New York, Author, 1971.

Purdue Clerical Adaptability Test — Form A (Revised)

Authors: C. H. Lawshe, Joseph Tiffin, and Herbert Moore

Variable: The Purdue Clerical Adaptability Test measures six specific skills required on certain clerical jobs.

Type of Measure: The clerical test is a paper and pencil device, suitable for administration to either individuals or groups. There are six subsections, each of which is timed, and the entire series takes forty-seven and one-half minutes. Scoring is done by hand with the use of a key.

Source from which Measure may be Obtained: University Book Store, 360 State Street, West Lafayette, Indiana 47906.

Description: The clerical adaptability test consists of six subsections, including spelling, computation, checking, word meaning, copying, and arithmetical reasoning. Although all six subsections may be administered to any one subject, in the screening and selection of personnel, it may be feasible to administer only those sections which are applicable to the particular job being filled. Raw scores may be converted to percentile ranks with the use of the tables provided in the manual.

NORMS: Norm tables are based on 3,970 clerical applicants to Purdue University, as well as 650 applicants to eight industrial companies. Combined samples are provided for the norm interpretations since raw score differences were nominal. No other differentiation for the norms is stated. Furthermore, it is advisable for the user to evolve company or institutional norms wherever possible.

VALIDITY AND RELIABILITY: Evidence is provided for content, concurrent, and predictive validity. Content validity is determined through judgments of the relationship of the job samples and the items in the clerical adaptability test. Predictive validity should be investigated by each user. Studies report that favorable supervisory ratings of employees, six months after hiring, correlated significantly with high scores obtained by those employees on three subsections of the clerical adaptability test, and low job performance supervisory ratings of employees, also six months after hiring, correlated significantly with low scores obtained by those employees on three subsections of the clerical adaptability test. Concurrent validity was determined by isolating subjects who performed critical operation of clerical personnel in eight firms. The results indicated that the more critical the operation performed is, the higher the probability that the score of the subject performing that operation will exceed the median value on the subsections of the clerical adaptability test.

Split-half reliability coefficients, based on 168 applicants, ranged from .97 on copying to .79 on reasoning.

BIBLIOGRAPHY:

Lawshe, C. H., Tiffin, J., and Moore, H.: *Manual of Instructions to accompany Purdue Clerical Adaptability Test.* West Lafayette, University Book Store, 1956.

The Purdue Industrial Mathematics Test

AUTHORS: C. H. Lawshe and Dennis H. Price

VARIABLE: The Purdue Industrial Mathematics Test measures achievement in simple and basic arithmetic and computational skills.

Type of Measure: The mathematics test is a paper and pencil device, suitable for administration to either individuals or groups. It is timed for twenty-five minutes. Scoring is done by hand with the use of a key.

Source from which Measure may be Obtained: University Book Store, 360 State Street, West Lafayette, Indiana 47906.

Description: The mathematics test is available in two parallel forms, A and B, and consists of thirty-two items. Its use extends to the assessment of arithmetic and computational skills needed by subjects in those skilled trades which include, but are not limited to, tasks such as setup, layout, maintenance, and design. It may also be used in apprenticeship and trade training programs. Raw scores may be converted to percentile ranks with the use of the table provided in the manual.

Norms: Tentative norms are based on 188 vocational trade school students, 150 trade apprentices, and 1,374 industrial supervisors. Scores are reported in percentiles as well as standard scores.

Validity and Reliability: The manual does not indicate validity data.

A reliability study carried out on 125 college students, based on intercorrelation of forms A and B, yielded a coefficient of .82.

Bibliography:

Lawshe, C. H. and Price, D. H.: *Preliminary Manual: The Purdue Industrial Mathematics Test,* West Lafayette, University Book Store, 1946.

SCAT-STEP — Series II — Levels 1 and 2

Author: Cooperative Test Division, Educational Testing Service

Variable: The SCAT-STEP — Series II measures a student's ability to do academic work in the major domains of the high school and college programs.

Type of Measure: The SCAT-STEP — Series II is a battery of eight paper and pencil subtests, suitable for administration to either individuals or groups. Each subtest is individually timed, and the entire series may take anywhere from four and three-quarter to five and one-half hours to complete. Scoring may be done manually or by machine or by the Cooperative Tests and Services scoring service.

Source from which Measure may be Obtained: Educational Testing Service, Cooperative Test Division, Princeton, New Jersey 08540.

Description: The SCAT-STEP — Series II is a comprehensive battery of subtests which were evolved by incorporating the Cooperative School and College Ability Test and the Sequential Tests of Educational Progress. Levels 1 and 2 are intended for use with students in grades 9 to 14 and measure the subject's capability to do academic work at the high school and college level. The SCAT-STEP program is flexible enough to allow schools to select that aspect of it which is most appropriate. Its purpose is to provide teachers with information to effect proper evaluations and prescriptions for their students in a wide variety of curriculum areas. General capability is assessed by the SCAT part of the program; verbal, quantitative, and total scores are obtained. The STEP series includes subtests in reading, mechanics of writing, English expression, and mathematics which are all two-part tests, and science and social studies which are one-part tests.

Norms: Normative data for SCAT forms 1A and 1B were based on college freshmen and sophomores, and forms 2A and 2B were standardized on students in high school grades 9 to 12. The samples were designed to reflect equal proportions of high school students being selected, regardless of institutional affiliations, such as public or parochial schools. At the college level, two types of institutions were selected: two year institutions and four year institutions, excluding professional and Ph.D. granting schools. Normative samples are extensive and are reported in a preliminary edition of a *Book of Norms* (1970). Scores are reported in percentile bands and ranks and stanines for the SCAT verbal, quantitative, and total scores; the same information is available for STEP scores in reading, English expression, mathematics concepts, science, and social studies.

VALIDITY AND RELIABILITY: The SCAT-STEP Supplement (1962) reports significant correlation values of .49 for SCAT verbal scores of eleventh grade students with their English grades and .52 for twelfth grade students, for six schools; a .86 correlation value for SCAT verbal scores with Scholastic Aptitude Test (SAT) verbal scores of 560 twelfth grade students; and a .78 correlation value of SCAT quantitative scores with SAT mathematics scores for 513 students. An entire manual is provided with validity study information and results. In addition, a long and comprehensive bibliographical listing of validity studies is also provided in annotated form.

Reliability coefficients, computed by Kuder-Richardson formula 20, ranged from .88 to .90 for form 1A and from .92 to .94 for form 1B for the STEP total, verbal, and quantitative scores. The lowest reliability coefficients, computed by Kuder-Richardson, were found to be .90 for reading, .90 for English expression, .87 for mathematics concepts, .83 for science, and .83 for social studies. Reliabilities for forms 2A and 2B are also reported.

BIBLIOGRAPHY:

Buros, O. K.: Test number 347.

Cooperative Test Division, Educational Testing Service: *SCAT-STEP — Series II, Teacher's Handbook — Preliminary Edition.* Princeton, Author, 1970.

______ : *SCAT-STEP — Series II, Book of Norms — Preliminary Edition.* Princeton, Author, 1970.

______ : *SCAT-STEP Supplement: Test Performance in Urban Schools.* Princeton, Author, 1963.

______ : *SCAT-STEP Supplement.* Princeton, Author, 1962.

______ : *Cooperative Sequential Tests of Educational Progress, Teacher's Guide.* Princeton, Author, 1959.

______ : *SCAT-STEP Supplement.* Princeton, Author, 1958.

______ : *Cooperative Sequential Tests of Educational Progress, Technical Report.* Princeton, Author, 1957.

Stanford Achievement Test — High School Battery

AUTHORS: Eric F. Gardner, Jack C. Merwin, Robert Callis, and

Richard Madden

Variable: The Stanford Achievement Test (SAT) assesses educational achievements of students in today's schools.

Type of Measure: The SAT is a battery of ten paper and pencil subtests, suitable for administration to either individuals or groups. Each subtest is individually timed, and the entire series takes seven hours and twenty minutes. Scoring may be done manually or by IBM machine.

Sources from which Measure may be Obtained: Harcourt Brace Jovanovich, 757 Third Avenue, New York, New York 10017.

Description: The SAT — High School Battery is available in three parallel forms, W, X, and S. The battery is designed to test student achievement in reading, spelling, English, numerical competence, mathematics, social studies, and science, as well as in the specialized courses relating to the college preparatory, business, and technical curriculums. The results of the SAT may serve as an evaluator of potential student performance as either working adults or college students in that they measure the knowledge expected to have been accumulated by the student. The English, numerical competence, mathematics, reading, science, social studies, and spelling subtests are available together in a single test booklet; whereas, the arts and humanities, business and economics, and technical comprehension subtests are available in separate booklets only. In addition, the aforementioned seven subtests are available each in their own separate booklets, except that English and spelling are combined into one. The time limits for each subtest are generous enough so that they may be considered tests of power rather than speed. Raw scores from either forms W or X may be converted into standard scores or percentile rank.

Norms: The standardization of the SAT was determined in 1965 and included 22,699 students from fifty-eight schools in thirty-nine school systems, representing nine geographic regions of the United States. Special plans were designed and implemented to ensure equal representation of socioeconomic status of the standardization sample, based upon 1963 enrollments as well as median years of education and income for each of the nine regions. The scores of all 22,699 students were entered into the basic set of norms which are used to convert raw scores to standard scores. Norms are available for the total standardization population by grade, for college preparatory students by grade, and for special groups in mathematics, science, business and economics, and technical comprehension. Form S has not yet been normed.

Validity and Reliability: Content validity was determined through examination of course of study and textbooks in use with consultation by experts in varied subject matter areas. Item statistics evidence appropriateness of various test items which have the ability to discriminate among grade levels in which a given content area should have been mastered. Most of the SAT subtests correlate significantly with the Otis — Gamma, yielding values ranging from .60 to .70; lower correlation values were found with few SAT subtests. Construct validation evidence, through a factor analytic procedure, established the existence of three factors: Factor A — English, spelling, reading, arts and humanities, and social studies; Factor B — science and technology; and Factor C — mathematics.

Split-half reliability coefficients, obtained on form X administered to 12th graders in a standardization program, were found to range from .87 to .95 for the various subtests.

Bibliography:

Buros, O. K.: Test number 27.

Gardner, E. F., Merwin, J. C., Callis, R., and Madden, R.: *Stanford Achievement Test-High School Battery, Manual.* New York, Harcourt Brace Jovanovich, 1965.

Understanding Communication

Author: Thelma Guinn Thurstone

Variable: The Understanding Communication test measures comprehension of verbal material.

Type of Measure: The test is a paper and pencil device, suitable for administration to either individuals or groups. It is timed for fifteen minutes. Scoring is done by hand with the use of a key.

Source from which Measure may be Obtained: Education-Industry Service, 1225 East Sixtieth Street, Chicago, Illinois 60637.

Description: Understanding Communication is a test of verbal comprehension which excludes the considerations of reading speed, vocabulary, and word fluency and concentrates purely on the subject's understanding of words. The test has forty multiple choice items to which the subject responds by selecting one of four possible words or groups of words which permits the item sentence to read correctly. Use of the test has proven effective in the selection of personnel in industry and business where information regarding a subject's understanding of written material is desired. Raw scores may be converted to standard scores by using the table provided in the manual.

Norms: Presently, norms are based on 517 industrial employees classified as: 80 professionals and executives, 244 skilled and semi-skilled, and 193 unskilled. (Neither sex nor age is specified.)

Validity and Reliability: A correlation value of .75 was obtained from the scores of 200 school children in the eighth grade on the Understanding Communication test with scores of a general scholastic achievement test. Correlation of the Understanding Communication scores with those of a verbal reasoning test yielded a value of .52 for a group of 193 unskilled employees, whereas the correlation for a group of forty-five professional and executive employees was .48, using the same verbal reasoning test. The combined correlation for these two groups is .63.

A split-half reliability coefficient of .91 was obtained for a group of 300 students who took the test.

Bibliography:

Thurstone, T. G.: *Understanding Communication (Verbal Comprehension), Test Administration Manual.* Chicago, Education-Industry Service, 1959.

The Wide Range Achievement Test — Level II

Authors: Joseph F. Jastak and Sarah R. Jastak

Variable: The Wide Range Achievement Test (WRAT) — Level II assesses a students capability in various school subject areas.

Type of Measure: The WRAT is a series of three subtests. The first two are oral, and the third is paper and pencil as well as oral. It is suitable for administration to either individuals or groups. Each subtest is individually timed, and the entire series takes about thirty minutes to complete. Scoring is done by hand with the use of a key.

Source from which Measure may be Obtained: Guidance Associates, 1526 Gilpin Avenue, Wilmington, Delaware 19806.

Description: The WRAT is useful for a wide variety of purposes, such as in the assessment of school achievement of adult learners, in rehabilitation programs, as well as in the assessment of capabilities for job placement in business industry. Level II is suitable for use with subjects from age twelve through adulthood and is intended to be used with intelligence tests and behavior adjustment inventories as a supplemental device. There are three subtests: reading, which requires recognition and naming of letters and the pronunciation of words; spelling, which includes copying marks resembling letters, writing the name, and writing words from dictation; and arithmetic, which includes reading number symbols, solving oral number problems, and performing written computations. Raw scores may be converted to percentile ranks or standard scores by using the tables provided in the manual.

Norms: The normative sample was concentrated in the Middle Atlantic States but extended to groups in the South and Far West. The adult norms include over three hundred males and females from age twenty-five to sixty-five and also include persons between the ages of sixteen and twenty-five. Norm tables are divided generally by ten year age ranges, for example, twenty-five to thirty-five, thirty-five to forty-five, and so on. Scores are reported in percentiles and grade equivalents.

Validity and Reliability: Numerous validity studies have been carried out, including correlation of WRAT test results with teachers' rating of students, correlation of different tests with the WRAT, and correlation with intelligence ratings. Factor analytic studies have also been carried out to determine the construct validity of the WRAT for individuals aged sixteen and over. Finally, investigations yielded values ranging from .54 to .87 in correlating the WRAT subtests of reading, spelling, and arithmetic with the Wechsler Adult Intelligence scales of verbal, performance, and total; this study was based on 300 subjects per WRAT subtest.

Split-half reliabilities were generally found to be .90 and higher, based on varied age groups and different subtests.

Bibliography:

Buros, O. K.: Test number 36.

Jastak, J. F. and Jastak, S. R.: *Manual: The Wide Range Achievement Test.* Wilmington, Guidance Associates, 1965.

GROUP 3 — COGNITIVE PROCESS MEASURES

Closure Flexibility

Authors: L. L. Thurstone and T. E. Jeffrey

Variable: Closure Flexibility measures an individual's capability to hold a picture in mind despite distraction; it also measures temperament.

Type of Measure: Closure Flexibility is a paper and pencil test, suitable for administration to either individuals or groups. The test is timed for ten minutes. Scoring is done by hand with the use of a key.

Source from which Measure may be Obtained: Industrial Relations Center, 1225 East Erie Street, Chicago, Illinois 60637.

Description: Closure Flexibility is one of a series of tests which are designed to yield a profile of scores on basic mental abilities. This test measures what has been identified by Thurstone as the "second closure factor", the ability to perceive a given figure which is "hidden" or embedded in a larger, more complex drawing, diagram, or figure. The test consists of forty-nine items, each of which is comprised of a stimulus figure on one side of the page followed by a row of four alternative figures. Some of the alternative figures contain the stimulus figure in its original size and orientation. A subject responds by indicating those figures which contain the stimulus. In a study by Pemberton (1951) on 154 subjects, it became evident that, in addition to measuring a subject's "second closure factor" capability, Closure Flexibility yielded variables related to temperament, including sociability, conventionality, theoretical interest, and drive for achievement. Assessment of this last variable is supported by the results of an earlier study by L. L. Thurstone (1944) which discriminated between a small group of "campus leaders" and a larger group of undergraduate students. The temperament variables yielded by this test might apply in discriminating among industrial occupational groups, as well as clinical patients or subjects in analysis, whereas the closure score itself can be used to identify subjects with mechanical aptitude and analytical ability.

Norms: Norms, collected in most cases prior to June of 1962, are based on the test performance of 1,105 male industrial employees, classified into the following occupational groups: professionals, middle and upper executives, junior executives, salesmen, foremen, and hourly. Norms are based on the combined scores of all six groups.

Validity and Reliability: The present form of the Closure Flexibility test is a refinement of the earlier Gottschaldt Figures Test. Determination of the validity of Closure Flexibility is based on results obtained with the Gottschaldt test. Thurstone, in early studies of perception, found that the perceptual factor, on which Gottschaldt Figures had its highest loading, was associated with his reasoning factor. Since then, further confirmatory evidence has been found. Other studies by Thurstone (1949), and Pemberton (1951) confirm the validity of the Closure Flexibility test with tests of analytical and inductive reasoning. The correlations varied between .59 and .63. Pemberton (1951) further found that high scorers tended to be socially retiring, not dependent on social convention, and to have both theoretical interests and a need to achieve.

In a study by Thurstone (1944), a split-half reliability coefficient of .78 was found, while Pemberton (1951) reports a corrected split-half reliability of .94 on the present form of the test.

BIBLIOGRAPHY:

Buros, O. K.: Test number 435.

Botzum, W. A.: A Factorial Study of the Reasoning and Closure Factors. Unpublished Ph.D. dissertation. Department of Psychology, University of Chicago, 1950.

Pemberton, C. L.: A Study of the Speed and Flexibility of Closure Factors. Unpublished Ph.D. dissertation. Department of Psychology, University of Chicago, 1951.

Thurstone, L. L.: A Factorial Study of Perception. *Psychometric Monographs,* No. 4. Chicago, University of Chicago Press, 1944.

——— : Mechanical Aptitude III: Analysis of Group Tests. *Report of the Psychometric Laboratory.* No. 35. Chicago, The Psychometric Laboratory, University of Chicago, 1949.

——— and Jeffrey, T. E.: *Closure Flexibility (Concealed Figures), Test Administration Manual.* Chicago, Industrial Relations Center, 1965.

Closure Speed

AUTHORS: L. L. Thurstone and T. E. Jeffrey

VARIABLE: Closure Speed measures an individual's ability to see what appears to be a disorganized or unrelated group of parts as a meaningful whole.

TYPE OF MEASURE: Closure Speed is a paper and pencil test, suitable for administration to either individuals or groups. It is timed for three minutes. Scoring is done by hand.

SOURCE FROM WHICH MEASURE MAY BE OBTAINED: Industrial Relations Center, 1225 East Sixtieth Street, Chicago, Illinois 60637.

DESCRIPTION: Closure Speed is a test which consists of twenty-four items. Each item is an incomplete picture drawn in black on a white background. The subject responds by indicating what the picture is and gives a description in the space provided. Specifically, the test yields information regarding a subject's ability to perceive a meaningful picture from an apparently unrelated group of parts. This ability as identified by Thurstone (1944) is the "first closure factor". The Closure Speed test may be used in identifying mechanical aptitude and interest, as well as in assessing a subject's ability to reason analytically. Although it is used mainly in government and industry, its application extends to subjects of all ages, including school students, wherever assessment of the closure factor is desired.

NORMS: Norms are based on 1,252 male industrial employees, classified into the following occupational groups: professionals, middle and upper executives, junior executives, salesmen, foremen, and hourly employees.

VALIDITY AND RELIABILITY: Many investigators have shown a relationship between perception and personality. Pemberton (1951, 1952) in investigating the relationship of performance on this test to both temperament and mental abilities with 154 college students to whom she gave four temperament and interest schedules and twenty-five tests of perceptual, verbal, and reasoning ability, one of which was the Closure Speed test, found that the Closure Speed scores had low, but positive and consistent correlations with the following tests of inductive reasoning ability: Number Series, .21; Letter Series, .28; Figure Classification, .32; and False Premises, .15. She also reported that Closure Speed test scores had a moderate positive correlation of .49 with results of the Flags test (a space thinking test). Thurstone (1951), in studying the relationship of closure speed and mechanical aptitude, found that results on the Closure Speed test differentiated between criterion groups who had a high and low degree of mechanical interest and aptitude.

A study by Pemberton (1951) yielded a reliability value of .67 for parallel forms of the test. The tests were administered to twenty-four students on different days.

BIBLIOGRAPHY:

Buros, O. K.: Test number 436.

Pemberton, C. L.: A Study of the Speed and Flexibility of Closure Factors. Unpublished Ph.D. dissertation. Department of Psychology, University of Chicago, 1951.
_____ : The Closure Factors Related to Other Cognitive Processes. *Psychometrika,* XVII, 267-88, September, 1952.
Thurstone, L. L.: A Factorial Study of Perception. *Psychometric Monographs,* No. 4, 78-80. Chicago, University of Chicago Press, 1944.
_____ : An Analysis of Mechanical Aptitude. *Report of the Psychometric Laboratory.* No. 62. Chicago, The Psychometric Laboratory, University of Chicago, January, 1951. Unpublished.
_____ and Jeffrey, T. E.: *Closure Speed, Test Administration Manual — Revised, 1966.* Chicago, Industrial Relations Center, 1966.

Continuous Letter Checking and Continuous Symbol Checking

AUTHOR: H. Reuning

VARIABLE: The Continuous Letter Checking and Continuous Symbol Checking tests (CLC and CSC) assess the ability of an individual to concentrate and work fast at a reasonably steady rate.

TYPE OF MEASURE: The CLC and CSC are paper and pencil tests, suitable for administration to either individuals or groups. They are timed together for one hour. Scoring is rather complex and takes about thirty minutes per test; it is done by hand with the use of two keys.

SOURCE FROM WHICH MEASURE MAY BE OBTAINED: National Institute for Personnel Research, Johannesburg, South Africa.

DESCRIPTION: The CLC and CSC tests confront the subject with a routine work activity. They are presented in the form of an eight page pad. Each page contains a table of 150 sets of four letters or symbols printed in rows and columns. The subject is required to compare rows of either four capital letters (CLC) or four symbols (CSC) and to determine for each item how many letters or symbols were changed from one row to the next. The task is uninterrupted, lasts one hour, and requires that the subject work as accurately and quickly as possible. The changes in one's output within the one hour period provides information on the subject's ability to overcome monotony resulting from routine work. Similarly, the level at which the work is performed, that is the making of mistakes and/or corrections and the rate at which the subject adapts to the task, is also measured. The CLC and CSC would be most useful in the screening and placement of employees who would engage in repetitious clerical and mechanical activities. The CLC is suitable for use with persons at the high school level or at least beyond twelve years of age. The CSC is suitable for persons at all educational levels and also for illiterates.

NORMS: Norms for the CLC are derived from testing teacher trainees who were regarded as a representative sample of the average and above average South African matriculant. Norms for the CSC are not stated in the manual.

VALIDITY AND RELIABILITY: Validity is not reported. However, procedures of a rather complex nature are provided to determined individual accuracy and stability.

BIBLIOGRAPHY:

Reuning, H.: *Test Administrator's Manual: Continuous Letter Checking and Continuous Symbol Checking — Preliminary Edition.* Johannesburg, South Africa, National Institute for Personnel Research, 1972.

Experimental Comparative Prediction Batteries — High School and College Levels

AUTHOR: John W. French

VARIABLE: The Experimental Comparative Prediction Batteries (CPB) predicts an individual's success in academic and nonacademic courses important in high school and college guidance.

TYPE OF MEASURE: The CPB is a battery of seven paper and pencil subtests, suitable for administration to either individuals or groups. Each of the subtests is individually timed, and the entire series takes approximately three hours. Scoring may be done manually or by machine.

SOURCE FROM WHICH MEASURE MAY BE OBTAINED: Educational Testing Service, Princeton, New Jersey 08540.

DESCRIPTION: The CPB is a battery of pure factor subtests, including induction, integration, visualization, meaningful memory, number facility, spatial orientation, and the interest index. These were evolved from extensive research into the isolation of distinctive traits. Detailed descriptions are provided in the manual for each of the subtests. The battery for the high school level supplies relevant data to aid the student and counselor in selecting a college or noncollege curriculum, while the college level battery is intended to allow for guidance in selection of major subjects, as well as occupations for students. Unlike the various aptitude tests which only estimate a student's success in education beyond college, the CPB yields information directly related to the selection of college and noncollege courses and provides a more realistic basis for selection of an educational or occupational future. Although the CPB is experimental in nature, many of the pure factor tests included in it have been utilized previously, and separate studies have been conducted on the reliability and validity of these subtests. In addition, data has been generated on normative samples for many of the subtests.

NORMS: Norms for the CPB are not yet available, per se, but do exist to some extent in the individual subtests. However, given the nature of the instrument to provide prediction of success in a wide variety of curriculum areas, the user is encouraged to develop relevant and appropriate norms.

VALIDITY AND RELIABILITY: Validity studies, correlating the varied CPB subtests with major college courses, are reported extensively for thirteen major subject areas on over seventeen hundred students at the college level. Other validity correlation values are reported for high school males and females separately, showing relationships of the CPB subtests with course grades in twelve academic and seven nonacademic areas for males and in twelve academic and two nonacademic areas for females. These values generally are in the range between .20 and .40 for samples between 80 and 900 subjects.

Reliability estimates are included but are not deemed to be reliabilities for the varied subtests.

BIBLIOGRAPHY:

Buros, O. K.: Test number 674.

French, J. W.: *Manual for Experimental Comparative Prediction Batteries — High School and College Level.* Princeton, Educational Testing Service, 1964.

Flags — A Test of Space Thinking

AUTHORS: L. L. Thurstone and T. E. Jeffrey

VARIABLE: The Flags test assesses the ability to see a rigid configuration changed into different positions.

TYPE OF MEASURE: Flags is a paper and pencil test, suitable for administration to either individuals or groups. It is timed for five minutes. Scoring is done by hand with the use of a key.

SOURCE FROM WHICH MEASURE MAY BE OBTAINED: Industrial Relations Center, 1225 East Sixtieth Street, Chicago, Illinois 60637.

DESCRIPTION: The Flags test consists of twenty-one items, each of which requires six responses. Every item presents a stimulus flag with six flags to the right of it, each positioned in the same (S) or opposite (O) direction or side as the stimulus flag. The subject responds by drawing a line through the "S" or "O" underneath each flag to indicate whether it is the same as or opposite to the stimulus flag. Although seemingly easy, the test's short timing measures the speed with which a subject can visualize the object when it is moved into different positions. This test intends to assess that which is identified by Thurstone (1941) as the "first space factor". In disclosing this first space factor, the Flags test would be useful in the selection of individuals with high mechanical interest and aptitude. Raw scores may be converted into standard scores.

NORMS: At the present time, norms are based on 278 male industrial employees classified into the following occupational groups: 47 professionals, 15 executives, 42 junior executives, 58 foremen, and 116 hourly employees.

VALIDITY AND RELIABILITY: A review of seven factor analytic studies, in which an older version of the Flags test was used, indicated that the primary loadings (correlations) are on the first space factor. The first space factor was identified by

Thurstone (1951) in his study of mechanical aptitude. Flags was not included in this research, although several other tests of the first space factor were. These findings suggest that the present version of the test will also be an efficient assessment of this factor. At the present time, other validity studies of the later version of Flags may be available. Tests of the first space factor have been found to discriminate between high and low mechanical interest and experience groups.

No reliability data are stated.

Bibliography:

Thurstone, L. L.: An Analysis of Mechanical Aptitude. *Report of the Psychometric Laboratory*. No. 62, Chicago, The Psychometric Laboratory, University of Chicago, January, 1951. Unpublished.

Thurstone, L. L. and Jeffrey, T. E.: *Space Thinking (Flags), Test Administration Manual*. Chicago, Industrial Relations Center, 1959.

——— and Thurstone, T. G.: Factorial Studies of Intelligence. *Psychometric Monographs*. No. 2. Chicago, University of Chicago Press, 1941.

Goldman-Fristoe-Woodcock Test of Auditory Discrimination

Authors: Ronald Goldman, Macalyne Fristoe, and Richard W. Woodcock

Variable: The Goldman-Fristoe-Woodcock Test of Auditory Discrimination (G-F-W) measures the ability of an individual to discriminate speech sounds.

Type of Measure: The G-F-W, which consists of two subtests, is an auditory device, most suitably administered in an individual situation. It is timed for seven and one-half minutes. Scoring is done by hand at the time of administration.

Source from which Measure may be Obtained: American Guidance Service, Publisher's Building, Circle Pines, Minnesota 55014.

Description: The G-F-W consists of thirty items broken into three parts. Part one is the training procedure and familiarizes the subject with the word-picture association concept used in the second and third parts; it permits the examiner to establish whether or not the subject possesses the ability to make the necessary associations. Part two, the quiet subtest, assesses the subject's auditory discrimination without background noise. Part three, the noise subtest, assesses the subject's auditory discrimination with distracting noise in the background. The test thereby permits assessment of auditory discrimination under ideal as well as distracting conditions. Part one is presented orally, and parts two and three are administered by means of a magnetic tape player. An error analysis matrix provides for a summary of error performance with respect to certain speech sounds. Used by a trained speech clinician, the G-F-W would be most useful in clinical settings for rehabilitation and counseling. Raw scores may be converted into percentile ranks or standard scores by using the tables provided in the manual.

NORMS: Norms are provided separately for the two subtests, for subjects ranging in age from three years, eight months to over seventy. The standardization sample ranged in age from three to eighty-four and included 745 subjects. Sex differences are not specified.

VALIDITY AND RELIABILITY: Concurrent validity yielded a point biserial correlation coefficient of .68 for clinical judgment with scores on the quiet subtest on twelve subjects, while a correlation of .72 was obtained for clinical judgment with scores on the noise subtest for the same twelve subjects. Content, concurrent, and construct validity data are presented in the manual. Content validity is inferred by judgment that the G-F-W subtests are close simulations of real life situations. The items, as well as the test material, are familiar to most subjects. Construct validity studies are also reported. For example, the change in score performance with age shows decreasing error scores into the twenties, a leveling into the forties, and a gradual increase in errors with older subjects.

Test retest reliabilities, performed on seventeen subjects over a two-week interval, were found to be .87 for the quiet subtest and .81 for the noise subtest. Internal consistency reliabilities for a clinical sample of 242 subjects were .87 on the quiet subtest and .68 on the noise subtest.

BIBLIOGRAPHY:

Buros, O. K.: Test number 938.

Goldman, R., Fristoe, M., and Woodcock, R. W.: *Goldman-Fristoe-Woodcock*

Test of Auditory Discrimination. Circle Pines, American Guidance Services, 1970.

Perceptual Speed

Authors: L. L. Thurstone and T. E. Jeffrey

Variable: The Perceptual Speed test is a measure of an individual's speed in perceiving and comparing visual figures.

Type of Measure: Perceptual Speed is a paper and pencil test, suitable for administration to either individuals or groups. It is timed for five minutes. Scoring is done by hand with the use of a key.

Source from which Measure may be Obtained: Industrial Relations Center, 1225 East Sixtieth Street, Chicago, Illinois 60637.

Description: Perceptual Speed is one in a series of tests designed to establish a profile of a subject's primary mental abilities as defined by Thurstone (1938). This test concerns the area of visual thinking. Specifically, perceptual speed may be defined as the speed with which an individual can compare a series of visual figures and then either choose two which appear similar or identical, or find a stimulus design incorporated within distracting material. The test is available in two parallel forms, A and B, each consisting of 140 items. Each item contains one stimulus figure and five alternative answer figures. The subject responds by indicating one of the five which appears the same as the stimulus. A suggested use for the Perceptual Speed test would be in the selection and placement of clerical workers, proofreaders, key punch operators, visual inspectors, and other occupations requiring a certain degree of perceptual speed. Please note, however, that it is advisable for the user to validate the test for the particular occupational groups within the organization for which it is intended. Raw scores may be converted to standard scores or percentile ranks.

Norms: Norms for the test were based on 297 industrial personnel tested prior to June of 1962. The normative samples were classified into the following occupational groups: professionals, middle and upper executives, junior executives, salesmen, foremen, and hourly workers. A second set of norms, based on 251 government clerical employees, is also presented. Age range for the latter group is from nineteen to seventy-eight. The characteristics of the two normative samples are fully described in the manual, including information on education, occupation, responsibilities, and income (sex is not specified).

Validity and Reliability: One investigation in 1966 yielded significant correlation values for Perceptual Speed test scores and the subscores on the General Clerical Test ranging from .32 to .55. A comparison of test scores on the Perceptual Speed test for the top rated one third clerical employees with the bottom rated one third, established that the top rated third scored significantly higher than the bottom rated third. A similar comparison for a supervisory group versus a non-supervisory group, in which the first group represented the upper range of clerical performance, showed significantly higher scores on the Perceptual Speed test for the supervisory group.

A split-half reliability coefficient of .98 was obtained in one use of the test and a reliability coefficient of .92 in another investigation. The reliabilities between immediate presentations of forms A and B, for eighty-eight male industrial personnel, yielded values of .80 and above.

Bibliography:

Buros, O. K.: Test number 444.

Thurstone, L. L.: *Primary Mental Abilities.* Chicago, University of Chicago Press, 1938.

Thurstone, L. L. and Jeffrey, T. E.: *Perceptual Speed (Identical Forms), Test Administration Manual — Revised 1966.* Chicago, Industrial Relations Center, 1966.

Word Fluency Test

Author: Raymond J. Corsini

Variable: The Word Fluency Test measures the speed with which an individual is able to make verbal associations.

Type of Measure: Word Fluency is a paper and pencil test, suitable for administration to either individuals or groups. It is timed for ten minutes. Scoring is done by hand.

Source from which Measure may be Obtained: Education-Industry Service, 1225 East Sixtieth Street, Chicago, Illinois 60637.

Description: Word Fluency assesses that primary mental ability known as the "word fluency factor" (Thurstone, 1941) in which verbal comprehension and vocabulary do not play a significant part in determining the score. The test sheet is headed with five category titles, and each row of five boxes is headed by a letter. The subject responds by writing in each of the category boxes, one word that begins with the stimulus letter. There are eighty boxes to be filled, and the total score is simply the total number of boxes in which the subject has written acceptable responses. The rule for determining acceptability of responses is to be lenient in case of misspellings as long as it is clear that the word fits the category. The use of this test extends to identifying and selecting personnel for positions or tasks which require a high degree of verbal fluency.

Norms: Norms for this test are reported only for a combined group of 528 male industrial personnel, classified into the following occupational areas: 75 laborers, 160 engineers and chemists, 60 executives and middle management, 45 white collar and junior executives, 89 foremen, and 99 salesmen. The range in score for all of these groups is sufficiently wide so that the test will discriminate very well among individuals in these groups.

Validity and Reliability: Validity was determined partly through correlation of various groups' scores on the Word Fluency Test with scores on Corsini and Rench's Verbal Reasoning Test. Correlations of the two tests, for six norm groups, varied from .10 to .30. For example, the group of forty-two foremen's scores yielded a correlation value of .55. A comparison of scores on the Word Fluency Test with Thelma G. Thurstone's Understanding Communication Test yielded correlation values for the six norm groups ranging from -.02 to +.50 with a correlation value of .56 for the total group of 445 subjects. This latter finding indicates that the Word Fluency Test is a potent measure of mental abilities.

Test retest, over a one month interval and based on a group of forty-eight men employed in varied occupations, yielded a reliability estimate of .78. Other results of reliability, using Kuder-Richardson formula 21, yielded a correlation of .78. Reliability estimates for the norm groups, again using K-R 21, yielded correlation values of: .74 for laborers; .75 for engineers and chemists; .67 for executives and middle management; .68 for white collar and junior executives; .84 for foremen; .75 for salesmen; and a total correlation of .84.

BIBLIOGRAPHY:

Corsini, R. J.: *Word Fluency Test, Test Administration Manual.* Chicago, Education-Industry Service, 1959.

Thurstone, L. L.: Primary Mental Abilities. *Psychometric Monographs #4.* Chicago, University of Chicago Press, 1941.

Chapter 5

PERSONALITY ASSESSMENT

GROUP 1 — GENERAL PERSONALITY MEASURES

The Adjective Check List

Authors: Harrison G. Gough and Alfred B. Heilbrun

Variable: The Adjective Check List (ACL) assesses over twenty personality traits.

Type of Measure: The ACL is a paper and pencil inventory, suitable for administration to either individuals or groups. It is untimed and typically takes ten to fifteen minutes to complete. Scoring may be done manually or by machine.

Source from which Measure may be Obtained: Consulting Psychologist Press, Inc., 577 College Avenue, Palo Alto, California 94036.

Description: The ACL includes 300 adjectives that are typically found in describing attributes of a person. Its primary usage lies in either self evaluation or as an instrument employed by raters or observers in an environment where recording of personality attributes is needed. The ACL measures twenty-four personality traits, including defensiveness, self confidence, self control, lability, personal adjustment, and "need" scales which include achievement, dominance, endurance, order, intraception, nurturance, affiliation, heterosexuality, exhibition, autonomy, aggression, change, succorance, abasement, deference, and counseling readiness. The ACL, which has its foundation in the "need press" theories of Murry, isolates the strongest traits in a subject. A complete and full description is provided for the twenty-four scales. The application of the ACL is limited only by the inventiveness of the user.

Norms: Norms are provided separately for males and females and by the number of adjectives checked.

Validity and Reliability: Numerous studies have reported on the relationship of the ACL with the Edwards Personal Preference Schedule, the Bennett Mechanical Comprehension Test, Chapin Social Insight Test, General Information Survey, Gottschaldt Figures, Guilford Creativity, Minnesota Paper Form Board, Terman Concept Mastery, and Wesman Personnel Classification Test, as well as the California Psychological Inventory and the Minnesota Multiphasic Personality Inventory. For the correlation of the ACL with the EPPS, ten of the coefficients were reported to be significant where the scales were similarly matched between the two inventories. Significant positive correlations were found for the self confidence scale of the ACL with the Guilford Creativity battery and the Terman Concept Mastery Test, as well as for the lability and personal adjustment scales of the ACL with the General Information Survey, Gottschaldt Figures test and Terman Concept Mastery Test. These are only a few examples of the findings based on a sample of 100 males.

Test retest correlations for the ACL scales over varying intervals of time ranged from .45 to .90 for ten weeks, from .31 to .75 for six months, and from .25 to .77 for five and one-half years. The number of cases varied from 34 to 100 male college students, adult males, and medical students.

Bibliography:

Buros, O. K.: Test number 38.

Gough, H. G. and Hielbrun, A. B.: *The Adjective Check List, Manual.* Palo Alto, Consulting Psychologists Press, 1965.

California Test of Personality — Forms AA and BB

Authors: Louis P. Thorpe, Willis W. Clark, and Ernest W. Tiegs

Variable: The California Test of Personality assesses an individual's balance between personal and social adjustment.

Type of Measure: The personality test is a paper and pencil device, suitable for administration to either individuals or groups. It is untimed and typically takes sixty-five minutes to complete. Scoring may be done manually or by machine.

Source from which Measure may be Obtained: CTB/McGraw-Hill, Del Monte Research Park, Monterey, California 93940.

Description: The personality test identifies and reveals a subject's traits relating to personal and social adjustment. It is available in two parallel forms AA and BB, each of which consists of 180 items. The subject responds by indicating "yes" or "no". Item responses yield information regarding the subject's types of tendencies in thinking, feeling, and acting, thereby disclosing undesirable individual adjustments. The test is divided into two parts: personal adjustment which covers the areas of self reliance, sense of personal worth, sense of personal freedom, feeling of belonging, withdrawing tendencies, and nervous symptoms; and social adjustment which covers the areas of social standards, social skills, antisocial tendencies, family relations, school relations, occupational relations, and community relations. The data obtained from test results can be used by job supervisors and counselors in ascertaining the mental health of a person. This is particularly true of the personal, social, and total adjustment scores. Researchers may also utilize this inventory to provide information in a wide variety of educational and industrial programs. Median scores on each specific item furnish valuable information for those who are in charge of evaluation, curriculum making, and supervision of instruction. Data would be useful for employment considerations also.

Norms: Norms are based on 3,133 adults in education and industry, from six states with a wide geographical spread. The racial composition of the normative sample includes 85 percent Caucasians and 15 percent Mexican, Negro, and other races. Sex differences in scores were found, but they are so negligible that norms are not separated by sex. Finally, a publication entitled the *Summaries of Investigations, Number One* provides normative data for special groups, such as adult evening school enrollees, industrial employees, adult stutterers, delinquents versus nondelinquents, pupils versus parents, among others.

Validity and Reliability: The California Test of Personality has been investigated extensively to determine its validity. Studies have shown it to be as thorough as an interview or teacher or parent rating in describing the personal and social adjustment of a subject. Inherent in its construction is that differences should be found between better adjusted subjects tolerating more self-damaging statements than less well adjusted subjects. Studies in this latter area have confirmed the ability of the test to discriminate better-adjusted from less well-adjusted subjects. The *Summaries of Investigation, Number One* includes ninety studies describing research uses of the California Test of Personality.

Reliability values, computed by Kuder-Richardson, varied, for the adult forms, from .82 to .96 for the subscales and yielded a value of .97 for total adjustment score.

Bibliography:

California Test Bureau, A Division of McGraw-Hill Book Company: *Summaries of Investigations, Number One — Enlarged Edition: California Test of Personality*. Author.

Thorpe, L. P., Clark, W. W., and Tiegs, E. W.: *Manual: California Test of Personality*. Monterey, CTB/McGraw-Hill, 1953.

Chromatic Differential Test

Authors: Arthur B. Sweney and Jack D. Bowles

Variable: The Chromatic Differential Test (CDT) determines objectively an individual's attitudes towards other people and institutions.

Type of Measure: The CDT is an oral test, most suitably administered in an individual situation. It is timed, and scoring is done by hand at the time of administration.

Source from which Measure may be Obtained: Test Systems, Inc., P. O. Box 18432, Wichita, Kansas 67209.

Description: The CDT consists of several color templates.

Each template has six colors graduated by hue and brightness. There are ten acetate response templates, each of which is labeled with an important personal construct, such as, likes and dislikes, emotional states, self, significant persons, and important institutions. The subject responds by choosing, by hue, the color template which he or she most closely associates with the stimulus (person, emotion, institution, and so on). There is an order of presentation which is as follows: preferences, emotions, persons, institutions, and self concept, and these are the constructs which yield an assessment of the subject's attitudes. Scoring is accomplished by counting the number of spaces, according to hue of color, between the constructs. Scales of interpretation allow judgment on like versus dislike patterns, alienation versus cultural anchorage, emotional associations, emotional evaluation, self rejection, and familial patterns. The usefulness of this inventory could be found in environments where verbal facility of the subject is limited. It's application extends to use in institutions, industry or academia, where measurement of attitudes is desired. Extensions of the inventory through use of other related attitudinal constructs is noted by the authors.

Norms: Norm tables include samples of college and other males and females. The norms are reported for seventy-five general college students with scores reported in stens (standard tens) with a mean of five and one-half and a standard deviation of two.

Validity and Reliability: Both content and concurrent validity studies are reported, and construct validity data is also provided. A factor analysis on the CDT yielded six factors from the scales of the inventory: father, mother, depression, hostility, self, and negative affect. Other uses of the inventory are summarized in a research section of the manual.

Split-half reliability coefficients, calculated for the ten response templates and the constructs of mother, father, self, and several others, ranged from .57 to .76.

Bibliography:

Sweney, A. B. and Bowles, J. D.: *Handbook for the Chromatic Differential Test*. Wichita, Test Systems, 1972.

The Differential Value Profile — Form A

Author: Walter Thomas

Variable: The Differential Value Profile (DVP) assesses an individual's personality traits.

Type of Measure: The DVP is a paper and pencil inventory, suitable for administration to either individuals or groups. It is untimed and typically takes forty-five minutes to complete. Scoring is done by hand with the use of a stencil.

Source from which Measure may be Obtained: W. Clement and Jessie V. Stone Foundation, 111 E. Wacker Drive, Suite 510, Chicago, Illinois 60601.

Description: The DVP includes 134 statements to which the subject responds by choosing one of four alternatives, from "strongly agree" to "strongly disagree". Six dimensions are assessed, specifically: aesthetic — perceiving one's environment; humanitarian — love for people; intellectual — emphasizing the rational and cognitive; material — perceiving one's environment in "dollar signs"; power — perceiving objects, persons, and events in relation to one's own power and authority; and religious — having great faith in God. Most of the DVP items are keyed for two directions. For example, if a subject agrees with a statement, he or she is scored toward one value and if the subject disagrees, he or she is scored toward an alternative value. However, some items do not set one value against another and are, therefore, keyed in only one direction. The DVP is intended for use in educational research and guidance applications, such as, assessing change in student values over four years of college (results published by the United States government-supported *Project on Student Values*, Grand Rapids, Michigan). Designed primarily for subjects at the college level, it's usefulness has been extended to include individual counseling and clinical applications. The DVP is also available in a more simplified form for use at junior and senior high school levels.

Validity and Reliability: Validity studies are reported including content, construct, and concurrent methods. Content validity was arrived at through judges' assessments of the dimension being measured by each item. A high level of agreement was achieved in which over 50 percent of the items were unanimously placed in the same dimension by the ten judges. All of the correlations among the judges' ratings were significant. Construct validity information is also presented. Finally, concurrent validity studies were carried out with groups of college students, by the dimensions of sex and two types of colleges: church and public related. Significant differences were obtained in all but one of the stated hypotheses, pointing to clear differences in values of students in different college environments.

Kuder-Richardson estimates of reliability on the six scales yielded correlations ranging from .75 to .88. Test retest, over a ten day time interval, yielded reliability coefficients ranging from .83 to .94 on the six subscales, based on administration to 100 subjects.

Bibliography:

Buros, O. K.: Test number 69.

Thomas, W.: *The Differential Value Profile — Form A.* Chicago, W. Clement and Jessie V. Stone Foundation, 1972.

Edwards Personal Preference Schedule

Author: Allen L. Edwards

Variable: The Edwards Personal Preference Schedule (EPPS) is a broad measure of personality dimensions and traits.

Type of Measure: The EPPS is a paper and pencil inventory, suitable for administration to either individuals or groups. It is untimed and typically takes forty minutes to complete. Scoring may be done manually or by machine.

Source from which Measure may be Obtained: The Psychological Corporation, 304 East Forty-fifth Street, New York, New York 10017.

Description: The EPPS is designed for a wide range of uses in the fields of research and counseling and extends to diagnostic assessments in environments where counseling is provided, in that some or all of the variables may be utilized, as well as to identification of personal attributes necessary for consideration in job promotions. It measures fifteen variables, including, achievement, deference, order, exhibition, autonomy, affiliation, intraception, succorance, dominance, abasement, nurturance, change, endurance, heterosexuality, and aggression. Detailed descriptions are provided in the manual which include specific behavioral characteristics of the fifteen dimensions. The EPPS consists of 225 pairs of statements. The subject responds by indicating which one of the two statements describes his or her usual behavior or preference. Each pair of statements is constructed to be parallel in social desirability, thereby allowing the responses to weigh on the personality variables alone. A high score on a particular variable indicates that this variable is descriptive of the subject. Raw scores may be converted to percentile ranks by using the tables provided in the manual.

Norms: Normative data has been developed for two groups of subjects: college students consisting of 749 women and 760 men ranging in age from fifteen to fifty-nine; and adults who were household heads including 4,932 women and 4,031 men. A breakdown of the adult sample, by age, family income, education, size of city of residence, and census region is available in a publication by Koponen (1957).

Validity and Reliability: Various studies have been made comparing personality trait ratings and scores on the variables of the EPPS. In one study, subjects were asked to rank themselves on the fifteen personality variables, without knowing their corresponding scores on the EPPS. Definitions of the variables were provided in terms of the statements appearing in the EPPS. The self-rankings of some subjects agreed perfectly with their rankings based on the EPPS scores. In other cases, there was little agreement between the self rankings and scores obtained on the EPPS. Differences in these findings are due to factors such as the wording of the items, the breadth and depth of descriptions, and so forth. However, they do indicate a tendency to reflect real behavioral traits. Further validity studies with the Guilford-Martin Personnel Inventory and the Taylor Manifest Anxiety Scale indicated concurrent validity coefficients in the desired directions with EPPS variables. For example, the correlation values of the EPPS aggression scale with the Guilford-Martin Personnel Inventory Scales of cooperativeness and agreeableness were both significant at -.37 and -.51, respectively.

Split-half reliability coefficients ranged from .61 to .87 for the fifteen variables. Test retest reliability, based on eighty-nine college students over a one-week time interval, yielded coefficients ranging from .74 to .88 on all variables.

BIBLIOGRAPHY:

Buros, O. K.: Test number 72.

Edwards, A. L.: *Manual — Revised 1959: Edwards Personal Preference Schedule*. New York, The Psychological Corporation, 1959.

Koponen, A.: The Influence of Demographic Factors on Responses to the Edwards Personal Preference Schedule. Unpublished doctoral dissertation. Columbia University, 1957.

Eysenck Personality Inventory

AUTHORS: H. J. Eysenck and Sybil B. G. Eysenck

VARIABLE: The Eysenck Personality Inventory (EPI) and its earlier version, the Maudsley Personality Inventory, measures personality in terms of two independent dimensions:

extraversion-introversion (E) and neuroticism-stability (N).

Type of Measure: The EPI is a paper and pencil inventory, suitable for administration to either individuals or groups. It is untimed and typically takes ten to fifteen minutes to complete. Scoring may be done manually or by machine.

Source from which Measure may be Obtained: Educational and Industrial Testing Service, P. O. Box 7234, San Diego, California 92107.

Description: The EPI is available to two parallel forms, A and B. Each intends to assess the individual's behavioral personality. There are fifty-seven items in the inventory to which the subject responds by answering "yes" or "no". In addition to the "E" scale, recognizable as a continuum of the outgoing, uninhibited sociability of an individual, and the "N" scale, indicative of a continuum of overreactive emotional behavior, the EPI includes a "lie" scale, which alerts the scorer to a subject's attempt at faking responses. Application of the EPI extends to the selection and placement of industrial personnel (Cooper and Payne, 1967) where an individual's personality might effect performance in certain positions, such as, in a routine work situation; or in educational guidance and counseling, such as, in the instance of a certain level of neuroticism affecting a student's ability to learn; as well as in supplementing a test battery to round out assessment of an individual's overall personality and in clinical settings as an aid in diagnosis and treatment of certain behavioral patterns. Scores may be converted to percentile ranks with the use of the tables in the manual.

Norms: Normative data is based on 1,003 cases, for form A, and 239 cases, for form B, tested at various colleges and universities throughout the United States. This limited sample indicates the desirability of constructing local norms for college students. Reference group norms are extensive with working classes, professionals, housewives, sales personnel, medical students, abnormal neurotic and psychotic groups among the thirty-one areas identified.

Validity and Reliability: The validity studies include data on construct and concurrent validity. This data indicates that significant relationships exist for the EPI with the Minnesota Multiphasic Personality Inventory (MMPI), the Adjective Check List (ACL), and the California Personality Inventory (CPI), among others. For example, a significant correlation exists on the exhibition scale of the ACL with the "E" scale of the EPI, in addition to a significant correlation of the dominance and sociability scales of the CPI with the "E" scale of the EPI. These are only a sampling of the research findings.

Test retest reliability, for groups of twenty-seven and ninety-two subjects over time intervals of nine months and one year, respectively, yielded coefficients ranging from .92 to .94 for the group of twenty-seven and from .84 to .88 for the group of ninety-two. Split-half reliabilities, based on normals, neurotics, and psychotics, ranged from .75 to .91 on the two scales of the EPI.

BIBLIOGRAPHY:

Buros, O. K.: Test number 76.

Cooper, R., and Payne, R.: Extraversion and Some Aspects of Work Behavior. *Personnel Psychology*, 45-57, 1967.

Eysenck, H. J. and Eysenck, S. B. G.: *Manual: Eysenck Personality Inventory*. San Diego, Educational and Industrial Testing Service, 1968.

Famous Sayings Test

AUTHOR: Bernard M. Bass

VARIABLE: The Famous Sayings Test (FS) assesses four areas of personality: hostility (HO), fear of failure (FF), social acquiescence (SA), and acceptance of conventional mores (CM).

TYPE OF MEASURE: The FS is a paper and pencil test, suitable for administration to either individuals or groups. It is untimed and typically takes thirty minutes to complete. Scoring may be done manually or by machine.

SOURCE FROM WHICH MEASURE MAY BE OBTAINED: Psychological Test Specialists, Box 1441, Missoula, Montana 59801.

Description: The FS intends to provide schools and institutional, business, and industrial personnel specialists with an instrument designed for speedy personality assessment. It consists of 131 items, each of which confronts the subject with a generality in the form of a famous saying, a proverb, an adage, or an aphorism. The subject responds by indicating agreement, disagreement, or uncertainty. Scores obtained on the FS discriminate as follows: a high "HO" score identifies the aggressive individual who believes in acting on his or her own, who is suspicious of people in general, and who has no time for persons with low intelligence levels: a high "FF" score reveals the individual who believes in trying his or her best to succeed, who is ambitious and desires fame and achievement, and who believes in the pitfalls of carelessness; a high score in "SA" identifies the person who will agree with literally anything; a high "CM" score reveals an individual who is a total conformist, who believes in being generous, forgiving, obedient, virtuous, and loyal, among others.

Norms: Approximately two thousand subjects, from different educational levels, regions of the United States, and occupational groups, were examined. Norms for each of the four scales are given, and summary scales are available for salesmen, sales applicants, factory supervisors, school teachers, student nurses, penitentiary inmates, and college and high school students. Advisability of developing of local norms is stressed.

Validity and Reliability: Validity studies yielded information establishing low intercorrelations among the subscales; this points to the independence of these scales. The CM, HO, and FF scales differentiated significantly between salesmen and nonsalesmen, as well as between inmates and noninmates, albeit not in the same manner. Also, significant correlation of the CM subscale of the FS with the Guilford-Zimmerman sociability subscore is reported. Extensive validity data is presented by Bass (1958).

Reliability estimates range from .69 for HO to .92 for SA,

with social acquiescence being the only scale which is long enough in its own right to achieve a respectable reliability without the need for additional evidence from other related tests or screening. However, reliability is adequate for screening purposes.

Bibliography:

Bass, B. M.: Famous Sayings Test: General Manual. *Psychological Reports.* Monograph Supplement 6. Reprinted June, 1968. Missoula, Psychological Test Specialists, 1958.

Gordon Personal Inventory

Author: Leonard V. Gordon

Variable: The Gordon Personal Inventory (GPI) assesses four personality dimensions: cautiousness, original thinking, personal relations, and vigor.

Type of Measure: The GPI is a paper and pencil inventory, suitable for administration to either individuals or groups. It is untimed and typically takes ten to fifteen minutes to complete. There are two editions of the GPI, one a hand-scorable booklet and the other an IBM answer sheet.

Source from which Measure may be Obtained: Harcourt Brace Jovanovich, 757 Third Avenue, New York, New York 10017.

Description: The GPI consists of twenty tetrads of descriptive phrases. The subject responds by choosing one phrase which is most, and one which is least, descriptive of himself or herself. The four traits of cautiousness, original thinking, personal relations, and vigor, are represented in each tetrad. The forced choice format permits each tetrad to yield four trait scores and is less susceptible to faking. The GPI is useful in assessing the adjustment potential of normal individuals in a wide variety of social settings, such as, in personnel placement. Raw scores may be converted to percentile ranks with the use of the tables in the manual.

Norms: Normative data is presented in percentile ranks for high school and college students, separately by sex, for each of the four traits. The high school norms are tentative, for they represent cases from schools in a limited geographical area. The college norms are based on students in nine schools with a wide geographical distribution. Also, norms for low level management males, second level management executive males, food salesmen, male insurance agent applicants, low level management females, and a wide variety of other samples, are available.

VALIDITY AND RELIABILITY: A wide variety of validity studies have been carried out, establishing the value of the GPI. The studies include salesmen, managers, supervisors, applicants for sales positions and others. Generally, results established significant correlations of GPI scores with rankings; other correlations were not significant with either one or more of the GPI traits measured. For example, Toorenaar found a significant correlation of the vigor scale of the GPI with ranking of class performance and field performance for seventy-eight salesmen. The rankings were carried out by eight instructors who normally worked with salespeople. The other three scales of the GPI were not significantly related to the ranking criteria. In a study by Gunderson on 162 incarcerated navy and marine subjects, the subscale of original thinking was significantly related with a dichotomous criterion of restoration success, that is, reincarcerated or not reincarcerated. None of the other subscales were related to this criterion.

Split-half reliability coefficients for all four traits ranged from .80 to .83 for college students and from .77 to .83 for high school seniors. Reliabilities, computed by Kuder-Richardson Case III formula, ranged from .79 to .84 on college students.

BIBLIOGRAPHY:

Gordon, L. V.: *Manual: Gordon Personal Inventory*. New York, Harcourt Brace Jovanovich, 1963.

(Please note that the manual references neither Toorenaar nor Gunderson.)

Gordon Personal Profile

Author: Leonard V. Gordon

Variable: The Gordon Personal Profile (GPP) assesses four personality dimensions: ascendancy, responsibility, emotional stability, and sociability.

Type of Measure: The GPP is a paper and pencil inventory, suitable for administration to either individuals or groups. It is untimed and typically takes seven to fifteen minutes to complete. There are two editions of the GPP, one a hand-scorable booklet and the other an IBM answer sheet.

Source from which Measure may be Obtained: Harcourt Brace Jovanovich, 757 Third Avenue, New York, New York 10017.

Description: The GPP consists of eighteen tetrads of descriptive phrases. The subject responds by choosing one phrase which is most, and one which is least, descriptive of himself or herself. The four traits of ascendancy, responsibility, emotional stability, and sociability, are represented in each tetrad. The forced choice format permits each tetrad to yield four trait scores and is less susceptible to faking. The GPP is useful in assessing an individual's personal adjustment and effectiveness in social situations, such as, in placement of personnel in positions requiring a person who is comfortable working in face to face circumstances or in positions that may require an individual to make numerous decisions. The GPP's use also extends to counseling and research. Raw scores may be converted to percentile ranks with the use of the tables in the manual.

Norms: Normative data was collected on high school, college, industrial, and general adult groups. The high school group is primarily located in the East, whereas the college group has a wide geographical distribution. Significant sex differences, found to exist on some of the traits, provided the basis for separate norms. The industrial group is comprised of low-level management and is available for men and women separately. Also, norm groups for manufacturing foremen, salesmen, female clerks, and second level management executive males are provided. Further percentile rank information is provided on both the male and female groups.

Validity and Reliability: Construct validity studies yielded information on the independence of the four personality dimensions. Studies have also yielded significant correlations of test scores of the GPP with peer ranking of the same traits on male and female samples. Significant correlations were found for trait scores with a criterion of "success" (defined as a sense of responsibility) in a supermarket environment with ninety-nine supervisory personnel; the criterion of success was arrived at through ratings by two supervisors (Brown and Landsberger, 1959). Finally, other studies are reported on a wide variety of samples, testifying to the validity of the GPP. The sample groups include management, armed services, foremen, and others.

Split-half reliability on college students ranged from .84 to .88 for the four traits. Reliabilities, computed by Kuder-Richardson Case III formula, ranged from .74 to .85 for the four traits. Test retest, on 200 college students over a one week interval, yielded reliability coefficients ranging from .84 to .87 for all four traits, and a test retest of eighty-eight high school students, over a three month interval, yielded reliabilities ranging from .80 to .87 for all four traits.

Bibliography:

Brown, A. W.: A Sense of Responsibility at Work: Its Measurement and Correlates. Unpublished Master's thesis. Cornell University, 1959. (Resume in *Occupational Psychology, 34*, January 1960.)

Gordon, L. V.: *Manual: Gordon Personal Profile*. New York, Harcourt Brace Jovanovich, 1963.

Minnesota Multiphasic Personality Inventory

Authors: S. R. Hathaway and J. C. McKinley

Variable: The Minnesota Multiphasic Personality Inventory (MMPI) assesses those personality characteristics which affect personal and social adjustment.

Type of Measure: The MMPI is a paper and pencil inventory, suitable for administration to either individuals or groups. It is untimed and may take from forty-five to ninety minutes to complete. It is available for individual administration in two card sort forms, one complete and one shortened version. Scoring may be done manually or by machine.

Source from which Measure may be Obtained: The Psychological Corporation, 304 East Forty-fifth Street, New York, New York 10017.

Description: The MMPI is designed to yield objective information regarding the personality traits which are relative to the personal and social adjustment of individuals. It consists of 550 items, covering a wide range of categories, from subject's physical condition to moral and social beliefs. The subject responds by indicating agreement, disagreement, or uncertainty. The items are structured over ten subscales, including, hypochondriasis, depression, hysteria, psychopathic deviate, masculinity-femininity, paranoia, psychasthenia (obsessive-compulsive), schizophrenia, hypomania (overresponsive), social introversion. In addition to these subscales, validation scales are also structured within the inventory: lie, validity, and other corrections, to identify a subject's intent or ability to fake responses. Uses of the MMPI extend to clinical assessment, research, and vocational and rehabilitation counseling. Also, the MMPI can be employed to provide a broad-based perspective of an individual's personality.

Norms: Norms were based on a cross-section of the Minnesota population, ranging in age from sixteen to fifty-five and including both sexes. Also included is data on 250 precollege and college students, representing a wide cross-section of college entrance applications. Additional studies by Goodstein and Dahlstrom (1956), drawing samples from the Midwest, have yielded scores on the MMPI close to the original values established for the MMPI almost twenty years prior.

Validity and Reliability: Validity data on the MMPI is so extensive that each situation in which the inventory could be used must be specifically investigated. For data on the specific studies, the reader must be thoroughly versed in clinical diagnosis and measurement. A reference for uses of the MMPI is *An MMPI Handbook: A Guide to Use in Clinical Practice and Research.*

In two test retest studies by Hathaway and McKinley (1942), using the card form on a group of forty normals over a three day interval and on a group of forty-seven normals over a one year interval, reliabilities ranged from .57 for the hysteria scale to .83 for the hypomania scale. Reliabilities, reported by Cottle (1950) using the card and group forms alternately over a one week interval on one hundred normals, ranged from .46 for the lie scale to .91 for the masculinity-femininity scale. Finally, a study by Holzberg and Alessi (1949) on thirty normals over a three day interval, yielded reliabilities ranging from .52 for the psychopathic deviate scale to .93 for the validity scale.

Bibliography:

Buros, O. K.: Test number 104.

Cottle, W. C.: Card versus booklet forms for the MMPI. *Journal of Applied Psychology, 34*:255-259, 1950.

Dahlstrom, W. G. and Welsh, G. S.: *An MMPI Handbook: A Guide to Use in Clinical Practice and Research.* Minneapolis, The University of Minnesota Press, 1960.

Goodstein, L. D. and Dahlstrom, W. G.: MMPI differences between parents of stuttering and nonstuttering children. *Journal of Consulting Psychology, 20*:365-370, 1956.

Hathaway, S. R. and McKinley, J. C.: A multiphasic personality schedule (Minnesota): III. The measurement of symptomatic depression. *Journal of Psychology, 14*:73-84, 1942.

______ and ______ : *Minnesota Multiphasic Personality Inventory, Manual, revised.* New York, The Psychological Corporation, 1967.

Holzberg, J. D. and Alessi, S.: Reliability of the shortened MMPI. *Journal of Consulting Psychology, 13*:288-292, 1949.

Omnibus Personality Inventory — Form F

Authors: Paul Heist and George Yonge

Variable: The Omnibus Personality Inventory (OPI) assesses attitudes, values, and interests of individuals in order to derive information about their personality traits.

Type of Measure: The OPI is a paper and pencil inventory, suitable for administration to either individuals or groups. It is untimed and typically takes fifty minutes to complete. Scoring may be done manually or by machine.

Source from which Measure may be Obtained: The Psychological Corporation, 304 East Forty-fifth Street, New York, New York 10017.

Description: The OPI is a wide-ranging personality measure. It contains 385 items designed to assess differences among subjects regarding attitudes, opinions, and feelings. The items are anchored in one or more of the fourteen scales which include thinking introversion, theoretical orientation, aestheticism, complexity, autonomy, religious orientation, social extraversion, impulse expression, personal integration, anxiety level, altruism, practical outlook, masculinity-femininity, and response bias. The subject responds by indicating agreement or disagreement with each item. The uses of the OPI extend to identification and selection of different types of individuals, as well as the measurement of change of certain personality characteristics of individuals over a period of one or more years. Application of the OPI also includes identification and description of certain groups of individuals, such as a student body entering a school. A detailed description of each of the fourteen scales is provided in the manual along with several examples of OPI profiles with accompanying interpretations.

Norms: The norms for the OPI were developed on over seven thousand freshmen from a wide geographical spread of both public and private men's and women's colleges and universities. Institutions, such as graduate schools, institutes of technology and of art, as well as junior colleges were included. Scores are reported as standard scores with a mean of fifty and a standard deviation of ten. Sex differences were found on most of the subscales, but norm tables are presented with the groups combined.

Validity and Reliability: Validity studies are reported correlating the OPI with the Allport-Vernon-Lindzey Study of Values, the Strong-Vocational Interest Blank, the Guilford-Zimmerman Temperament Survey, the Opinion, Attitude, and Interest Survey, the Myers-Briggs Type Indicator, the Kuder Preference Record, the California Psychological Inventory, the Miller Analogies, the Scholastic Aptitude Test, the Activities Index, the Edwards Personal Preference Schedules, among other variables. The findings were generally significant and in desired directions. The remaining criteria include life satisfaction goals, ideal job requirements, educational goals, and other life expectations. One correlational finding, for example, shows a significant relationship for the OPI thinking introversion subscale with the Strong-Vocational Interest Blank occupational score for those occupationally oriented toward abstract ideas and concepts. A second example is the correlation of .37 for the OPI autonomy subscale and the EPPS need for autonomy subscale for ninety-eight subjects.

Internal consistency reliability coefficients, computed by Kuder-Richardson formula 21, ranged from .67 to .89 on all subscales for the norm samples. Another internal consistency study yielded reliabilities ranging from .65 to .91 on all subscales for 400 students. Test retest, over intervals of three and four weeks, yielded subscale reliabilities ranging from .79 to .94 for sixty-seven women and from .84 to .93 for seventy-one men.

Bibliography:

Buros, O. K.: Test number 116.

Heist, P. and Yonge, G.: *Omnibus Personality Inventory — Form F, Manual.* New York, The Psychological Corporation, 1968.

Personal Orientation Inventory

Author: Everett L. Shostrom

Variable The Personal Orientation Inventory (POI) assesses the values and behaviors related to the development of self-actualization.

Type of Measure: The POI is a paper and pencil inventory, suitable for administration to either individuals or groups. It is untimed and typically takes thirty minutes to complete. Scoring may be done manually or by machine.

Source from which Measure may be Obtained: Educational and Industrial Testing Service, Box 7234, San Diego, California 92107.

Description: The POI consists of 150 two alternative items. Items are scored, first, for the two basic scales of inner directed support (127 items) and time competence (23 items) and, second, for ten subscales which assess the elements of self-actualization. Time competence assesses the degree to which an individual lives in the past, present, or future. The inner direction support subscale assesses the subject's mode of reaction as either self or other oriented. The ten subscales of the POI include: self-actualizing value; existentiality, which is the ability to react without regard to certain principles; feeling reactivity which is the sensitivity of an individual to his or her own needs; spontaneity or the ability to be oneself; self-regard or belief in one's own worth; self-acceptance; nature of man, which measures one's view of masculinity and femininity; synergy, or the ability to function easily with others; acceptance of aggression; and capacity for intimate contact. In addition to being a useful tool in individual counseling and psychotherapy, application of the POI extends to general use by colleges, business and industry, and counseling agencies. Raw scores may be converted to standard scores with the use of the tables in the manual.

Norms: Norms are available for college students and also for certain occupational and clinical groups. The college group includes those entering college, freshmen, juniors, and seniors. The occupational and clinical groups include supervisors, student nurses, service organization volunteers, high school students, hospitalized psychiatric patients, delinquent males, alcoholic males, and psychopathic felons.

Validity and Reliability: Results of one study indicate that the POI significantly discriminated between two groups of individuals judged as self-actualized and nonself-actualized in eleven of the twelve subscales. The judgments were made by certified clinical psychologists. Another study, in a clinical setting, showed that all scales of the POI differentiated significantly among a hospitalized sample of psychiatric patients, a self-actualized sample, and a sample of normal adults. Additional studies report the relationship between the POI subscales and the Minnesota Multiphasic Personality Inventory. Results indicate that there are many areas of significant agreement between subscales of the POI and the MMPI. Finally, among other studies, the correlations of the POI with the Eysenck Personality Inventory are also reported. Many other correlation values are reported as being significant.

Test retest, on forty-eight college students over a one-week interval, yielded reliability coefficients of .71 and .84 for time competence and inner direction, respectively. Reliability coefficients for all subscales ranged from .55 to .85.

Bibliography:

Buros, O. K.: Test number 121.

Shostrom, E. L.: *Manual: Personal Orientation Inventory.* San Diego, Educational and Industrial Testing Service, 1966.

Personal Values Abstract

Author: Harrison G. Gough

Variable: The Personal Values Abstract assesses three personality dimensions: modernity, socialization, and femininity.

Type of Measure: The abstract is a paper and pencil inventory, suitable for administration to either individuals or groups. It is untimed, and scoring is done by hand.

Source from which Measure may be Obtained: Consulting Psychologists Press, 577 College Avenue, Palo Alto, California 94306.

Description: The abstract consists of ninety-seven items to which the subject responds by indicating agreement or disagreement. The items intend to assess the subject's personality in three areas: modernity, indicative of the self-assured, outgoing personality; socialization which identifies the self-disciplined, responsible individual; and femininity which relates to the nurturing behavior in an individual. The three scales of the Personal Values Abstract are taken from the California Psychological Inventory (CPI) and may be used in counseling and guidance among other environments.

Norms: Norms are based on over five hundred males and over forty females. Means and standard deviations for each sex and scale are provided.

Validity and Reliability: These are not stated; however, the reader is referred to the CPI for descriptive information as well as statistical data on these three scales.

Bibliography:

Gough, H. G.: *Personal Values Abstract from the California Psychological Inventory.* Palo Alto, Consulting Psychologists Press, 1970.

Sixteen Personality Factor Questionnaire — Forms A and B

Authors: Raymond B. Cattell and Herbert W. Eber

Variable: The Sixteen Personality Factor Questionnaire (16 PF) provides an assessment of an individual's personality traits.

Type of Measure: The 16 PF is a paper and pencil inventory, suitable for administration to either individuals or groups. It is untimed and typically takes sixty minutes to complete. Scoring may be done manually or by machine.

Source from which Measure may be Obtained: Western Psychological Services, 12031 Wilshire Boulevard, Los Angeles, California 90025.

Description: The 16 PF is a broad-based personality measure, developed by factor analytic methods to devise meaningful scales of personality. It contains 187 multiple choice items and is available in two parallel forms, A and B. There are from ten to thirteen items which treat each of the sixteen factors. The factors include reserved versus outgoing, less intelligent versus more intelligent, affected by feelings versus emotionally stable, humble versus assertive, sober versus happy-go-lucky, expedient versus conscientious, shy versus venturesome, tough minded versus tender minded, trusting versus suspicious, practical versus imaginative, forthright versus shrewd, placid versus apprehensive, conservative versus experimenting, group dependent versus self-sufficient, undisciplined self-conflict versus controlled, and relaxed versus tense. It can be used by counselors who may select one or more of the scales for interpretation. In addition, it is possible for the user to break the sixteen factors down into four, less specific subscales: anxiety, extraversion, alert poise, and independence. The 16 PF has proven a valuable measure in clinical, industrial, and educational settings, yielding specific personality predictions. Raw scores may be converted into standard scores.

Norms: Norms tables are provided in the following groups, for ages fifteen to seventy, separately for men and women: high school students, juniors and seniors; university and college undergraduate students; and general adult population, including wide ranges in age, education, occupation, and race. Norms are reported as stens (standard tens) with a distribution over ten equal interval standard scores.

Validity and Reliability: External criterion yielded a correlation value of .60 for the 16 PF as the predictor with a criterion of school achievement. Other studies showed a correlation of .50 with earnings in salesmanship. The reader is referred to the *16 PF Handbook* for more specific validity study data.

Test retest, over a six day interval, for 146 adults yielded reliability coefficients ranging from .76 to .93 for all subscales, using forms A and B. Test retest, over a two month interval for 132 students, yielded reliability coefficients ranging from .63 to .88 for all subscales, using forms A and B.

Bibliography:

Buros, O. K.: Test number 139.

Cattell, R. B. and Eber, H. W.: *Manual for Forms A and B: Sixteen Personality Factor Questionnaire.* Champaign, Institute for Personality and Ability Testing, 1962.

Cattell R. B. and Eber, H. W. and Tatsudka, M. M.: *Handbook for the 16PF Questionnaire.* Champaign, 1970.

Institute for Personality and Ability Testing: *Tabular Supplement No. 1 to the 16 PF Handbook.* Champaign, Author, 1970.

Study of Values

Authors: Gordon W. Allport, Philip E. Vernon, and Gardner Lindzey

Variable: The Study of Values is designed to isolate and assess six basic interests or motives in personality: theoretical, economic, aesthetic, social, political, and religious.

Type of Measure: The study is a paper and pencil inventory, suitable for administration to either individuals or groups. It is untimed and is both self-administered and scored within one hour. Scoring may be done manually or by machine.

Source from which Measure may be Obtained: Houghton Mifflin Company, 53 West Forty-third Street, New York, New York 10036.

Description: The study consists of forty-five items based upon familiar situations. Each item has either two or four alternative answers. Each of the six values is treated with twenty answers. The study yields six scores which show the individual's positions in the six value areas. The Study of Values has proven useful as a tool in classroom demonstration, in counseling, vocational guidance and selection, and in research.

Norms: Norms are based on a college population, including liberal arts majors with a wide geographical distribution. Specialized norms for technically trained groups are presented separately in the manual. Users of the study should note the differences in sex norms for both college and occupational groups. The occupational groups include: engineering, business, medical and education students; individuals in personnel and guidance; Air Force officers; clergy; social workers; laboratory technicians; and others. These groups include male and/or female samples. Norms for high school students are also available.

Validity and Reliability: Validity studies, performed with older forms of the study, indicated that the scores obtained by students in college were predictive of occupational careers five to fifteen years after graduation (Mawardi, 1952). Another study showed that special college education produced changes in value profiles in expected directions (Newcomb, 1943).

Split-half methods yielded a mean reliability coefficient of .90 for all scales. Test retest, over one and two month intervals, yielded mean reliability coefficients of .89 and .88, for two samples of thirty-four and fifty-three subjects, respectively.

Bibliography:

Allport, G. W., Vernon, P. E., and Lindzey, G.: *Manual: Study of Values.* 3rd Ed. Boston, Houghton Mifflin Company, 1960.

Buros, O. K.: Test number 146.

Mawardi, B. H.: The Allport-Vernon Study of Values as a Tool in Vocational Guidance with Liberal Arts College Women. Unpublished Master's thesis. Wellesley College Library, 1952.

Newcomb, T. M.: *Personality and Social Change: Attitude Formation in a Student Community.* New York, Dryden Press, 1943.

Test of Basic Assumptions — Form X

Authors: James H. Morrison and Martin Levit

Variable: The Test of Basic Assumptions (TBA) assesses the basic personality traits of an individual.

Type of Measure: The TBA is a paper and pencil inventory, suitable for administration to either individuals or groups. It is untimed and typically takes sixty minutes to complete. Scoring is done by hand.

Source from which Measure may be Obtained: James H. Morrison, 9804 Woodward Avenue, Overland Park, Kansas 66212.

Description: The TBA assesses the subject's attitudes toward four "life areas"; organization of effort and problem solving; human abilities and the individual, general philosophy of life; and economics and business. It consists of twenty items, each of which has three alternatives. The subject responds by choosing one alternative with which he or she most disagrees and one with which he or she most agrees. The three alternatives each deal with one of the basic assumptions underlying the test, dealing with the realism, idealism, and pragmatism of the subject. Conflict within an individual can be explored through the number and type of agreement or disagreement as determined by each of the four life areas. Among the TBA's uses are: assessment of subject's nonrational thinking process for the prediction of behavioral patterns, especially in clinical settings; determination of an individual's basic assumptions in organizational settings, in light of the individual's ability to influence the functions of the organization; assessment and selection of employees, by determining "successful" behavioral patterns; and in individual counseling, especially when used to give the subject a better understanding of his or her thoughts or actions.

Norms: Normative data is based on a study of 116 managers in the Minneapolis-St. Paul area in 1967. No other descriptive information is provided. Note: The Test of Basic Assumptions — Form X is published for experimental and research use, only, to expedite standardization" (Morrison, 1959, p.3).

Validity and Reliability: Two criteria scales are included that relate the Test of Basic Assumptions to the Allport-Vernon-Lindzey Study of Values (STV) and the Gordon Study of Interpersonal Values (SIV). Generally, correlation values of the TBA and the STV were in the range of from -.25 to +.25 for each of the subscales based on 116 subjects. No other interpretive data is stated.

Reliability coefficients, computed by Kuder-Richardson formula, were .73, for a group of industrial supervisors on the "agree" answers and .73, .59, and .80 for realist, idealist, and pragmatist, respectively.

Bibliography:

Buros, O. K.: Test number P:268.

Morrison, J. H.: *Manual — Form X — Test of Basic Assumptions.* Overland Park, J. H. Morrison, 1959.

_____ : *Manual Supplement: Form X — Test of Basic Assumptions.* Overland Park, J. H. Morrison, 1968.

GROUP 2 — SPECIFIC PERSONALITY MEASURES

The A-S Reaction Study

Authors: Gordon W. Allport and Floyd H. Allport

Variable: The A-S Reaction Study assesses the orientation of individuals' abilities to overpower their peers or to be overpowered by them.

Type of Measure: The reaction study is a paper and pencil inventory, suitable for administration to either individuals or groups. It is untimed and typically takes twenty minutes to complete. Scoring is done by hand.

Source from which Measure may be Obtained: Houghton-Mifflin Company, 53 West Fifty-third Street, New York, New York 10036.

Description: The reaction study assesses the subject's personality as being ascendant or submissive by presenting a number of typical situations in which the subject may have been during his or her life. The subject responds by indicating the one of several alternatives which best describes his or her usual behavior in the situation presented. Since most people will react differently at varied times and conditions, all the responses chosen will not indicate either absolute ascendance or submission in the subject. Enough situations are presented, however, to ascertain which type of reaction is predominant. The study is available in two forms, one for men containing thirty-three items, and one for women containing thirty-four items. The two forms are not interchangeable. Suggested uses for the study include: individual counseling in helping one overcome extreme ascendance or submission; vocational counseling in directing the ascendant or submissive subject toward those careers which might be best suited to his or her personality; and selection and placement of personnel where the ascendant or submissive leanings in one's personality would have a direct bearing on job performance. It is advisable that the scores and interpretations yielded by the study be used in conjunction with other information obtained from interviewing and screening; they should not be considered as conclusive evidence of the subject's potential performance in a given area.

Norms: Norms are based on 2,578 cases for the form for men and 600 cases for the form for women. The normative sample was derived from the three upper level college classes in institutions over a wide geographical spread and, therefore, represent a broad sampling of students, with the exception of freshmen. Norms and interpretations of scores are presented separately by sex. A study by Cooper (1930) found no significant differences in scores of Negroes and whites.

Validity and Reliability: Validity cannot be so clearly defined for this inventory since suitable criterion for validation is not available. However, correlating the ratings of individual's ascendance or submission with A-S Reaction Study scores yielded values ranging from .29 to .79 (neither the number of subjects, nor the characteristics of the rating system is stated in the manual). Other data on the use of the A-S Reaction Study established increasing ascendance scores for subjects with increasing amounts of executive responsibility. Bender (1928), among others, established a correlation of .35 for the A-S Reaction Study scores with extraversion-introversion scales.

Approximate split-half reliabilities are reported as .85 for the men's form and .90 for the women's form. Test retest reliabilities were found to be .78 for both forms; (neither the number of cases nor the time interval for these values is stated in the manual).

Bibliography:

Allport, G. W. and Allport, F. H.: *The A-S Reaction Study, Manual of Directions, Scoring Values, and Norms.* 2nd ed. — revised. Boston, Houghton Mifflin Company, 1967.

Bender, I.: Ascendance-submission in relation to certain other factors in personality. *Journal of Abnormal and Social Psychology, 23*:137-143, 1928.

Cooper, P.: Notes on psychological race differences. *Social Forces, 8*:425 f, 1930.

Ruggles, R. and Allport, G. W.: Recent Applications of the A-S Reaction Study. *Journal of Abnormal and Social Psychology, 34*:518-528, 1939.

Defense Mechanism Index

Authors: Authur B. Sweney and M. Jerold May

Variable: The Defense Mechanism Index (DMI) measures the conflict and defenses within an individual.

Type of Measure: The DMI is a paper and pencil inventory, suitable for administration to either individuals or groups. It is untimed and typically takes sixty minutes to complete. Scoring is done by hand with the use of a stencil.

Source from which Measure may be Obtained: Test Systems, Inc., 4300 Janesville, Wichita, Kansas 67220.

Description: The DMI consists of 288 items and is available in three forms, B, C, and F. The subject responds by indicating one of four alternatives, from "strongly agree" to "strongly disagree". The items measure behavioral patterns theoretically related to defenses and ego conflicts. There are twelve defense behaviors being measured with incidental information secured from the relationship of defenses to basic ego conflicts. The ego conflict scales measured include aggression versus fear of retaliation, blame avoidance versus blame acceptance, dominance versus submission, dependency versus independency, expression versus repression of sexual needs, fortitude versus immediate gratification, faith in God versus faith in man, heterosexual versus other roles, individuality versus needs for social acceptance, judgment versus immediate action, kindness versus selfish actions, and expression of love versus fear of rejection. The measurement obtained from these scales is the extent to which the subject is attracted or repelled by them, that is, the degree to which there is conflict. The adaptive defense scales measured are rationalization, compensation, negative affect, humor and positive affect, perceptual defense, autism. The maladaptive defenses are projection, repression, phantasy, paleologic, dissociation, and reaction formation. The result of scoring every item permits isolation of the source of conflict, as well as determination of whether the defense being used is either adaptive or maladaptive. It is well to note that the DMI does not intend to assess all areas of conflict or modes of defense, but it only attempts to sample some of these. A great deal more research will be necessary before the DMI can be structured comprehensively.

Norms: Normative data is available on normals, delinquents, college students, mental hospital samples, and samples of general population categorized by sex. Other norms are available for different forms of the test.

Validity and Reliability: Several validity studies are reported; one establishes the relationship between the defense mechanism ratings (Hill, 1966) and scores on the DMI. Correlation values ranged from .25 for the autism subscale to .70 for the negative affect subscale (N not indicated). Other studies show the abilities of the conflict subscale as a predictor of normal and delinquent boys using form C of the DMI and as a discriminator between college and mental hospital samples.

Split-half reliability coefficients for adaptive defense scales DMI form E (an earlier form) ranged from .66 to .82 and for maladaptive defense scales, from .68 to .82. Split-half reliability for DMI ego conflict scales ranged from .48 for perceptual defense to .86 for phantasy.

BIBLIOGRAPHY:

Buros, O. K.: Test number 63.

Hill, W. M.: Two instruments for the measurement of ego mechanisms. Unpublished dissertation. Texas Tech., August, 1966.

Sweney, A. B. and May M. J.: *DMI, Handbook and Interpretation Manual.* Wichita, Test Systems, Inc., 1970.

Depression Adjective Check Lists

AUTHOR: Bernard Lubin

VARIABLE: The Depression Adjective Check Lists (DACL) provide a measure of self-reported depressive moods.

TYPE OF MEASURE: The DACL is a series of seven paper and pencil check lists, suitable for administration to either individuals or groups. It is untimed and typically takes three minutes to complete each list. Scoring is done by hand with the use of a key.

SOURCE FROM WHICH MEASURE MAY BE OBTAINED: Educational and Industrial Testing Service, P. O. Box 7234, San Diego, California 92107.

DESCRIPTION: The DACL is a series of seven lists, A to G, of adjectives to which the subject responds by checking those words which best describe how he or she feels at the particular moment. The primary purpose of the lists is to diagnose depression in the subject. Use of the DACL is especially feasible in clinical settings where a self-reported reading of depression of either depressed or nondepressed patients is desired. Parallel forms of the DACL exist within the seven check lists; forms A to D comprise set one, and forms E to G comprise set two.

NORMS: Norms were established in the following groups: 856

high school, college, and male and female graduate students, the majority of whom were college students; 61 senior citizens, primarily females who were volunteers in a senior citizen center; and 78 female adolescent delinquents, residing in a residential treatment center; and several groups of psychiatric patients, exceeding 250 male and female subjects, diagnosed as either depressed or not depressed.

VALIDITY AND RELIABILITY: Validity evidence, using the DACL and characteristics of age, sex, and education of normal and psychiatric patients, showed the DACL's ability to differentiate significantly among normals, nondepressed patients, and depressed patients, using all seven lists. Further validity evidence is presented, showing a correlation of .71 for psychiatrists' ratings with total DACL scores, for seventy-three male and female subjects. Validity evidence is also established through presentation of significant correlation values of the DACL scores with scores on the Zung Depression Scale. Finally, data is presented correlating the DACL with the Minnesota Multiphasic Personality Inventory, and a discussion and presentation of data establishes the relationship between the DACL and sex, age, education, and the mental health classification of the subject.

Internal consistency reliabilities ranged from .79 to .90 for the seven lists for both male and female groups. Split-half reliabilities ranged from .82 to .93 for normals on the seven lists and from .86 to .93 for patients, also on the seven lists.

BIBLIOGRAPHY:

Buros, O. K.: Test number 65.

Lubin, B.: *Manual for the Depression Adjective Check Lists.* San Diego, Educational and Industrial Testing Service, 1967.

Ego Strength Q-Sort Test

AUTHOR: Russell N. Cassel

VARIABLE: The Ego Strength Q-Sort Test (ESQT) is concerned

in which individuals perceive their life value orientations.

Type of Measure: The evaluation is a paper and pencil device, suitable for administration to either individuals or groups. It is untimed. Scoring is done by hand with the use of a key.

Source from which Measure may be Obtained: Psychometric Affiliates, P.O. Box 3167, Munster, Indiana 46321.

Description: The evaluation provides a determination of the subject's procedure of valuation, as either a moralist, a realist, or an individualist. Information from the test can be used in counseling as well as in occupational placement. The test encompasses modes of valuating, significant to the culture existing in the United States today. The moralist valuates the characteristics of a certain mode of behavior, regardless of consequences resulting from the pattern. The realist valuates the consequences of a certain mode of behavior, rather than the structural characteristics of that behavior.

> *Individualist valuation*, on the other hand, focuses specifically on the psychological significance of the behavior in question for the performer. Behavior enlargement, the development of as many behavior potentialities as possible on the part of every individual are positively valuated. Behavior limitation, the elimination of psychological and/or interactional alternatives are negatively valuated (p. 1, manual).

Norms: Normative data is based on a general population samples of 192 students, including a small Negro group.

Validity and Reliability: Validity was determined through peer ranking of students on the three value scales of realism, moralism, and individualism. Correlations are reported on samples of varying size but indicate that for some of the value areas, significant relationships were established between student scores on The Evaluation Modality Test and the peer rating of the students in the three value areas.

Reliability data is not stated in the manual.

Bibliography:

Engelmann, H. O.: *The Evaluation Modality Test, Manual of Instructions.* Munster, Psychometric Affiliates, 1956.

Fear-Anxiety Profile — Form C

Author: Arthur B. Sweney

Variable: The Fear-Anxiety Profile (FAP) provides an assessment of types of reactions to threat, fear, and anxiety.

Type of Measure: The FAP is a paper and pencil inventory, suitable for administration to either individuals or groups. There are four subtests, and only the first is timed. The entire series typically takes sixty minutes to complete. Scoring is done by hand with the use of a stencil.

Source from which Measure may be Obtained: Test Systems, Inc., P. O. Box 18432, Witchita, Kansas 67218.

Description: The FAP assesses fear as the recognition of physical danger, as well as feelings of threatened security or self-respect, and it assesses anxiety as the subject's failure either to acknowledge the threat or to eliminate the source of threat by not dealing with it properly. In addition to yielding a profile, defining a subject's areas of fear and anxiety, the FAP also provides information regarding the subject's behavior toward and manner of dealing with these dangers or fears. Suggested uses of the FAP include assessment of patients in clinical settings or individual analysis, as well as counseling of students. The FAP includes four subtests. Part I, memory, asks the subject to memorize a number of threat words and then to recognize them within a group of other words. Part II, paired words, consists of eighty triads of words to which the subject responds by choosing one of two alternative words which he or she associates with the stimulus word. Part III, uncommon knowledge, contains two subtests: the first measures perceptual distortion and the second, information on dangers. In perceptual distortion, sixty items reflect material which is beyond the realm of common knowledge.

The subject responds by choosing one of the multiple choices which he or she feels is the correct answer. Information on dangers also contains sixty multiple choice items, but these are factually based, and the number of correct responses indicates the subject's familiarity with that area. Scales included in the subtests are death, assault, emotional control, social rejection, impotence or sex role inadequacy, marital rejection and jealousy, parental rejection, jail and civil authority, hospital, illness and injury, finances and poverty, and war. Detailed descriptions of each scale are provided in the manual. Raw scores may be converted to stanines.

Norms: The norm tables were developed on college students and a general population. No breakdown by sex is provided, since scores have not been found to significantly differentiate male versus female variance.

Validity and Reliability: Neither of these is stated in the manual.

Bibliography:

Sweney, A. B.: *FAP Manual.* Wichita, Test Systems, Inc., 1972.

Fear Survey Schedule — Preliminary Edition for Research Purposes

Authors: Joseph Wolpe and Peter J. Lang

Variable: The Fear Survey Schedule (FSS) identifies reaction to sources of maladaptive and emotionally related behavior in individuals.

Type of Measure: The FSS is a paper and pencil inventory, suitable for administration to either individuals or groups. It is untimed. The manual does not give any information regarding the scoring of this instrument.

Source from which Measure may be Obtained: Educational and Industrial Testing Service, P. O. 7234, San Diego, California 92107.

Description: The FSS yields information regarding a subject's unpleasant reactions, that is, those which are fear tinged or fear related. The information is useful in eliciting the degree and types of the subject's fears. It's value lies in determining the applicability of behaviorally related desensitization techniques to deal with phobias and phobic reactions. The FSS contains 108 items to which the subject responds on a five point scale by indicating whether the item causes him or her to feel fear: "not at all", "a little", "a fair amount", "much", or "very much".

Norms: Male and female college students, in excess of one thousand, provide the norm sample. Means and standard deviation are reported for the FSS scores, by sex.

Validity and Reliability: Validity evidenced in the first seventy-three items of the FSS was found to be significant when the FSS phobic score and total fear score were correlated with the neuroticism scale of the Maudsley Personality Inventory.

No reliability data is stated in the manual.

Bibliography:

Buros, O. K.: Test number 80.

Wolpe, J, and Lang, P. J.: *Manual for the Fear Survey Schedule.* Preliminary edition for research purposes. San Diego, Education and Industrial Testing Service, 1969.

IPAT Anxiety Scale Questionnaire

Authors: Raymond B. Cattell and Ivan H. Scheier

Variable: The IPAT Anxiety Scale Questionnaire is a brief, nonstressful assessment of anxiety.

Type of Measure: The anxiety scale is a paper and pencil inventory, suitable for administration to either individuals or groups. It is untimed and typically takes five to ten minutes to complete. Scoring is done by hand with the use of a key.

Source from which Measure may be Obtained: Educational and Industrial Testing Service, P. O. Box 7234, San Diego, California 92107.

Description: The anxiety scale is designed to yield, in a brief and objective manner, clinical data regarding an individual's anxiety level. It is appropriate for subjects age fourteen through the adult range. It consists of forty multiple choice items to which the subject responds by indicating one of three alternative answers which is most descriptive of him or her. The scale assesses five anxiety domains: defective integration, lack of self-sentiment; ego weakness, lack of ego strength; suspiciousness or paranoid insecurity; guilt proneness; and frustrative tension of Id pressure. The scales provide a score which indicates overt or conscious anxiety and covert or hidden anxiety. The anxiety scale scores could be diagnostic as well as evaluative for the purpose of charting changes in anxiety with therapy or remediation. In addition to the Anxiety Scale Questionnaire, IPAT has recently made available the IPAT 8-Parallel-Form Anxiety Battery designed especially for repeated testing of subjects' anxiety levels over varying periods of time. Raw scores may be converted to stens (standard tens) or percentiles with the use of the tables in the manual.

Norms: Norms are provided for twenty-three groups, including a variety of neurotics, psychotics, character disorders, and physically disabled subjects. Also, there are almost three thousand normative cases available, classified under three main headings: general adult population; college students; and teenage high school students. Each of these is presented separately by sex and with both sexes combined.

Validity and Reliability: Construct validity is estimated at +.85 to +.90 for the total scale. These values were obtained by correlating the items with the total scores of the five domains assessing anxiety. Also reported are values ranging from .30 to .40, correlating clinical judgment of anxiety level with IPAT scores. Another study cited the significant differences in scores of normals and scores of normals with anxiety hysteria on the IPAT anxiety-hysterics scale. The latter group averaged twenty points higher on the hysterics scale than the normals.

Test retest, over a two year interval on 170 medical students, yielded reliability coefficients ranging from .47 to .71, with a mean reliability of .60. In comparison with a general adult population, the reliability should be about .70, that is, slightly higher than that of a medical student group. Over two years, changes did occur in the student group's anxiety level, although a very strong tendency exists to maintain one's initial anxiety scores. The actual dependability (immediate retest) reliability figures, over a one week time interval, based on seventy cases in IPAT files, were .89 and .82 for the covert and overt subscales, respectively.

Bibliography:

Cattell, R. B. and Scheier, I. H.: *Handbook for the IPAT Anxiety Scale Questionnaire — Self Analysis Form.* Champaign, Institute for Personality and Ability Testing, 1963.

Scheier, I. H. (editor): *Recent Data on IPAT Anxiety Tests: Information Bulletin No. 13.* Champaign, Institute for Personality and Ability Testing, 1967.

IPAT Humor Test of Personality

Authors: Raymond B. Cattell and Donald L. Tollefson

Variable: The IPAT Humor Test of Personality assesses an individuals ego-defense mechanism.

Type of Measure: The humor test is a paper and pencil inventory, suitable for administration to either individuals or groups. It is untimed and typically takes thirty-five to forty minutes to complete. Scoring is done by hand.

Source from which Measure may be Obtained: Institute for Personality and Ability Testing, 1602 Coronado Drive, Champaign, Illinois 61820.

Description: The humor test is available in two forms, A and B. Form A uses eight pairs of items (jokes) for assessing thirteen factors. This yields 104 items in a forced choice design. Form B is comprised of ten pairs of items (jokes) per factor, giving a total of 130 items. The subject responds by indicating which of the jokes of each pair is funnier. The thirteen factors include anxious considerateness versus debonair, sexual and general uninhibitedness, dry wit versus good natured play, compensation versus tough self-composure, theatricalism versus cold realism, among others. Elaborate descriptions are provided to fully depict the meaning of each of the thirteen factors. Because it is considered to be an objective personality assessment, as well as a rough indication of intelligence level, the humor test is suitable in screening subjects for these dimensions, that is, personality, especially persons who are not easily tested with the usual personality inventory, such as, older persons or persons who are testwise. Raw scores may be converted to standard scores with the use of the tables in the manual.

Norms: Normative data is based on high school and college students, by sex. The number of subjects in all groups exceeded eleven hundred.

Validity and Reliability: Validity data reflects the fact that the items in the humor test have a commonality in one factor only. Therefore, the validity can be assumed to be a derivative of the reliability of the factor. No other validity data is reported. Content judgments were taken to ensure that each factor was as funny, or as dull, as every other factor.

Split-half reliabilities, based on 151 students, ranged from .19 to .49 for form A and from .18 to .49 for form B, separately for the thirteen factors. Test retest, over a two week interval for 151 subjects, yielded reliability coefficients ranging from .20 to .54 for form A and from .29 to .55 for form B for the thirteen factors.

Bibliography:

Buros, O. K.: Test number P. 119.

Cattell, R. B. and Tollefson, D. L.: *Handbook for the IPAT Humor Test of Personality.* Champaign, Institute for Personality and Ability Testing, 1963.

Institute for Personality and Ability Testing. *The IPAT Humor Test of Personality, Supplement of Norms.* Champaign, Author, 1966.

The Manson Evaluation

Author: Morse P. Manson

Variable: The Manson Evaluation is designed to identify alcoholics and potential alcoholics.

Type of Measure: The evaluation is a paper and pencil inventory, suitable for administration to either individuals or groups. It is untimed and typically takes ten to twenty minutes to complete. Scoring is done by hand with the use of a key.

Source from which Measure may be Obtained: Western Psychological Services, Box 775, Beverly Hills, California 90213.

Description: The evaluation intends to; 1) reveal those persons whose behavior and characteristics and personality indicate that they are potential alcoholics or have severe alcoholic problems; 2) identify the nonalcoholic who has characteristics usually found in alcoholics; and 3) obtain an understanding of the psychodynamics of the alcoholic or potentially alcoholic personality in order to assist in the rehabilitation of these people. Clinical studies indicate that alcoholics have psychoneurotic and psychopathic traits. Seven of them are anxiety, depressive fluctuations, emotional sensitivity, resentfulness, incompleteness, aloneness, shallow interpersonal relationships. There are seventy-two items in the evaluation.

Norms: The norms were developed through comparison of 126 alcoholics with 157 nonalcoholics. Both of the groups were comparable in intelligence, age, and socioeconomic levels. An analysis of the original items, believed to differentiate alcoholics from nonalcoholics, resulted in the selection of the test items.

Validity and Reliability: Validity was determined by four methods: selection of highly diagnostic items, correct prediction or diagnosis of subjects, highly significant score differences obtained on the evaluation by alcoholic versus nonalcoholic groups, and use of the phi coefficient to establish the fact that alcoholics consistently obtained higher scores on the evaluation than nonalcoholics. The first two methods showed that 79 percent of the male group and 84 percent of the female group were correctly identified by the Manson Evaluation.

Reliability coefficients, computed by the shorter approximation of the Kuder-Richardson formula, were found to be .94 and .94 for male and female groups, respectively.

Bibliography:

Manson, M. P.: *Manual: The Manson Evaluation.* Beverly Hills, Western Psychological Services, 1965.

The Minnesota T-S-E Inventory

Authors: Catherine Evans and T. R. McConnell

Variable: The Minnesota T-S-E Inventory (TSE) assesses three types of extraversion-introversion traits: thinking, social and emotional.

Type of Measure: The TSE is a paper and pencil inventory, suitable for administration to either individuals or groups. It is untimed and typically takes twenty to thirty minutes to complete. Scoring is done by hand with the use of a stencil.

Source from which Measure may be Obtained: Educational Testing Service, Princeton, New Jersey 08540.

Description: The TSE was designed to identify the introvert or extravert on three levels: thinking, social and emotional behavior. It consists of 150 questions to which the subject responds by indicating how often his or her behavior corresponds to the question asked: always, frequently, occasionally, seldom, or never. The use of the TSE extends to clinical research settings for either individual or group appraisal, including diagnosis as well as monitoring behavior changes during and after therapy and assessing varied occupational and student groups.

Norms: Norms are based on 400 college men and 600 college women. In addition, descriptive data is available for men and women who were born shortly after 1900.

Validity and Reliability: Validity studies were conducted on college students using the TSE extraversion-introversion scores with criteria, such as, choice of curricula, interests as measured by the Kuder Preference Record, artistic interest as expressed by preference for naturalistic or nonnaturalistic pictures, scholastic aptitude, academic success, vocabulary success, and student teaching success. Many of these studies report significant findings which attest to the validity of the TSE. For example, significant differences are found between thirty-five engineering and fourteen mathematics majors on the thinking Introversion-Extroversion scale of the TSE. Significant differences were obtained between the extreme quartiles on the TSE on honor point ratios (grades) of education students, as well as significantly higher scores on the TSE scale for successful life insurance salesmen compared with the men in the general norm group.

Split-half reliabilities, based on 396 education seniors, were found to be .91 for the thinking scale, .88 for the social scale, and .75 for the emotional scale. Test retest, based on 101 college of education students, yielded reliability coefficients of .89 for thinking, .84 for social, and .88 for emotional; time interval was not stated in the manual.

Bibliography:

Evans, C. and McConnell, T. R.: *Manual: The Minnesota T-S-E Inventory.* Revised ed. Princeton, Educational Testing Service, 1957.

Motivation Analysis Test — High School Battery

Authors: Raymond B. Cattell, John L. Horn, and others

Variable: The Motivation Analysis Test (MAT) assesses an individual's interests and drives, specifically, motivations, sentiment, and value systems.

Type of Measure: The MAT is a battery of four paper and pencil subtests, suitable for administration to either individuals or groups. It is untimed and typically takes fifty-five to sixty-five minutes to administer. Scoring may be done manually or by machine.

Source from which Measure may be Obtained: Educational and Industrial Testing Service, P. O. Box 7234, San Diego, California 92107.

Description: The MAT, available in forms A and B, is a battery of four subtests, including uses with forty-eight items, estimates with fifty-six items, paired words with forty-eight items and information with fifty-six items. The test is structured over ten subscales to assess five drives — mating, assertiveness, fear, narcism-comfort and pugnacity-sadism, and five sentiments — self-concept, super ego, career, sweetheart-spouse and home parental. Use of the MAT extends to selection and guidance counseling in education, psychological clinics and industrial personnel work. In addition, when used in conjunction with both ability and personality measures, the MAT raises the accuracy of selection and prediction for college and occupational achievement, and combined with the psychiatric interview, it can increase the reliability of conclusions regarding personality dynamics. The range of derived scores from the MAT, such as, conflict, interest, integrated and unintegrated scores, enhance its applicability to research.

Norms: Norms were developed on 866 college students (60 percent men), 156 servicemen, and a variety of industrial positions, such as, nursing and skilled and semiskilled. These latter groups include 412 men and 413 women. Norms are also available for users of the test in Australia.

Validity and Reliability: Validity data reportedly answered two questions: Do the basic factors of the test exist as independent unities? and, with what precision does the battery measure these factors? Data indicated that the factors do exist as independent unities through extensive research studies on adults. In answer to the second question, correlations of MAT scores with the Sixteen Personality Factor (16 PF) scale indicates relationships to be very low. The highest correlation value is with the self-sentiment scales of the 16 PF and the MAT. Further data shows relationship with crystallized intelligence and age and supports the inherent validity of the MAT to provide a general indicator of intelligence when no other is available. A study by Noty has found significant uses of the difference in integrated and unintegrated scores in the selection of executives. These scores reflect level of conflicts of subjects and are derived from the MAT.

As estimates of reliability, dependability coefficients, based on 156 Air Force enlisted men, ranged from .51 to .81 over the ten subscales. Alpha coefficients, based on a general adult population of 227 subjects (Cattell and Horn, 1963), ranged from .33 to .71 over the ten subscales. Arbitrary split-half coefficients, based on 151 college students (Tollefson, 1961), ranged from .33 to .70 for all ten subscales. Finally, test retest, based on 101 college students over a five week interval (Tollefson, 1961), yielded reliability coefficients ranging from .39 to .69 for the ten subscales.

Bibliography:

Buros, O. K.: Test number 110.

Cattell, R. B. and Horn, J. L., and others: *Handbook for the Motivational Analysis Test.* Champaign, Institute for Personality and Ability Testing, 1964.

_____ and _____: An integrating study of the factor structure of adult attitude-interests. *Genet. Psychological Monographs, 67*:89-149, 1963.

Tollefson, D. L.: Differential responses to humor and their relation to personality and motivation measures. Unpublished doctoral dissertation. Urbana, University of Illinois Library, 1961.

(Please note Noty is not referenced in the manual.)

Myers-Briggs Type Indicator

Author: Isabel Briggs Myers

Variable: The Myers-Briggs Type Indicator attempts to ascertain an individual's basic preferences.

Type of Measure: The indicator is a paper and pencil inventory, suitable for administration to either individuals or groups. It is untimed and typically takes fifty-five minutes to complete. Scoring may be done manually or by machine.

Source from which Measure may be Obtained: Educational Testing Service, Princeton, New Jersey 08540.

Description: The indicator contains separate measures for assessing each of the four basic preferences of: extraversion or introversion; sensing or intuition; thinking or feeling; and judgment or perception. It includes 166 items in a forced choice format; there are controls for the effect of omissions and item corrections for social desirability. Use of the indicator extends to counseling in high schools and the adult learning environment, college admissions, psychotherapy, and marriage counseling, as well as selection and placement of business and industrial personnel. Raw scores may be converted to percentile ranks with the use of the tables in the manual.

Norms: Normative data is based on college preparatory high school students and noncollege preparatory high school students. Also included are liberal arts college students and engineering college students. Norms are presented separately by sex and in percentiles.

Validity and Reliability: Extensive validity data is reported, covering the relationship of the indicator to Gray Wheelwright (an instrument measuring the same dimensions as the Myers-Briggs), the Strong Vocational Interest Blank, the Allport-Vernon-Lindzey Study of Values, the Edwards Personal Preference Schedule, faculty ratings, turnover in utility jobs, measures of creativity and scholastic performance, among others. Generally, the majority of correlation values are significant. These findings lead one to infer the existence of meaningfulness in the Myers-Briggs over a wide variety of applications.

Split-half reliabilities of each index for various samples ranged from .44 to .89 for males with a number of cases ranging in size from 30 to 100 and from .75 to .94 for females. Split-half reliabilities for each index for six samples of 100 subjects ranged from .66 to .91 for males and from .74 to .93 for females.

Bibliography:

Myers, I. B.: *Manual: The Myers-Briggs Type Indicator.* Princeton, Educational Testing Service, 1962.

Neuroticism Scale Questionnaire

Authors: Ivan H. Scheier and Raymond B. Cattell

Variable: The Neuroticism Scale Questionnaire (NSQ) measures the degree of neuroticism in adults and adolescents.

Type of Measure: The NSQ is a paper and pencil inventory, suitable for administration to either individuals or groups. It is untimed and typically takes five to ten minutes to complete. Scoring may be done manually with the use of a key or by machine.

Source from which Measure may be Obtained: Western Psychological Services, 12031 Wilshire Boulevard, Los Angeles,

California 90025.

Description: The NSQ assesses those six personality dimensions which are considered to be highly discriminant between clinically judged neurotics and normals. It is structured over six factors, including, overprotection, depressiveness, submissiveness, worry, ergic tension, and ego weakness (the last three factors yield one score — anxiety). The inventory consists of forty items to which the subject responds by indicating "yes", "no", or "uncertain" as to whether the item pertains to him or her. Use of the NSQ extends to clinical environments in which a rapid assessment is needed in order to diagnose a potential anxiety condition or other neurotic trait. Further use extends to research in which anxiety may play a part in effecting the performance of subjects.

Norms: Norms are based on 1,068 male and female subjects from teenage through the adult range, in varying occupations and geographical locations. These subjects are considered to be cases from the general population. Norms are presented separately by sex, because research suggests differences in varied male and female subscores. Males in the norm group had a mean age of thirty-three and an average of thirteen years of schooling; females had a mean age of thirty-one and an average of eleven and one-half years of schooling. Furthermore, sten values (standard ten with a mean of 5.5) are reported for twenty-one criterion groups, including, neurotics — all types, anxiety reaction neurotics, psycho- and sociopaths, delinquents, alcoholics, narcotics users, male homosexuals, schizophrenics — chronic and differentiated, among others. The number of cases varied from twelve to over six hundred.

Validity and Reliability: Two types of validity are reported. Concept validity is the correlation of the items in a given scale with the factor (concept or dimension) they are designed to measure. The validities reported were estimated through the known relationship of the reliability of each scale to its potential validity value. Concrete validity is the correlation of the test with life performances and categories, in short, with a "pointed out" criterion in everyday life. Significant differences in total NSQ scores were found between 102 clinically judged neurotics and the norm group from the general population. Other studies are also reported which attest to the ability of the NSQ to differentiate between clinical groups and normals.

Split-half reliabilities ranged from .47 to .70 for the subscales and yielded a .67 value for the total neuroticism score. These are based on a sample of normals only: 200 men and 100 women. The reliability of the components is lowered by the brevity of the scales, although the number of cases was adequate.

Bibliography:

Scheier, I. H. and Cattell, R. B.: *Handbook for the Neuroticism Scale Questionnaire*. Champaign, Institute for Personality and Ability Testing, 1961.

Reid Report

Author: John E. Reid

Variable: The Reid Report is designed to test and assess an individual's honesty.

Type of Measure: The report is a paper and pencil inventory, suitable for administration to either individuals or groups. It is untimed. Scoring is done by John E. Reid and Associates only.

Source from which Measure may be Obtained: John E. Reid and Associates, 600 South Michigan Avenue, Chicago, Illinois 60605.

Description: The Reid Report is a comprehensive honesty test. Its use is most valuable in the discrimination and selection of potential employees, especially those applicants whose job functions would include the unsupervised handling of money and/or merchandise. Its application also extends to its use as a supplement to the polygraph (lie detector) test. It is broken into three sections. The first is a questionnaire to which the subject responds by indicating "yes" or "no". This section yields a score regarding the subject's attitude toward measure of punitiveness. The second section is a personal data blank, covering such biographical information as, previous employment, education, personal history (including marital status and addresses over past ten years), financial history and indebtedness, medical and social history (including questions regarding alcohol and drug use, psychotherapy, gambling practices, and police-related experiences, such as arrest and conviction of a number of theft-related crimes). The third section is a questionnaire to which the subject again responds by indicating "yes" or "no"; however, in this section, the "yes" responses are admissions of guilt of crimes committed. Typically, the Reid Report would be administered at the place of potential employment. A member of the John E. Reid and Associates staff would then score part one and analyze and evaluate both the biographical and crime admissions sections and, on the basis of the three, give a final determination of "recommended" or "not recommended".

Norms: Normative information is reflected in several studies by Ash (1970, 1971, 1974). The data presented in these studies shows means and standard deviation scores for recommended and nonrecommended subjects, by race, age, and sex. One study by Ash (1970) notes that blacks score slightly higher (more honest) than whites. Also provided are means and standard deviations for felons and employment applicants, divided by race.

Validity and Reliability: Validity data was determined through use of the Reid Report and the polygraph evaluation. Significant chi square analyses indicated a high degree of correspondence between individuals recommended by the Reid Report and by the polygraph evaluation. The hit ratio of agreement between the polygraph and the Reid Report scores was 65 percent, whereas the miss ratio was less than 20 percent.

Reliability, computed by Kuder-Richardson formula 20, yielded values ranging from .78 to .93 on sample sizes of from twenty-one to eight hundred subjects. This data is presented by race and age grouping.

Bibliography:

Ash, P.: Validation of an instrument to predict the likelihood of employee theft. Proc. of the Seventy-eighth Annual Convention of the APA. Vol. 5, 579-580, 1970.

______ : Screening employment applicants for attitudes toward theft. *Journal of Applied Psychology*, *55*:161-164, 1971.

______ : Criminal Justice and Behavior: Convicted Felons' Toward Theft. Official publication of the American Assn. of Correctional Psychologists. March, 1974.

Buros, O. K.: Test number 132.

Reid, J. E. *Reid Report*. Chicago, John E. Reid and Associates, 1974.

SAQS Chicago Q Sort

Author: Raymond Corsini

Variable: The SAQS Chicago Q Sort measures the agreement between one's perception of self with that of an ideal self.

Type of Measure: The SAQS is a card sort inventory, suitable for administration to either individuals or groups. It is untimed and typically takes ten to fifteen minutes to complete. Scoring is done by hand with the use of a score sheet for coding choices.

Source from which Measure may be Obtained: Psychometric Affiliates, P. O. Box 3167, Munster, Indiana 46321.

Description: The SAQS consists of fifty personal adjectives, presented on a ten by five rectangular pattern. The subject responds by organizing the adjectives in the order of his or her perception of how others perceive him or her. Consequently a subject may sort the cards for himself or herself (SS), for another person (A), for another person's perception of himself or herself (SAA), for another person's perception of the subject (SAS), or for another person's perception of another person (SAB), among others. Any two sorts may be correlated to obtain an index of the similarity of congruence of the two sorts, including one's own perception of self. The score sheet codes choices and then assigns weights to the responses. The correlations are computed by using a "Conversion Table for Transforming the Sums of the Differences" between each sort into a Pearsonian correlation coefficients. Suggested uses for the SAQS include determining similarities between personalities, preferences among people, similarities among persons in a group, empathic ability of a person, marriage counseling, among others.

Norms: A conversion table of differences and correlations is presented, although age, sex, and occupations are not specified.

Validity and Reliability: The SAQS does not appear to have generalizable validity, since it is a self-perception ipsative scale. However, a correlation of .75 for twenty subjects was found with the Burgess' General Satisfaction of Self and Concept of Mate's Happiness Test scores. The Terman Personal History and the Burgess Personality Test are reported to correlate well with the Burgess Happiness Test. In a multiple correlation, using three adjustment and personality inventories, it appeared that the SAQS was contributing some variance in addition to the other instruments, indicating marital happiness. The SAQS also appeared to contribute some variance in a battery using other inventories, especially where information about the congruences of attitude and perception are important.

Test retest, over a one week interval based on twenty-seven women and thirty-one men, yielded reliabilities of .81 for women and .79 for men.

Bibliography:

Corsini, R.: *Manual of Instructions: SAQS Chicago Q Sort.* Munster, Psychometric Affiliates, 1956.

———: Understanding and Similarity in Marriage. *J. Apn. Soc. Psychol., 32*:327-332, 1956.

The S-I Inventory

Author: A. H. Maslow and others

Variable: The S-I (Security-Insecurity) Inventory assesses an individual's emotional security, revealing inner conscious feelings.

Type of Measure: The S-I is a paper and pencil inventory, suitable for administration to either individuals or groups. It is untimed and typically takes ten minutes to complete.

Scoring is done manually with the use of a key.

Source from which Measure may be Obtained: Consulting Psychologists Press, 577 College Avenue, Palo Alto, California 94306.

Description: The S-I measures psychological or emotional security. Its value lies in work being done with large groups, especially in research surveys in selected groups, or comparison groups. Uses also extend to identifying individuals in need of psychological counseling. It consists of seventy-five personal questions to which the subject responds by indicating agreement, disagreement, or uncertainty.

Norms: Distribution of scores is available for men and women, in different high schools and colleges, and includes descriptive data on men and women in prisons. The college samples are from state and private schools for both men and women as well as coeducational.

Validity and Reliability: Correlation of the S-I with various criteria is as follows: the Minnesota Multiphasic Personality Inventory scales ranged from .05 to .41 (the highest value of .41 was found between the S-I and psychasthenia); the Otis Intermediate I.Q., .09; high school grade average, .008; Sims Score Cards (socioeconomic status), .10; Thurstone Neurotic Inventory, .68 based on 117 subjects; Bernreuter (neurotic), .58 based on fifty-nine subjects; Allport Ascendance-Submission, .53 based on forty-five subjects.

Test retest, over a two week interval for 62 subjects, yielded a reliability of .84. Split-half reliabilities were found to be .86 and .91 for two groups of 100 subjects.

Additional validity and reliability data is reported in the manual.

Bibliography:

Maslow, A. H. and others: *Manual for the Security-Insecurity Inventory.* Palo Alto, Consulting Psychologists Press, 1952.

Survey of Personal Values

Author: Leonard V. Gordon

Variable: The Survey of Personal Values (SPV) assesses the traits that typify an individual's behavior.

Type of Measure: The SPV is a paper and pencil inventory, suitable for administration to either individuals or groups. It is untimed and typically takes fifteen minutes to complete. Scoring is done by hand with the use of a stencil.

Source from which Measure may be Obtained: Science Research Associates, 259 East Erie Street, Chicago, Illinois 60611.

Description: The SPV consists of thirty sets of triads. A forced choice format is used. The subject responds by choosing one statement which is most important and one which is least important to him or her. For each triad, three of the six value dimensions are assessed. The scales measured in the SPV include practical mindedness, achievement, variety, decisiveness, orderliness, and goal orientation. The statements in the triads are equalized for social desirability. Uses of the SPV include personnel selection, promotion and transfer, vocational guidance, individual counseling, among others. Raw scores may be converted to percentile ranks with the use of the tables provided.

Norms: Normative data is based on samples of over two thousand male and female college students in thirteen colleges and universities across major regions of the country. Most of the students were liberal arts majors in their freshmen and sophomore years. The high school norms are based on male and female high school students from urban California.

Validity and Reliability: Correlation values, based on the relationship between the SPV scales and the Survey of Interpersonal Values (SIV) scales for a sample of 279 college students, ranged from -.51 to +.45. Many of these values are reported as statistically significant, but generally one can infer that the SPV is an assessment device independent of the interpersonal values measured by the SIV. The significant relationships reported are to be expected between the two scales. Other correlation values are reported in the desired directions for the SPV and the Gordon Personal Profile. Other studies report correlation of the SPV with the Study of Values, the Work Environment Preference Schedule, and the

Crowne-Marlow Need for Approval, among other personality and cognitive measures. Finally, cross-cultural studies between the American and Japanese high school and college students' performance on the SPV are also reported, including means and standard deviations, as well as significant differences between the two samples (N = 1,000).

Reliabilities, based on 167 college students and computed by Kuder-Richardson Case III formula, ranged from .72 to .92 for all six scales of the SPV. Test retest, over varying intervals from seven to ten days based on ninety-seven college students, yielded reliability coefficients ranging from .74 to .92 for the six scales.

Bibliography:

Buros, O. K.: Test number 148.

Gordon, L. V.: *Survey of Personal Values, Manual.* Chicago, Science Research Association, 1967.

Tennessee Self Concept Scale

Author: William H. Fitts

Variable: The Tennessee Self Concept Scale (TSCS) assesses an individual's self-perception and concept.

Type of Measure: The TSCS is a paper and pencil inventory, suitable for administration to either individuals or groups. It is untimed and typically takes ten to twenty minutes to complete. Scoring may be done manually or by the publisher.

Source from which Measure may be Obtained: Counselor Recordings and Tests, Box 6184 Acklen Station, Nashville, Tennessee 37212.

Description: The TSCS consists of one hundred items that are self-descriptive statements. The subject employs these statements in order to construct a picture of himself or herself by responding to them on a five point scale from "completely true" to "completely false". The TSCS is available in a counseling form and a clinical and research (C and R) form. The counseling form yields fewer scores than the C and R form, since it treats fewer variables in the self concept domain. The C and R form is a more complex device. It is generally not appropriate for self interpretation or direct feedback to the subject as is the counseling form. The counseling form yields the following scores: self-criticism, positive, variability, distribution, and time. The positive score yields other subscores, such as, identity, self-scales factor, behavior, physical self, moral ethical self, personal self, family self, and social self. The C and R form yields, in addition to the counseling form scores, true-false ratio, net conflict, total conflict scores, and empirical scales, as well as the number of deviant signs score. The uses of the TSCS extend to individual counseling, clinical assessment and diagnosis, research in behavioral science, and personnel selection, among others.

Norms: Normative data is based on a group of 626 subjects from various parts of the country, from age twelve to sixty-eight, with equal numbers of both sexes, including Negroes and whites representative of all social, economic, intellectual, and educational levels from grade 6 through the Ph.D. level. Subjects were obtained from high school and college classes and employers at state institutions, among others. Scores are reported on profile forms using a standard score system.

Validity and Reliability: Validity data is extensive. For example, studies are reported showing the ability of the TSCS to clinically discriminate among patient groups, such as, job applicants, paranoid schizophrenics, depressive reactions, and emotionally unstable personalities on selected subscales of the TSCS (Huffman, 1964). Correlation of the TSCS with both the Minnesota Multiphasic Personality Inventory (McGee, 1960) and the Edwards Personal Preference Schedule is also reported. The correlations with the MMPI are in the desired direction, while values for the EPPS are low but can be explained through the difference in nature of the two scales. Correlation studies with other personality measures are also reported.

Test retest, over a two week period based on sixty college students, yielded reliabilities ranging from .60 to .92 for all subscores. In a study by Congdon (1958), using a shortened version of the TSCS on psychiatric patients, a reliability coefficient of .88 was obtained for the total positive score.

Bibliography:

Buros, O. K.: Test number 151.

Congdon, C. S.: Self theory and chlorpromazine treatment. Unpublished doctoral dissertation. Vanderbilt University, 1958.

Fitts, W. H.: *Manual: Tennessee Self Concept Scale.* Nashville, Counselor Recordings and Tests, 1965.

Huffman, T. B.: Relationships between the self concept and three psychopathological types. Master's thesis in preparation. University of Tennessee, 1964.

McGee, R. K.: Personal Communication, 1960.

Wahler Self Description Inventory

Author: H. J. Wahler

Variable: The Wahler Self Description Inventory (WSDI) measures the way in which respondents emphasize either favorable or unfavorable traits in the process of self evaluation.

Type of Measure: The WSDI is a paper and pencil inventory, suitable for administration to either individuals or groups. It is untimed and typically takes twenty minutes to complete. Scoring is done by hand with the use of a key.

Source from which Measure may be Obtained: Western Psychological Services, 12031 Wilshire Boulevard, Los Angeles, California 90025.

Description: The WSDI assesses the subject on two scales. The Fa scale contains twenty-four desirable items depicting favorable personal characteristics. The Uf scale contains forty-two items considered to be undersirable, depicting unfavorable personal characteristics. Application of the WSDI extends to screening and evaluation of subjects in clinical settings, as well as indicating the extent of success of treatment. It is suitable for administration to adolescents as well as adults.

Norms: Data was generated on a sample of males and females, including students and patients. The data is reported in over twenty score ranges that indicate level of frequencies and decile of favorable and unfavorable scores. Subjects were selected from an adult psychiatric clinic and had a mean age of twenty-nine and an average of tenth grade education for both males and females. Subjects in the college norm group consisted of over one hundred sophomores.

Validity and Reliability: Validity studies indicate significant differences in responses to most items for students versus patients. Cross-validation samples indicate a high proportion of "hits" or correct classifications for both the favorable and unfavorable items in comparing two contrasting groups of students and patients.

Four studies, using Kuder-Richardson formula 20, yielded reliabilities in a range from .85 to .90 for the Fa scale and from .92 to .99 for the Uf scale, for student and patient samples, separated by sex.

Bibliography:

Wahler, H. J.: *Wahler Self Description Inventory: Manual.* Los Angeles, Western Psychological Services, 1971.

GROUP 3 — PERSONALITY ADJUSTMENT MEASURES

Business Judgment Test

Author: Martin M. Bruce

Variable: The Business Judgment Test assesses an individual's empathy or "feel" for the generally accepted ideas and opinions regarding desirable courses of action in relation to and with people.

Type of Measure: The judgment test is a paper and pencil device, suitable for administration to either individuals or groups. It is untimed and typically takes ten to fifteen minutes to complete. Scoring is done by hand with the use of a key.

Source from which Measure may be Obtained: Western Psychological Services, 12031 Wilshire Boulevard, Los Angeles, California 90025.

Description: The judgment test consists of twenty-five multiple choice items to which the subject responds by choosing the one of four alternatives which best describes what his or her behavior would be in a given situation. It samples various types of social or interpersonal situations common to the business world and assesses the subject's awareness of what the majority feels are proper courses of action; "proper", in this instance, has been predetermined by the opinions of the "general" business population. Suggested uses of the test include personnel selection, as well as training of personnel to be employed or promoted to managerial positions (Kirkpatrick, 1959). The user who applies this test in an industrial setting is cautioned to do so in light of the particular organization's philosophy, as good business judgment in the weighting scheme may not be fully applicable to all firms.

Norms: Four sets of norms are offered. They include a general business population of 3,225 cases, 95 percent male and 80 percent in white collar vocations, with an age range of nineteen to sixty-one years, with a wide geographical spread, including 4 percent from Canada. The group has a wide education range, including from sixth grade to the Ph.D. level, and from occupational areas, such as, research and development and sales, among others. The second group included eighty-nine members of a middle management group, twenty-one of whom completed college, ranging in age from twenty-six to fifty-two. The third was a group of fifty supervisors, ranging in age from twenty-five to early fifties; and the last group included 1,113 sales applicants with age ranging from twenty-two to forty-five, 20 percent of whom were Canadian.

Validity and Reliability: In one investigation, correlating the scores of thirty-two office personnel with ratings of their "business judgment" by two supervisors yielded a value of .43, representing a moderate indication of criterion-related validity. Another study, which established an interrater reliability value of .71, found that when the ratings of the managers were correlated with scores on the Business Judgment Test of twenty-two foremen, a correlation value of .55 was obtained. It appears as if there is some indication of the actual behavior of examinees as seen by members of management. Validity studies are also reported on subjects in a Canadian company using the Business Judgment Test.

Test retest, over varying intervals of two to three weeks based on eighty-two subjects, yielded a reliability coefficient of .81. Split-half reliability was found to be .85. Test retest, over varying intervals of one to three months based on a group of 200 subjects, yielded a reliability coefficient of .81, high enough to warrant confidence in consistency of measurement.

Bibliography:

Bruce, M. M.: *Examiner's Manual: Business Judgment Test.* Revised. Los Angeles, Martin M. Bruce, Ph.D. Publishers, 1969.

Buros, O. K.: Test number 1059.

Kirkpatrick, D. L.: Techniques for evaluating training programs — part 2 — learning. *Journal of American Social Training Directors, 13*:21-26, 1959.

The Chapin Social Insight Test

Author: Harrison G. Gough

Variable: The Chapin Social Insight Test assesses the degree of perceptiveness that an individual uses in both evaluating others and predicting what they will say or do.

Type of Measure: The insight test is a paper and pencil device, suitable for administration to either individuals or groups. It is untimed and typically takes thirty minutes to complete. Scoring is done by hand.

Source from which Measure may be Obtained: Consulting Psychologists Press, 577 College Avenue, Palo Alto, California 94306.

Description: The insight test consists of twenty-five multiple choice items, each of which presents a problem or situation. The subject responds by using insight in analyzing each situation, assuming the reason for it, predicting the outcome of it, or predicting the individual's, involved in the situation, reaction to it. Usefulness of the test might lie in the screening and selection of persons applying to psychiatry, psychology, or social work in educational training programs, as well as in the assessment of person in leadership positions in political, social, industrial, or religious settings.

Norms: Normative data, reported as means and standard deviations, is available for both males and females. The male sample includes bank managers, graduate students in psychology, industrial research scientists, college students in liberal arts and engineering, middle level business executives, medical students, military officers, and high school students. The female sample includes graduate students in psychology, medical students, liberal arts college students, and high school students. The total number of males exceeds one thousand; females exceed four hundred.

Validity and Reliability: Correlations of the Social Insight Test with other instruments, including Arthur Stencil Design Test, Bennett Mechanical Comprehension Test, College Vocabulary Test, General Information Survey, Ghiselli Analysis for Relationships Test, How Supervise? Test, Terman Concept Mastery Test, and Wesman Personnel Classification Test, ranged from .24 to .40 on sample sizes ranging from 35 to 297. For example, a correlation value of .36 on 145 cases is obtained between the Social Insight Test and the Terman Concept Mastery Test. Other studies are reported which establish the relationship of the Social Insight Test to: Barron-Welsh Art Scale, $r = .19$ for 246 subjects; California Psychological Inventory scales; and the Minnesota Multiphasic Personality Inventory.

Split-half reliability, based on a sample of one hundred adult males, was found to be .78. Item to total score point biserial correlations for the original forty-five items of the test yielded median coefficients of .30 for men and .28 for women. By correcting to twenty-five items, estimated reliabilities of .71 and .68 were obtained.

Bibliography:

Buros, O. K.: Test number 51.

Gough, H. G.: *Manual: The Chapin Social Insight Test.* Palo Alto, Consulting Psychologists Press, 1968.

Diplomacy Test of Empathy

Author: Willard A. Kerr

Variable: The Diplomacy Test of Empathy measures an individual's ability to put himself or herself in another person's place, establish rapport, and anticipate emotional reactions, feelings and behaviors.

Type of Measure: The empathy test is a paper and pencil device, suitable for administration to either individuals or groups. It is untimed and typically takes ten to fifteen minutes to complete. Scoring is done by hand with the use of a key.

Source from which Measure may be Obtained: Psychometric Affiliates, P. O. Box 1367, Munster, Indiana 46321.

Description: The empathy test consists of twenty-two multiple choice items which yield information regarding an individual's capability to understand others' feelings and tastes as well as his or her potential for reacting tactfully towards others. The empathy test would be most useful in the screening and selection of employment applicants, such as, for leadership or social relations positions in which a broad sense of understanding and/or empathy is required for effective job performance.

Norms: Normative data is based on approximately two hundred male employees from different industrial areas, ranging from routine workers, general business, and lower management to sales, sales managers, and upper management.

Validity and Reliability: One study comparing a group of fifteen promising foremen in a management training class with a group of twenty-eight student engineers showed a median score of forty-eight for the foremen and of forty-two for the students and yielded a tetrachoric coefficient of .67 between scores for the two groups. This study indicates the empathy test's ability to discriminate between two groups in the hypothesized direction. Other validity studies report a correlation of .31 of empathy test scores with average annual salary increase for 81 business personnel. Additional studies, indicating the relationship of empathy test scores and election to offices of leadership, yielded a correlation value of .40 between those two variables for 102 business personnel.

Split-half reliability was found to be .56 on 114 adults. This level permits some practical use of the instrument within limits.

Bibliography:

Kerr, W. A.: *Manual of Instructions: Diplomacy Test of Empathy*. Munster, Psychometric Affiliates, 1960.

EMO Questionnaire

Authors: George O. Baehr and Melany E. Baehr

Variable: The EMO Questionnaire is a measure of emotional stability which provides information about subjects' feelings toward their work or home environment.

Type of Measure: The EMO is a paper and pencil inventory, suitable for administration to either individuals or groups. It is untimed and typically takes twenty to thirty minutes to complete. Scoring is complex and may be done manually or by machine.

Source from which Measure may be Obtained: Industrial Relations Center, 1225 E. Sixtieth Street, Chicago, Illinois 60637.

Description: The EMO consists of 140 items, each describing an experience which might have occurred within the last month, such as, feelings in dealing with superiors or feelings related to level of energy. The subject responds by placing a check mark under an appropriate column heading: "no" indicates that this particular experience did not occur during the last month; it "pleased" him or her, "not affected", "troubled a little", and "troubled very much", all indicate that the experience did occur within the past month and how the subject felt about it. In addition to interpretation of scores based on the frequency of maladjustive responses to groups of items, the EMO assesses the summed intensity, as well as conformity, of responses. Use of the EMO extends to the screening and placement of potential employees; personality assessment in counseling settings by the identification of anxiety, insecurity, and emotional problems in subjects; as well as the screening and promotion of present employees into supervisory positions.

Norms: Up to the present, the results have been obtained almost exclusively on male subjects, although there does not seem to be any reason why the results should not apply to female subjects as well. Age of the subjects ranged from nineteen to fifty-eight, and the occupational areas varied to include sales, sciences, and research. Other normative samples included hospital patients who were mentally disturbed; they were all male with a mean age of forty-one.

Validity and Reliability: The majority of the scores from the EMO have shown an ability to significantly differentiate industrial versus hospital normative samples. Those indices which discriminate best between the criterion groups are the subscores which measure depression, projection, unreality and withdrawal, and the "Z" vector. Furthermore, the correlation between the patients' own evaluations of benefits derived from treatment with the shift in the intensity score of the EMO over a course of therapy yielded a correlation value of .66 for 66 subjects. Estimates of the correlation of a ward psychiatrist's evaluation of the benefits derived by 44 patients from therapy with the intensity score resulted in a value of .52. Further validity information is presented for both screening and placement, as well as for personality diagnoses. A summary of validity studies indicates ongoing research to ascertain the predictive validity of the instrument with new criterion groups in industry and emotionally disturbed patients.

Test retest, for a sample of 86 self-referred neurotic patients, over a twenty-four day interval, yielded a reliability coefficient of .84. Test retest, for a sample of 28 self-referred neurotic patients who had completed treatment and whose time interval was six hours between testings, yielded a reliability of .96.

Bibliography:

Baehr, G. E. and Baehr, M. O.: *EMO Questionnaire, Test Administration Manual.* Chicago, Industrial Relations Center, 1959.

The Empathy Test

Authors: W. A. Kerr and B. J. Speroff

Variable: The Empathy Test measures an individual's ability to understand and anticipate the reactions of others.

Type of Measure: The Empathy Test is a paper and pencil inventory, suitable for administration to either individuals or groups. It is untimed and typically takes from six to fifteen minutes to complete. Scoring is done by hand.

Source from which Measure may be Obtained: Psychometric Affiliates, P. O. Box 3167, Munster, Indiana 46321.

Description: The Empathy Test is designed to assess one's empathic ability or the ability to put oneself in another's place by anticipating the other's feelings, reactions, and behaviors. It is available in three parallel forms, A, B, and C. Each form consists of thirty-nine items broken into three sections. The first section, music, has fourteen items, each of which denotes a type of music, such as, polka, waltz, spiritual, and others. The second section, magazine, has fifteen items, each of which is the title of a magazine publication. The third section, annoying experience, has ten items, each of which presents a petty annoyance. In all three sections, the subject responds by ranking the items numerically, that is, by popularity in the first section, by circulation in the second section, and from most to least annoying in the third section. Suggested uses for the Empathy Test include the screening and selection of personnel for positions in which empathic ability is advantageous to, or necessary for successful job performance, such as, in sales or supervisory.

Norms: Normative data is available on groups ranging from college students to varied occupational areas. These norms include, union business agents, union members — male, male and female college of fine arts students, science and liberal arts majors, industrial supervisors, retail clerks, firemen, hospital volunteers, automobile salesmen, among others. The number of cases varies from a low of 32 for automobile salesmen to 432 for college men.

Validity and Reliability: Validity data was generated using Moreno's Sociometric technique on ninety-two college men who were asked to nominate, by a like-dislike criterion, other peers. Results showed a moderate correlation of .34 of interpersonal acceptance with empathic ability as measured by the Empathy Test. Significant relationships were found in comparing empathy scores with the number of campus activities participated in by college students. Three of the Kuder Preference scales, computational, persuasive, and clerical, are also significantly related to empathy scores with values ranging from .22 to .28, although no relationship was found when using varied aptitude and achievement devices. Other studies are also reported relating six criteria of union leadership with Empathy Test scores. These criteria were, for example, settling grievances, recruitment ranking on leadership by other union members. Correlation values yielded on these sixty-four subjects were generally in the .40 to .60 range.

Test retest, based on groups of 100 and 60 college students, yielded reliabilities ranging from .67 to .81 (time interval is not stated in the manual) for form A. A split-half reliability value of .89 was obtained on 124 male, skilled workers for form A. Intercorrelation of forms A and B, administered over a one year period on seventy plus college students, yielded a value of .83.

Bibliography:

Kerr, W. A. and Speroff, B. J.: *Manual of Instructions: The Empathy Test.* Munster, Psychometric Affiliates, 1955.

The Family Adjustment Test

Author: Gabriel Elias

Variable: The Family Adjustment Test (FAT) assesses family members' feelings of homeyness and homelessness.

Type of Measure: The FAT is a paper and pencil inventory, suitable for administration to either individuals or groups or for oral administration to individuals. It is untimed and typically takes thirty-five minutes to complete. Scoring is done by hand with the use of a key.

Source from which Measure may be Obtained: Psychometric Affiliates, P. O. Box 3167, Munster, Indiana 46321.

Description: The FAT is comprised of 114 items broken into ten subtests, including, attitudes toward mother, attitudes toward father, father-mother attitude quotient, oedipal, struggle for independence, parent-child friction-harmony, interparental friction-harmony, family inferiority-superiority, rejection of child, and parental qualities. In addition to the personal, family adjustment areas, the FAT provides a measure of homeyness, the feeling of being drawn toward one's family — a sense of belonging, and homelessness, the feeling of being repelled by one's family or the feeling that one's family members want to move away from the group. Obviously, the FAT is most valuable in family group counseling; however, it is also a useful tool in the screening and counseling of students, delinquents, and psychiatric patients.

Norms: Extensive use of the inventory has been performed with groups varying in dimensions of socioeconomic status, intelligence levels and race, in large cities as well as rural farm areas. Norms are presented for ages twelve through the adult range, separately by sex.

Validity and Reliability: No differences in scores have been found to indicate that race, income, or education are important variables to be considered in the use of this inventory. Specifically, studies of contrasting sex groups have yielded differences between males and females on the homeyness scale. Finally, significant differences were obtained between a comparison of juvenile delinquents and nondelinquents on the dimensions of homeyness and homelessness.

Corrected split-half reliability, based on groups of college students and juvenile delinquents, was found to be .97.

Bibliography:

Elias, G.: *Elias Family Opinion Survey, The Family Adjustment Test, Manual of Instructions*. Munster, Psychometric Affiliates, 1954.

The Forer Structured Sentence Completion Test

Author: Bertram R. Forer

Variable: The Forer Structured Sentence Completion Test

(FSSCT) is designed to detect personality problems in individuals.

Type of Measure: The FSSCT is a paper and pencil inventory, suitable for administration to either individuals or groups. It is untimed and typically takes sixty minutes to complete. Scoring must be done manually by a trained clinician.

Source from which Measure may be Obtained: Western Psychological Services, 12031 Wilshire Boulevard, Los Angeles, California 90025.

Description: The FSSCT is comprised of 100 partial sentences. The subject responds by completing each sentence, as quickly as possible, with the first thing that comes to mind. By employing very structured items, a wide coverage of the individual, attitude-value systems of evasiveness, individual differences and defense mechanisms will be detected. The FSSCT is available in forms M for men, W for women, B for boys, and G for girls. It is most useful as a diagnostic tool which enables the subject to express attitudes in certain areas already decided upon by the diagnostician. The scoring is complex and requires training in the use of sentence completion devices.

Norms: No normative data is reported in the manual. However, several classification systems are available for arriving at interpretations of responses.

Validity and Reliability: Although no empirical data is stated, the use of a device that employs a sentence completion approach does have utility in both diagnosis and therapy. Responses to such an instrument can be used with other information in order to seek insights into the traits of a subject, especially where more structured devices would be a handicap.

Bibliography:

Forer, B. R.: *Manual: The Forer Structured Sentence Completion Test.* Los Angeles, Western Psychological Services, 1957.

Fundamental Interpersonal Relations Orientation — Behavior

Author: William C. Schutz

Variable: The Fundamental Interpersonal Relations Orientation — Behavior (FIRO-B) assesses an individual's behavior towards others.

Type of Measure: The FIRO-B is a paper and pencil inventory, suitable for administration to either individuals or groups. It is untimed. Scoring is done by hand with the use of a template.

Source from which Measure may be Obtained: Consulting Psychologists Press, 577 College Avenue, Palo Alto, California 94306.

Description: The FIRO-B provides assessment of the subject's behavior toward other persons on three dimensions: inclusion or the individual's need to have good or positive relationships and interactions with others; control or the behavior of decision making between individuals; and affection or the subject's need for loving and affectionate relationships with others. Each of these dimensions is assessed on two scales: expressed behavior and wanted behavior. The FIRO-B would be useful: as a counseling aid, such as, to determine the ability of a subject to both desire and express inclusion, affection and control; or to identify individuals who have a balance between expressed and wanted behavior, such as, for the purpose of placing them in positions which demand these characteristics; or as an aid in vocational guidance, such as, in selecting occupations in which discrepancies between expressed and wanted behavior are desired factors.

Norms: Normative data is based on samples varying in size from sixteen, for nursing school students and nurses, to over one thousand, for Harvard freshmen. Norm groups also include traveling salesmen, business school graduates, medical students, college freshmen (females), navy personnel, educational administrators, creative architects, and teachers, among others. The sex of each norm group is specified.

Validity and Reliability: Numerous studies have been conducted with the FIRO-B in determining the effects of human relationship training, and its use as a psychiatric classification system and relationship of FIRO-B scores to other personal and biographical factors. The reader is referred to the extensive bibliography in the reference manual for articles reporting on the validity of the FIRO-B.

Reliability data is not stated in the manual but is available from the Guttman scaling computer program (GUTS) upon request from the publisher.

Bibliography:

Buros, O. K.: Test number 78a.

Schutz, W. C.: *The FIRO Scales, Manual.* Palo Alto, Consulting Psychologists Press, 1967.

Human Relations Inventory

Author: Raymond E. Bernberg

Variable: The Human Relations Inventory (HRI) measures social conformity as it is manifest in attitudes.

Type of Measure: The HRI is a paper and pencil inventory, suitable for administration to either individuals or groups. It is untimed. Scoring is done by hand with the use of a key.

Source from which Measure may be Obtained: Psychometric Affiliates, P. O. Box 3167, Munster, Indiana 46321.

Description: The HRI assesses societal conformity, in light of the cultural and social pressures placed upon it, by the acts and attitudes of the individual. It does this by confronting the subject with thirty-seven multiple choice items to which the subject responds by choosing one of five percentage figures. The real answers to the questions are not necessarily known. However, as the choices of the respondent lean to one extreme or the other, they reveal his or her need-value system. Attitude scales encompassed by the inventory items include moral values, positive goals, reality testing, ability to give affection, tension level, and impulsivity. The HRI might be useful in individual and group counseling. Raw scores may be converted to percentile ranks with the use of the tables in the manual.

Norms: The norm group is comprised of males and females, age eighteen and over, of different socioeconomic and religious backgrounds, with a wide variability of educational, intelligence and age levels, and from varied religions and cultures. Norms are available for senior high school students, college students, church goers, Los Angeles police, male prisoners, female prisoners, and reform school males.

Validity and Reliability: Validity was found, based on 160 male inmates in a California prison. The group had a median age of twenty-one years. A comparison of the mean scores of this group with a norm group of noninmates revealed a significant difference in the predicted direction between the two groups. Further validity studies found that the HRI discriminated significantly between delinquent and vocational high school males (Roys, 1955), while additional studies by Bassin (1957) found that a significant increase in scores on the HRI occurred in adult male probationers after group therapy.

A reliability value of .77 was found through using a youth prisoner group.

Bibliography:

Bassin, A.: Unpublished Ph.D. thesis, Sociology. New York University, 1957.

Bernberg, R. E.: *Human Relations Inventory, Manual of Instructions.* Munster, Psychometric Affiliates, 1959.

Roys, J.: Unpublished M.S. thesis, Psychology. Illinois Institute of Technology, 1955.

Life Interpersonal History Enquiry

Author: William C. Schutz

Variable: The Life Interpersonal History Enquiry (LIPHE) measures an individual's recall of information and impressions of parental relationships before he or she was six years old.

Type of Measure: The LIPHE is a paper and pencil inventory, suitable for administration to either individuals or groups. It is untimed and typically takes fifteen minutes to complete. Scoring is done by hand.

Source from which Measure may be Obtained: Consulting Psychologists Press, 577 College Avenue, Palo Alto, California 94306.

Description: The LIPHE is one of a series of instruments entitled the Fundamental Interpersonal Relations Orientation (FIRO) Scales. It addresses itself to the subject's early childhood, previous to the age of six. It poses parent-child-related questions which, allowing for distortion by such factors as the passing of time, attempt to assess relationships between so-called childhood actors and targets, as well as between ego and so-called adulthood actors and targets (targets typically being mother and father). In addition, items are constructed to measure the dimensions of inclusion, control, and affection, all on two levels: behavior and feelings. Use of the LIPHE extends to clinical settings in family therapy in which an understanding of the adult's perception of his or her childhood would be informative and useful in treating the interpersonal relationships within the family.

Norms: The author notes the LIPHE scores are unrelated to the usual characteristics of age, intelligence, socioeconomic measures, ethnic groups, marital status, or religious identification. Distribution of scores as well as descriptive measures are available from the publisher under the Guttman scaling computer program (GUTS).

Validity and Reliability: Construct validation studies yielded two factors: a relationship with father and a relationship with mother dimension. Predictive validity findings are also reported and indicate that for a group of school administrators, satisfaction with one's childhood relationship with one's father was a strong indication of administrative success.

Reliability data are not reported in the manual but are available from the GUTS program upon request from the publisher.

Bibliography:

Buros, O. K.: Test number 78.

Schutz, W. C.: *The FIRO Scales, Manual.* Palo Alto, Consulting Psychologists Press, 1967.

The Press Test

Authors: Melany E. Baehr, Raymond J. Corsini, and Richard Renck

Variable: The Press Test assesses an individual's capability to work under stress with accompanying distracting environmental conditions.

Type of Measure: The Press Test is a paper and pencil instrument, suitable for administration to either individuals or groups. There are three parts to the test, each of which is timed, and the entire series takes about four minutes to complete. Scoring is done manually by summing the number of responses.

Source from which Measure may be Obtained: Industrial Relations Center, 1225 East Sixtieth Street, Chicago, Illinois 60637.

Description: The Press Test is a three-part test which assesses the subject's response to a simulated, controlled, and stressful situation. The first part includes columns of words with the names of colors and four color names with four corresponding columns of circles. The subject responds by placing the first letter of each of the color words in the circle corresponding to that word. The difficulty of the task increases in the second and third parts, where the tasks become more confusing, such as, in part three, the stimulus word may be printed in a color other than the word, and the subject is required to place the first letter of the color of the ink in which the word is written in the appropriate circle. The test yields five subscores which may be converted to standard scores and percentiles with the use of the tables in the manual. The Press Test is most valuable in the screening and selection of suitable personnel for positions with a high stress load and where conflicting, confusing information must be dealt with quickly.

Norms: In its present form, the test has been used principally with male industrial subjects. The first norm group included seventy-two supervisory trainees. The present norm group comprises 291 industrial employees, including 92 engineers and chemists, 48 executives and middle management, 33 white collar and junior executives, 72 foremen, and 46 salesmen. Norms are presented for 914 male industrial personnel for Parts I, II, and III and discrepancy scores between

Part combinations.

Validity and Reliability: Validity as expressed through significant correlation with the Temperament Comparator (a validated temperament test) is presented. Evidence points to the validity of The Press Test as presented and explained in the manual. Further evidence is presented through the ability of The Press Test to significantly discriminate between various industrial groups. For example, significant differences were found between engineers and foremen, executives and foremen, and engineers and salesmen on Part I. Evidence states that Press Test scores are valid for selection of higher level personnel, such as, upper and middle management.

Test retest, over a one week interval on fifty-eight industrial personnel, yielded reliability coefficients ranging from .72 to .82 for each of the three parts of the test.

> "... reliabilities for the derived scores I minus II and III minus II are unsatisfactory." (p. 11, manual)

Bibliography:

Baehr, M. E., Corsini, R., and Renck, R.: *The Press Test, Test Administration Manual.* Chicago, Industrial Relations Center, 1967.

Buros, O. K.: Test number P.213.

The Purpose in Life Test

Authors: James C. Crumbaugh and Leonard T. Maholick

Variable: The Purpose in Life Test (PIL) isolates and assesses an individual's determination to find meaning and purpose in human existence.

Type of Measure: The PIL is a paper and pencil inventory, suitable for administration to either individuals or groups. It is untimed and typically takes ten to twenty minutes to complete. Scoring is done by hand.

Source from which Measure may be Obtained: Psychometric Affiliates, P. O. Box 3167, Munster, Indiana 46321.

Description: The PIL attempts to identify the subject's attitude regarding the meaning of life. It serves as a therapeutic device and may be used with patients in therapy programs, as well as with individuals seeking career direction. There are three parts. Part A has twenty items to be rated on a scale from one to seven. Numbers one and seven are extreme alternatives, while number four represents a neutral feeling with little judgment expressed. Part B is comprised of thirteen partial sentences to be completed freely by the subject. Part C intends for the subject to write a paragraph detailing his or her ambitions, aims, and goals in life. Only Part A is scored objectively; Parts B and C are interpreted clinically. Raw scores may be converted to percentiles.

Norms: Norms are based on 1,151 cases reported by Crumbaugh (1968). Although no other normative data is stated, it is reported that the test is pertinent to alcoholics, retired persons, and handicapped populations.

Validity and Reliability: One validity study established a relationship of .38 between the PIL and therapist ratings based on fifty subjects. Other empirically based studies showed interrelationships between the PIL and the subscales of the Minnesota Multiphasic Personality Inventory, while a subsequent study by Snavely (1962) showed a relationship of .57 with forty students between PIL and the Crowne Marlow Social Desirability Scale. Other validity studies employed the California Personality Inventory, the Personal Orientation Inventory, and a host of other personality measures.

Corrected split-half reliabilities were found to be .81 and .85 in two studies, respectively.

Bibliography:

Buros, O. K.: Test number 130.

Crumbaugh, J. C.: Cross-validation of Purpose-in-Life Test based on Frankl's concepts. *Journal of Individual Psychology, 24*:74-81, 1968.

——— and Maholick, L. T.: *Manual of Instructions for The Purpose in Life Test.* Munster, Psychometric Affiliates, 1969.

Snavely, H. R.: An unpublished special course project, Carleton College, 1962.

Social Intelligence Test

Authors: F. A. Moss, T. Hunt, K. T. Omwake, and L. G. Woodward

Variable: The Social Intelligence Test (SIT) assesses an individual's capabilities in the areas of social relationships.

Type of Measure: The SIT is a paper and pencil test, suitable for administration to either individuals or groups. There are several editions timed from thirty to forty-five minutes. Scoring is done by hand with the use of a key.

Source from which Measure may be Obtained: Western Psychological Services, 12031 Wilshire Boulevard, Los Angeles, California 90025.

Description: The SIT was first available in 1927, with a subsequent form published in 1929. It is at present available in the following editions: revised form — second edition (1949), short edition, and SP (special) edition. The 1949 edition includes five parts: 1) judgment in social situations, 2) recognition of the mental state of the speaker, 3) memory for names and faces, 4) observation of human behavior, and 5) sense of humor. The short edition and the SP both are published for industrial uses. These shorter forms reduce the time and complexity of administration while still retaining the parts useful in the industrial setting, such as, for possible selection and placement of sales and supervisory personnel. The short edition includes parts one, two, four, and five, and the SP edition includes only parts one and four.

Norms: Normative data for the SP edition and the revised edition is based on the following samples: high school seniors, college freshmen, college graduate students and employed adults. Norms for the short edition were based on: high school seniors, college freshmen and upper class college students. Employed adult norms as well as high school and college norms are based upon persons tested in the middle Atlantic states. Education level of adult cases is above high school. Occupations for the adult groups include administrative and executive, teaching, secretarial, sales manager, sales representative, engineering, nursing, and sales applicants. The number of cases varies from over two hundred for college graduates to several thousand employed adults. Norms are presented in percentiles for total test scores for each of the three editions.

Validity and Reliability: The early validation of the SIT by

Hunt (1928) established a .61 correlation value of the test scores with ratings by executives on how a sample of ninety-eight subjects dealt with people in a sales company. Also, significant differences in scores on the SIT were obtained for different levels of extracurricular activity of students. Finally, studies yielded significant differences among occupational groups, with higher scores for those occupations that deal with interrelationships among people.

Test retest, on 100 college sophomores (time interval is not stated in the manual), yielded a reliability of .89 for the total score. Split-half methods yielded correlation values ranging from .72 to .86 for the total score. These were carried out on varied forms of the test, and samples generally totaled around one hundred subjects.

Bibliography:

Hunt, T.: The Measurement of Social Intelligence. *Journal of Applied Psychology, 12*:317-34, 1928.

Moss, F. A., Hunt, T., Omwake, K. T., and Woodward, L. G.: *George Washington University Series — Social Intelligence Test, Manual.* Washington, D. C., Center for Psychological Service, 1955.

Survey of Interpersonal Values

Author: Leonard V. Gordon

Variable: The Survey of Interpersonal Values (SIV) assesses important values involving an individual's interrelationships with others.

Type of Measure: The SIV is a paper and pencil inventory, suitable for administration to either individuals or groups. It is untimed and typically takes fifteen minutes to complete. Scoring is done by hand with the use of an overlay stencil.

Source from which Measure may be Obtained: Science Research Associates, 259 East Erie Street, Chicago, Illinois 60611.

Description: The SIV attempts to assess those individual values deemed important to one's interrelationships. The values measured by the SIV include support, conformity, recognition, independence, benevolence, and leadership. It consists of thirty triads in a forced choice format. The subject responds by choosing one statement of three alternatives which is most important to him or her and one which is least important. Three of the six values are evaluated in each triad. All statements are balanced for social desirability. The SIV would be most useful as a supplement to a personnel selection battery, especially for positions requiring face to face relationships; in appraisal or vocational guidance; and in individual counseling.

Norms: Normative data is based on 1,075 men and 746 women, selected from colleges representing major regions of the country. Furthermore, descriptive data is provided for males and females separately, as well as for supervisory and trade personnel (N = 68).

Validity and Reliability: A factor analytic approach was used to develop the scales. Repeated factor analysis of data confirmed the existence of separate and independent scales in the SIV. In addition, validity studies have also shown low correlations of SIV scores with the subscores of the College Qualification Test: verbal, quantitative, total, science and social studies. Generally, these results indicate that the SIV is independent of intelligence. Correlation with the Gordon Personal Profile illustrated results that are generally expected to be found between the two instruments. For example, a significant correlation is found between the cautiousness subscale of the Gordon Personal Profile and the conformity subscale of the SIV, as well as between sociability subscale of the Gordon and recognition subscale of the SIV.

Test retest, over a ten day interval based on seventy-nine students, yielded reliability coefficients ranging from .78 to .89 for the six subscales. Reliabilities, estimated by Kuder-Richardson Case III formula, yielded values ranging from .71 to .86 for the six subscales.

Bibliography:

Gordon, L. V.: *SRA Manual for Survey of Interpersonal Values*. Chicago, Science Research Associates, 1960.

Test of Behavioral Rigidity (Research Edition)

Author: K. Warner Schaie

Variable: The Test of Behavioral Ridigity (TBR) assesses the capability of an individual to adjust to the stress arising from constant environmental change.

Type of Measure: The TBR is a paper and pencil device, suitable for administration to either individuals or groups. It is untimed and typically takes thirty minutes to complete. Scoring is done both by hand and by machine (the latter is used only for subtest III).

Source from which Measure may be Obtained: Consulting Psychologists Press, 577 College Avenue, Palo Alto, California 94306.

Description: The TBR includes three subtests: a capitals test, an opposites test, and a questionnaire. The subtests yield scores which result in three factor scores. The factor scores are: motor-cognitive rigidity which points to the subject's ability to change with minimum difficulty from activity to activity; personality-perceptual rigidity which measures a subject's ability to adjust easily to new environments as well as to changes in intellectual and situational patterns; and psychomotor speed which measures the rate of emission of familiar cognitive responses. The composite score of the three factors may be interpreted as a general estimate of the individual's flexibility. It is interesting to note that the scores yielded by this test may be a good indication of an individual's ability to function to the limit of his or her capabilities. A study by Schaie (1958a) indicated that the TBR could also be used effectively to determine the degree to which subjects in older age groups maintain their flexibility.

Norms: Normative data is based on 500 subjects drawn from the upper 75 percent of the United States socioeconomic status. Subjects ranged in age from twenty to seventy, divided into five-year groups with equal numbers of males and females. Norm tables are presented with a mean of fifty and a standard deviation of ten, by age groups (five years), by subtest and by composite scores.

Validity and Reliability: Validity data on the construct validity of the TBR is reported. This includes factor analyses studies which yielded three factors from the scales included in the inventory. Other data indicates that prison inmates have a significantly lower rigidity quotient than the general population (Konietzko, 1959).

Reliability data is not presented. However, the reader is urged to consult reference articles using this inventory, which may currently report such information.

Bibliography:

Konietzko, K.: An investigation of the concept of behavioral rigidity as applied to a penal population. Unpublished Ph.D. thesis, Temple University, 1959.

Schaie, K. W.: Rigidity-flexibility and intelligence: A cross-sectional study of the adult life span from 20 to 70 years. *Psychological Monographs, No. 9 (Whole no. 462). (a)*:72, 1958.

_____ : *Preliminary Manual: Test of Behavioral Rigidity — Research Edition.* Palo Alto, Consulting Psychologists Press, 1960.

WLW Personal Attitude Inventory

Author: Robert W. Henderson

Variable: The WLW Personal Attitude Inventory assesses individuals' self-perceptions and how they want others to see them.

Type of Measure: The WLW is a paper and pencil inventory, suitable for administration to either individuals or groups. It is untimed. Scoring is done by hand.

Source from which Measure may be Obtained: William, Lynde and Williams, Painesville Professional Center, Suite 401, Painesville, Ohio 44077.

Description: The WLW is available in three editions, three, five, and six. It is comprised of both positively and negatively stated items to which the subject responds by indicating whether or not the items are descriptive of him or her. There are six scales measured: emotional stability, friendliness, aggressiveness, humility and insight, reliability, and supervisory style. Some of the editions include additional scales, such as, considerate and democratic leadership. A subject's high or low score indicates that he or she is paying attention to identifying the positive (high) or negative (low) dimension aspects of the inventory and indicates that the dimension is of particular interest to the subject. The WLW can be used to identify strengths and weaknesses of the subject's psychological constitution, thus providing a foundation for discussion in personal analysis or individual counseling. The manual provides detailed descriptions of each of the scales measured by the inventory, as well as specific item examples.

Norms: Normative data is based on male middle management and ranges in group size from several hundred to almost several thousand, depending on the edition used.

Validity and Reliability: No validity information is stated in the manual.

Split-half reliabilities, determined for a middle management sample of 100 subjects, ranged from .73 to .79 for the six subscales.

Bibliography:

Buros, O. K.: Test number 158.

Henderson, R. W.: *Manual: WLW Personal Attitude Inventory*. Editions three, five and six. Painesville, William, Lynde and Williams, 1969.

Chapter 6

INTEREST AND VOCATIONAL MEASURES

California Occupational Preference Survey

Authors: Robert R. Knapp, Bruce Grant, and George D. Demos

Variable: The California Occupational Preference Survey (COPS) is used to identify an individual's occupational and professional interests.

Type of Measure: The COPS is a paper and pencil inventory, suitable for administration to either individuals or groups. It is untimed and typically takes thirty minutes to complete. Scoring may be done manually with the use of a stencil or by machine.

Source from which Measure may be Obtained: Educational and Industrial Testing Service, P. O. Box 7234, San Diego, California 92107.

Description: The COPS is aimed at vocational guidance on the basis of the subject's interest. It covers fourteen interest areas, including: science-professional and skilled; technical-professional and skilled; outdoor; business-professional and skilled; clerical; linguistic-professional and skilled; aesthetic-professional and skilled; and service-professional and skilled. There are 168 items covering activities in numerous occupations. The subject responds on a four point scale, from "like very much" to "dislike very much", and since a forced choice format is not used, the subject is able to state his or her degree of like or dislike on every item. The COPS is available in either a self-scoring form or a reusable booklet. It is useful as an aid in vocational counseling or as a supplement to an aptitude battery in planning for career selection.

Norms: Normative data was collected on samples of male and female college freshmen and upper-level high school students. These samples formed the basis for twelve of the scales. Raw scores are presented separately by sex, and profile sheets, based on percentile norms, are available for high school and college students.

Validity and Reliability: Several validity studies yielded information which indicates that individuals in a wide variety of occupations who are considered to have chosen their occupational fields do score highly on the respective scales of the COPS. Navy radiomen had their highest level on the technical skill scale, based on high school norms. Storekeepers scored highest on the clerical scale, bankers on the business professional scale, and so forth. A further study found general usefulness of the COPS with disadvantaged minority groups when scores were reported at and above the 75th percentile on one or more scales and were not depressed on all scales.

Test retest, over a one week interval for 113 students, yielded reliabilities ranging from .81 to .91 on the COPS scales. Split-half reliabilities, based on 290 high school students, were found to be in a range from .86 to .95. Test retest, over a one year interval and then over a two year interval for 182 students, yielded median reliabilities of .66 and .63, respectively.

Bibliography:

Buros, O. K.: Test number 1012.

Knapp, R. R., Grant, B., and Demos, G. D.: *Manual: California Occupational Preference Survey*. San Diego, Educational and Industrial Testing Service, 1971.

Gordon Occupational Check List

Author: Leonard V. Gordon

Variable: The Gordon Occupational Check List determines suitable occupations for an individual.

Type of Measure: The check list is a paper and pencil inventory, suitable for administration to either individuals or groups. It is untimed and typically takes twenty to twenty-five minutes to complete.

Source from which Measure may be Obtained: Harcourt Brace Jovanovich, 757 Third Avenue, New York, New York

10017.

Description: The check list is comprised of 240 items, each of which is related to a specific occupation. The subjects respond by indicating those activities that they would like to do in a full-time job and by circling those activities that they would most like to do. Items are categorized into the areas of business, outdoor, arts, technology, and service. These categories are broken into thirty related clusters. This allows the scorer to note the categories as well as the clusters marked most frequently by the subject. The implication flowing from the use of these results will allow specific occupational areas to be identified, for potential subject interest and, ultimately, selection. It is interesting to note that the items of the Gordon Occupational Check List coincide extensively with those listed in the third edition of the Dictionary of Occupational Titles (DOT), as both were evolved from the same source, including the Group and Level Schemata of Roe (1956).

Norms: Norms were evolved on 6,000 high school students, geographically spread throughout the United States.

Validity and Reliability: The breadth of the occupations covered in the check list was determined in a survey of high school students who added a few new occupations to the group already provided. Additional validity is reported showing difference in performance of males versus females on the fifth dimension of business through service. Finally, additional responses of users, to feasibility of the check list, indicated a high level of acceptability and meaningfulness of the information secured from its interpretation.

Test retest, over a one month interval for a group of twelfth grade males (N = 52) and females (N = 45), yielded reliability coefficients ranging from .88 to .94, for the number of items underlined. Within the same sample for the dimension of identical items underlined, the test retest reliabilities were .81 for males and .82 for females.

Bibliography:

Buros, O. K.: Test number 1019.

Gordon, L. V.: *Gordon Occupational Check List, Manual.* New York,

Harcourt Brace Jovanovich, 1963.
Roe, A.: *The Psychology of Occupations.* New York, John Wiley and Sons, 1956.
United States Government Printing Office: *Dictionary of Occupational Titles. Volume I — Definition of Titles.* 3rd ed. Washington, Author, 1965.
______ : *Dictionary of Occupational Titles. Volume II — Occupational Classification.* 3rd ed. Washington, Author, 1965.

Job Analysis and Interest Measurement

Author: Regis Walther

Variable: The Job Analysis and Interest Measurement (JAIM) assesses those personal qualities of an individual which effect job success or failure.

Type of Measure: The JAIM is a paper and pencil inventory, suitable for administration to either individuals or groups. It is untimed and typically takes sixty minutes to complete. Hand scoring keys are not available for the JAIM, therefore, scoring arrangements must be made with the Office of Special Tests, Educational Testing Service, Princeton, New Jersey or the author.

Source from which Measure may be Obtained: Educational Testing Service, Princeton, New Jersey 08540.

Description: The JAIM includes 125 multiple choice items which are oriented to values, preferences and behaviors of the subject in job-related situations. It measures determinates of job success or failure based on "personality difficulties" by providing measures on thirty-seven variables relating to job orientation, work content preferences, interpersonal behavior, formal organizational behavior, information analysis behavior, success criteria and personal history. A detailed description of each subscale is provided in the manual. Because its reliability is not yet established at a high enough level, the JAIM should not be used as the sole basis for decisions in selecting individuals. However, it has already proven useful in discriminating between high and low level performers within the same occupational groups.

Norms: Norms are based on a group of 4,361 males who took the United States Department of State Foreign Service Officer Examination in September of 1963. This sample consisted of predominantly college-educated subjects who had either a history or political science background in college, who ranged in age from twenty-one to twenty-four, and who were geographically spread throughout the United States. Norms are reported as standard scores.

Validity and Reliability: Clerical personnel in the foreign service were rated on job performance and then separated into groups of high and low performers. Correlations were obtained when scores on the JAIM were used to predict performance in a cross-validation study. The values of .60 for thirty-two secretaries and of .38 for thirty-one code clerks were reported between JAIM scores and job performance. Numerous studies establishing the ability of the JAIM to differentiate among varied occupational groups are also provided.

Test retest, over a two day interval for twenty-six clerical employees, yielded a mean reliability of .85 on thirty-one scales of form 162 (a preliminary form of the JAIM). Split-half reliabilities, determined on 100 subjects selected from the norm sample, ranged from .46 to .76 with a mean of .61 for the thirty-four scales.

Bibliography:

Buros, O. K.: Test number 95.

Walther, R.: *Job Analysis and Interest Measurement, Manual.* Princeton, Educational Testing Service, 1964.

Kuder Occupational Interest Survey

Author: G. Frederic Kuder

Variable: The Kuder Occupational Interest Survey (OIS) assesses an individual's vocational interests.

Type of Measure: The OIS is a paper and pencil inventory, suitable for administration to either individuals or groups. It is untimed and typically takes thirty minutes to complete. Scoring is usually done by machine, because manual scoring is difficult. (Please note that Science Research Associates provides free machine scoring of the OIS in any quantity.)

Source from which Measure may be Obtained: Science Research Associates, 259 East Erie Street, Chicago, Illinois 60611.

Description: The OIS assesses occupational interests by comparing the subject's scores on the 171 scales, structured within the inventory, with the established interests of individuals in certain occupations. There are one hundred triads in the OIS to which the subject responds by indicating one most preferred and one least preferred activity. The OIS scales include occupations and college majors as criterion and thereby achieve a better differentiation. The scales include seventy-seven occupational scores and twenty-nine college major scores for men and fifty-seven occupational scores and twenty-seven college major scores for women; twenty-eight of the women's scales were developed on male subjects. In addition, eight experimental scales were included as measures of masculinity-femininity, maturation of interests, and faking.

Norms: Normative data is extensive and includes assessment of individuals in over one hundred occupational fields. The nature of interest inventories demands comparison of one's score with the interest patterns of others upon which the occupation scores were formed. The occupational criterion group ranged from accountants to X-ray technicians and generally included 100 or more individuals who had attained a recognized status in their fields of endeavor. Generally, the subjects were between the ages of twenty-five and sixty-five, active at least three years in their fields, and typically were members of trade and professional organizations.

Validity and Reliability: Validity data attempted to determine the errors of classification by ascertaining the performance of criterion groups on scales other than their own. Studies indicate a low misclassification rate of 5 percent. Other data indicated that criterion group members generally achieved their highest scores in the occupational area that they represent. Few scores were further than one to two standard errors of measurement from their highest score.

Test retest, over a two week interval for four groups, two

high school and two college student groups, yielded reliability coefficients of .91 on both high school groups and of .90 on both college groups with a median reliability of .90; there were twenty-five subjects in each group. Test retest on ninety-two high school senior males and fifty college senior females yielded median reliabilities of .93 and .96 for the two groups, respectively.

Bibliography:

Buros, O. K.: Test number 1025.

Kuder, G. F.: *Kuder Occupational Interest Survey, General Manual.* Chicago, Science Research Associates, 1971.

Kuder Preference Record — Personal — Form A

Author: G. Frederic Kuder

Variable: The Kuder Preference Record assesses personal preferences which contribute to job satisfaction.

Type of Measure: The preference record is a paper and pencil inventory, suitable for administration to either individuals or groups. It is untimed and typically takes forty minutes to complete. Scoring may be done manually or by machine.

Source from which Measure may be Obtained: Science Research Associates, 259 East Erie Street, Chicago, Illinois 60611.

Description: The preference record assesses the subject's preference attitudes in five areas: being active in groups, familiar and stable situations, working with ideas, avoiding conflict, and directing (influencing) others. The five scales are independent of each other and of the scales in the Kuder Preference Record — Vocational. The preference record is available in two parallel forms, AH and AM, and intends to reveal the environment in which the subject prefers to work. It indicates, for example, how much one likes to partake in group activities, role preference in a group, interests in exploring new situations, whether or not the individual likes to be self-assertive, and whether one prefers working with ideas or things. This inventory would be most useful in the selection and placement of personnel when used as a supplement to an interest inventory, such as, the Kuder Preference Record —

Vocational. It may also be used in the vocational guidance of students.

Norms: The adult norms are based on 1,000 men and 532 women, ranging in age from twenty to sixty-five. The occupational composition of the groups included professional, clerical, service, skilled and unskilled workers, among others. The high school norms are based on 3,650 males and 3,924 females from high schools well distributed over the country. Also provided are mean scores for over forty male occupational groups and over ten female occupational groups on each of the five scales.

Validity and Reliability: Validity data is extensive. Studies using criteria, such as, personality, job satisfaction and academic grades are either reported in the manual or currently in progress to be reported in newer editions of the manual. Present evidence indicates that preferences measured are related to job satisfaction and suggests relationship to labor turnover and job performance. For example, significant differences were obtained on at least one of the Kuder scales for satisfied versus dissatisfied groups of male accountants and retail managers, among others, and for women who were grammar school teachers or housewives.

Reliabilities, computed by Kuder-Richardson Case IV formula and based on the normative group of men and women as well as other college and high school males and females, were found to range from .76 to .89 on all of the scales.

Bibliography:

Buros, O. K.: Test number P.139.

Kuder, G. F.: *Examiner Manual for the Kuder Preference Record — Personal — Form A.* Chicago, Science Research Associates, 1963.

Occupational Interest Inventory — Advanced

Authors: Edwin A. Lee and Louis P. Thorpe

Valiable: The Occupational Interest Inventory (OII) assesses the occupational interests and attitudes of an individual.

Type of Measure: The OII is a paper and pencil inventory, suitable for administration to either individuals or groups. It is untimed and typically takes thirty to forty minutes to complete. Scoring may be done manually or by machine.

Source from which Measure may be Obtained: CTB/McGraw-Hill, Del Monte Research Park, Monterey, California 93940.

Description: The OII is divided into two parts. Part I consists of 240 paired items. Each item measures an activity with vocational implications. There are forty items in each of the six major interest areas of personnel, social, natural, mechanical, business, the arts and sciences. Part II is comprised of thirty triads. Each triad concerns itself with one occupational field at a time but at different levels of interest, that is, low, medium, and high. The inventory yields three groups of scores arranged according to: the aforementioned six fields of interest; types of interest, including, verbal, manipulative, and computational; and levels of interests. There are ten scores obtained from the inventory enabling the subject to judge not only his or her interests in terms of vocational categories or fields, but also the level of interest. The OII may be used effectively in educational counseling, in youth and group guidance programs, as well as in selection of occupations. Raw scores may be converted to standard scores and percentile ranks with the use of the tables provided.

Norms: Norms are based on over twenty-five thousand inventories administered to high school and college students, veterans, and other adult groups. Norm tables are presented in percentiles and standard scores for each of the separate subscales.

Validity and Reliability: Extensive judgment available on the content validity of the inventory indicates the meaningfulness of the inventory items in depicting and measuring occupational interest. A construct validity investigation, using a factor analytic approach, yielded six factors identified as interest in people, natural, mechanics, business, aesthetic, and science. These findings coincide closely with the major interest areas and thereby provide a second level of utility to the inventory. Also, studies are reported establishing the correlations between the OII and the Strong Vocational Interest Blank for men. Significant correlation values are reported in this study as well as in a study showing the relationship between the Kuder Preference Record and the OII.

Test retest, over a one week interval for 177 subjects, yielded reliability coefficients ranging from .72 on the level of interest subscale to .94 on the type of interest — verbal subscale.

Bibliography:

Lee, E. A. and Thorpe, L. P.: *Manual: Occupational Interest Inventory.* Monterey, CTB/McGraw-Hill, 1956.

The Orientation Inventory

Author: Bernard M. Bass

Variable: The Orientation Inventory assesses satisfaction with one's job.

Type of Measure: The inventory is a paper and pencil instrument, suitable for administration to either individuals or groups. It is untimed. Scoring is done by hand with the use of a stencil.

Source from which Measure may be Obtained: Consulting Psychologists Press, 577 College Avenue, Palo Alto, California 94306.

Description: The inventory addresses itself to those personal attitudes of the individual which are most likely to affect job performance. By assessing the subject's attitudes toward problem solving and completion of tasks, the inventory is useful in the screening and placement of personnel, especially in positions where consistency, persistence, or technical background is required. There are twenty-seven triads to which the subject responds by choosing two of three alternatives indicating the one most and the one least preferred. The inventory yields three scores: self orientation or the degree to which one expects rewards regardless of job performance; interaction orientation or the degree to which one attempts to show a surface satisfaction about one's job and relationship to others; and task orientation which shows whether a person is interested in completing a job or solving a problem. Raw scores may be converted to standard scores or percentile ranks.

Norms: Normative data is based on 908 male and female college freshmen and sophomores in four different state universities. Norms are presented separately by sex.

Validity and Reliability: Significant differences were obtained in the three part scores of the inventory for supervisors' ratings of "best" employees versus "less than best" employees. The group was comprised of twenty-seven chemical plant supervisors. Further validity studies showed significant differences among three groups of foremen rated as top, middle, and low performers on selected subtest scores of the inventory. Other validity studies are reported on the ability of the inventory to differentiate among such groups as technical graduates engaged in research versus administration, safety and security supervisors versus line supervisors, and salaried personnel with and without technical training. Also, significant differences are reported between college women and secretaries on the subtest scores of self orientation and interaction orientation. Finally, correlation of peer ratings and inventory scores are also reported for management personnel. Many correlation values are reported as statistically significant.

Test retest, over a one week interval for eighty-four college students, yielded reliability coefficients of .73, .76, and .75 for the self-orientation interaction orientation, and task orientation scales, respectively.

Bibliography:

Bass, B. M.: *Manual: The Orientation Inventory*. Palo Alto, Consulting Psychologists Press, 1962.

Personnel Reaction Blank

Author: Harrison G. Gough

Variable: The Personnel Reaction Blank (PRB) assesses individual interests and attitudes.

Type of Measure: The PRB is a paper and pencil inventory, suitable for administration to either individuals or groups. It is untimed and typically takes fifteen minutes to complete. Scoring is done by hand with the use of a key.

Source from which Measure may be Obtained: Consulting Psychologists Press, 577 College Avenue, Palo Alto, California 94306.

Description: Application of the PRB is appropriate in the selection and placement of personnel, especially in occupations where diligence and restraint are important work qualities. It is interesting to note that although it is not a measure of intelligence, motivation, or interpersonal skills, the PRB provides data relative to the subject's effective performance of routine tasks. There are two parts of the PRB. Part I consists of a list of eighteen occupations to which the subject responds by indicating "like", "dislike", or "indifferent". Part II consists of seventy situational statements to which the subject responds by indicating "true" or "false" thereby revealing his or her personal reactions.

Norms: Norms are based on subjects selected from a wide geographical spread of cities and states and include groups of delinquent and nondelinquent males and females, high school, college, and medical students, department store applicants, supermarket employees, office workers, shop foremen and supervisors, bank officers and male and female research scientists. Norms are presented in groups varying in size from thirty-nine to over sixteen hundred subjects.

Validity and Reliability: One investigation evidenced the ability of the PRB to significantly discriminate between delinquent and nondelinquent males and delinquent and nondelinquent females. Further validity evidence was shown by correlations of ratings of effectiveness or quality of work with the PRB. A median correlation of .25 with the PRB scores for the five occupational areas was obtained. Finally, correlations of the PRB with the Adjective Check List, the California Psychological Inventory, and the Minnesota Multiphasic Personality Inventory are also presented.

Test retest, over a five year interval for twenty-six medical students, yielded a reliability coefficient of .56. Split-half reliabilities, for different male and female samples, were found to range from .65 to .95.

Bibliography:

Buros, O. K.: Test number P. 202.

Gough, H. G.: *Manual for the Personnel Reaction Blank.* Palo Alto, Consulting Psychologists Press, 1972.

Picture Interest Inventory

Author: Kurt P. Weingarten

Variable: The Picture Interest Inventory (PII) assesses an individual's fields and patterns of occupational interests.

Type of Measure: The PII is a paper and pencil inventory, suitable for administration to either individuals or groups. It is untimed and typically takes thirty to forty minutes to complete. Scoring may be done manually or by machine.

Source from which Measure may be Obtained: CTB/McGraw-Hill, Del Monte Research Park, Monterey, California 93940.

Description: The PII is comprised of two parts. Part I consists of fifty-three triads to which the subject responds by choosing two of three alternatives indicating the one liked most and the one disliked most. Part II consists of thirty picture items to which the subject responds by indicating "like" or "dislike". Two sets of scores are obtained. The first is fields of occupational interest, including interpersonal service, natural, mechanical, business, aesthetic, and scientific. The second includes the supplemental scales, including verbal, computational, and time perspective. Application of the PII would be most valuable when administered in conjunction with an aptitude measure. Its uses extend to vocational guidance of students as well as to occupational selection for adults. Raw scores may be converted to percentile ranks.

Norms: Norms are based on administration of the PII to approximately one thousand subjects, including male and female junior high, high school and college students from seventeen different states. Norms are presented in percentiles and standard scores, separately by sex, for each of the fields of interest in the three supplement scales.

Validity and Reliability: Extensive validity data is provided, including information on the content validity of the PII. Furthermore, empirical studies report relationships between selected subscales of the PII and teacher ratings. For example, the time perspective scale yielded a correlation value of .40, for 135 students from three schools, with teachers' ratings on time perspective for those students. Other concurrent validity studies interrelate the PII scales with the Strong Vocational Interest Blank for men's occupations. Significant empirical relationships, expected between selected scales and occupations, were found and generally confirm the PII as an inventory of occupational assessment. Further significant correlations are reported on the relationship between the PII and the Kuder Preference Records.

Test retest, over a one week interval for eighty-five twelfth grade students, yielded reliability coefficients ranging from .76 for the verbal and time perspective scores to .92 for the natural score.

Bibliography:

Weingarten, K. P.: *Manual: Picture Interest Inventory*. Monterey, CTB/McGraw-Hill, 1958.

Rating Scales of Vocational Values, Vocational Interests, and Vocational Aptitudes

Authors: George D. Demos and Bruce Grant

Variable: The Rating Scales of Vocational Values, Vocational Interests, and Vocational Aptitudes (rating scales VIA) are used to assist individuals in their career selection.

Type of Measure: The rating scales VIA are paper and pencil inventories, suitable for administration to either individuals or groups. They are untimed and typically take forty-five minutes to complete. Scoring is done by hand.

Source from which Measure may be Obtained: Educational and Industrial Testing Service, P. O. Box 7234, San Diego, California 92107.

Description: Each of the three scales consists of sixty activities to which the subject responds in the following manner. On the scale of vocational values, the subject rates the item from zero if the activity is not considered worthwhile to five if the activity is considered to be very much worthwhile. On the scale of vocational interests, the subject rates the item from zero if he or she feels dislike for the activity to five if the activity is liked very much. Finally, on the vocational aptitudes scale, the subject rates the item from zero if he or she has relatively no aptitude for the item to five if the subject feels that he or she has considerably more aptitude for the activity than most people. Each of the scales has a space for indicating uncertainty on any of the items, but this is discouraged. Twenty occupational areas are included in the scales, including administrative, animal, artistic, athletic, clerical, commercial, computational, creative, dramatic, executive, literary, manual, mechanical, musical, organizing, plant, scholastic, scientific, service and socializing. Scores are plotted on a profile sheet. Application of the rating scales VIA extends to use by vocational or personnel counselors who, by assessing the interrelationships among the scales, can direct the subject in proper career selection. Raw scores may be converted to percentile ranks.

Norms: Norms for the VIA stem from administration to 645 high school and college students and are presented in percentiles separately for males and females.

Validity and Reliability: Internal correlations are presented among the twenty vocational areas. Correlation values ranged from near zero to the .30 and .40 range for the vocational aptitudes scale. This attests to the relative independence of the scales. These values are also presented for the values and interests scales. No other empirical studies are cited in the manual.

Reliability data is not stated in the manual.

Bibliography:

Buros, O. K.: Test number 1033.

Demos, G. D. and Grant, G.: *Manual for Rating Scales VIA*. San Diego, Educational and Industrial Testing Service, 1966.

Sales Comprehension Test — Revised

Author: Martin M. Bruce

Variable: The Sales Comprehension Test assesses individual's sales capability.

Type of Measure: The sales test is a paper and pencil device, suitable for administration to either individuals or groups. It is untimed and typically takes fifteen to twenty minutes to complete. Scoring is done by hand and takes about two minutes.

Source from which Measure may be Obtained: Western Psychological Services, 12031 Wilshire Boulevard, Los Angeles, California 90025.

Description: The sales test assesses a subject's potential in the fields of retail, wholesale and direct consumer selling, all of which might cover a range of products from heavy capital goods to insurance. It yields information on the subject's comprehension of the basic concepts of selling. Use of this inventory extends to evaluation and selection of sales personnel as well as to counseling in vocational guidance. Please note, however, that as it is intended for use only as an aid, this test should be used only in conjunction with the information obtained from interviewing and other testing procedures involved in the decision-making process. The sales test is comprised of thirty multiple choice items to which the subject responds by choosing one of four alternative answers. Raw scores may be converted to percentile ranks with the use of the tables provided.

Norms: Norms are based on test data obtained from the administration of the sales inventory to forty different groups which included salesmen from a wide geographical spread across the United States. For example, groups of sales in general, aggressive sales, hardware, paint, electronics, among others are included. Normative data is also presented for male and female nonsales groups.

Validity and Reliability: Three studies yielded significant differences between sales and nonsales groups, pointing to inherent differences in their responses. A comprehensive study of over seventeen thousand insurance salesmen yielded data tentatively concluding that the Sales Comprehension Test would be a valid instrument with criteria of personnel turnover or production. Significant correlations were reported for Sales Comprehension Test scores with a criterion of production for a group of seventy-eight securities salesmen. The manual includes more than fifteen studies, several of which do not show significant differences in test scores of groups under study.

Test retest, over a ten week interval for 103 college students, yielded a reliability coefficient of .71 for the group. Test retest, over a two week interval for a group of ninety-six white collar employees, yielded a reliability coefficient of .81. Test retest, over varying intervals of one to two months for seventy-seven salesmen, yielded a reliability coefficient of .73. Finally, split-half reliability, based on sixty-seven sales managers, was found to be .88.

Bibliography:

Bruce, M. M.: *Examiner's Manual: Sales Comprehension Test.* Revised. New Rochelle, Martin M. Bruce, Ph.D., Publishers, 1971.

Sales Motivation Inventory

Author: Martin M. Bruce

Variable: The Sales Motivation Inventory assesses interests considered to be common among salesmen.

Type of Measure: The sales inventory is a paper and pencil device, suitable for administration to either individuals or groups. It is untimed and typically takes twenty to thirty minutes to complete. Scoring is done by hand with the use of a key.

Source from which Measure may be Obtained: Western Psychological Services, 12031 Wilshire Boulevard, Los Angeles, California 90025.

Description: The sales inventory includes seventy-five tetrads to which the subject responds by indicating one of the four alternative activities that he or she would prefer doing. The inventory thereby provides an assessment of the subject's interest in and motivation for sales work. "Sales" work, here, refers to occupations in which all or part of one's income is dependent upon one's efforts. Use of the inventory extends to aiding in the selection, guidance, and placement of sales personnel and should be supplemented with other information, such as, that obtained from interviewing. Raw scores may be converted to percentile ranks with the use of the tables in the manual.

Norms: Normative data is based on twelve samples. Sales samples include: paint, men's toiletries, insurance (Midwest), "successful" insurance, low-production insurance, State Farm Insurance Companies' general and sales applicants. Other samples include: nonsales applicants; men, ranging from semiskilled production workers to professionals with an age range of nineteen to fifty-one; female clerical; and women, including those applying for jobs of secretary, receptionist, clerk, librarian, bookkeeper, editorial writer, tabulating machine operator and office manager, ranging in age from eighteen to thirty-eight with a median education of one year of college completed.

Validity and Reliability: Validity data is extensive. Significant correlation values are reported for the Sales Motivation Inventory with the Otis Mental Ability Test, the Sales Comprehension Test, the Study of Values, the Kuder persuasive score and the Strong Vocational Interest Blank for occupations of real estate, life insurance and sales manager. Other studies are also reported in the manual establishing the relationship of the Sales Motivation Inventory to intelligence or ability measures.

Test retest reliabilities were found to be .83 for intervals varying from one week to six months for 64 subjects and .81 for forty-eight men for a long-range study where the shortest interval was twenty-five months. Split-half reliability was found to be .90 for 731 salesmen, nonsalesmen, and women. A second split-half study yielded a reliability value of .88.

Bibliography:

Bruce, M. M.: *Examiner's Manual: Sales Motivation Inventory.* New Rochelle, Martin M. Bruce, Ph.D., Publishers, 1965.

The Self Directed Search

Author: John L. Holland

Variable: The Self Directed Search (SDS) is intended to assist in the vocational counseling of individuals who do not have access to a professional counselor.

Type of Measure: The SDS is a paper and pencil inventory, suitable for administration to either individuals or groups. It is untimed and typically takes thirty to fifty minutes to complete. It is self-scored by hand.

Source from which Measure may be Obtained: Consulting Psychologists Press, 577 College Avenue, Palo Alto, California 94306.

Description: The SDS is most useful in vocational guidance of both high school and college students, as well as in counseling of adults for the purpose of redirecting their careers. The subject taking the SDS does so with full recognition of what is being assessed, how it is to be scored, profiled and interpreted, and literally obtains the results of the self-assessment immediately. The SDS yields a three-letter occupational code which is used to locate a suitable occupation in a booklet entitled, *The Occupations Finder.* This booklet contains 414 occupational titles and encompasses 95 percent of the labor force in the United States. The SDS is structured over six personality domains, including realistic, investigative, artistic, social, enterprising, and conventional. There are separate sections on occupational daydreams, activities, competencies, occupations, and self-estimates, all of which are used to determine the ranking of the six personality domains.

Norms: Normative data was collected on over seven hundred men and women at the University of Maryland. Means and standard deviations for each of the six personality domains and their combinations are provided. The key for comparison, however, is the more than four hundred occupational groups upon which data has been compiled through previous empirical studies. It is through this comparison that a subject may obtain a more refined, as well as realistic, picture of his or her vocational orientation.

Validity and Reliability: Extensive studies by the author have yielded low to moderate relationships between the six SDS subscales and the SDS items. Studies between SDS scores and student vocational behavior are in progress.

Internal consistency reliability coefficients, computed by Kuder-Richardson formula 20, ranged from .63 to .88 in activities, competencies and occupations for men from the norm group and from .53 to .85 in activities, competencies and occupations for women from the norm group.

Bibliography:

Holland, J. L.: *A Counselor's Guide for Use with The Self Directed Search.* Palo Alto, Consulting Psychologists Press, 1971.

______: *The Occupations Finder for Use with The Self Directed Search.* Palo Alto, Consulting Psychologists Press, 1972.

Strong-Campbell Interest Inventory — T325 (Merged Form)

Authors: Edward K. Strong and David P. Campbell

Variable: The Strong Campbell Interest Inventory (SCII) identifies an individual's interests and value patterns in order to provide an occupational orientation.

Type of Measure: The SCII is a paper and pencil inventory, suitable for administration to either individuals or groups. It is untimed and typically takes thirty minutes to complete. Scoring is done by machine by any one of several outside services.

Source from which Measure may be Obtained: National Computer Systems, 4401 West Seventy-sixth Street, Minneapolis, Minnesota 55435.

Description: The SCII is evolved from the merging of the Strong Vocational Interest Blanks (SVIB) for men and for women. It is comprised of 325 items to which the subject responds by indicating "like", "dislike", or "indifferent". The items are constructed on six occupational themes and yield scores indicating the subject's orientations towards realistic, investigative, artistic, social, enterprising and conventional values. Responses are analyzed on three levels: overall interest trend; degree of consistency of twenty-three basic interest areas; and the degree of similarity of responses to those of individuals employed in a wide range of occupations. The results are determined by eliciting responses of subjects toward over one hundred occupations, interests toward thirty-six school subjects, interests in fifty-one behavioral activities and interests in thirty-nine amusements, as well as preferences between thirty pairs of activities and fifteen personal characteristics. Among the many uses of the SCII are: counseling students in order to establish vocational interest for the purposes of course and/or career selection; employee counseling, such as, for determining the reason for dissatisfaction with one's job: personnel selection, when used to complement information obtained through interview and testing of potentially employable subjects; research purposes, such as, in the study of occupational characteristics, change in individuals, groups, institutions, or societal trends, or, among others, in the study of cross-cultural influences.

Norms: Norms are provided for the various parts of the SCII. The values scales were normed on a combined sample of 600 men and women. For each scale, the mean and standard deviation of this sample were set equal to fifty and ten, respectively. Other scales of the SCII, such as, the occupations, interpret scores along a dimension of "very similar" to "very dissimilar". Included in the norms is a study, conducted in 1973 by Andrulis, which generated norms for life insurance salesmen and saleswomen.

Validity and Reliability: Content, concurrent, and predictive validity studies are extensive. Content validity exists in the nature of the scales, as constructed concurrent validity exists in the ability of the SCII to discriminate among dislike occupations. Predictive validity studies generally establish that the interest patterns of subjects coincide with their eventual occupations.

Test retest, over a thirty day interval for a sample of thirty-five women and sixty-seven men, yielded a reliability coefficient of .88 for the six general occupational themes. Test retest, over a two week interval for 106 women and 74 men, yielded a median value of .91 for the six themes.

BIBLIOGRAPHY:

Andrulis, R. S.: Renorming the SCII for Life Insurance Men and Women (Norms only) in the *Strong Vocational Interest Blank, Manual for the Strong Campbell Interest Inventory — T325 (Merged Form).* Stanford, Stanford University Press, 1974.

Buros, O. K.: Test numbers 1036 and 1037.

Campbell, D. P.: *Strong Vocational Interest Blank, Manual for the Strong-Campbell Interest Inventory* — T325 (Merged Form). Stanford, Stanford University Press, 1974.

Vocational Apperception Test — Advanced Form

AUTHORS: Robert B. Ammons, Margaret Newman Butler, and Sam A. Herzig

VARIABLE: The Vocational Apperception Test — Advanced Form (VAT:ADV) assesses an individual's vocational interests and attitudes.

TYPE OF MEASURE: The VAT:ADV is an oral test in which the examiner displays eight or ten stimulus cards. It is individually administered. It is untimed and typically takes twenty-five to forty minutes to complete. Scoring is done by hand at the time of administration.

SOURCE FROM WHICH MEASURE MAY BE OBTAINED: Psychological Test Specialists, Box 1441, Missoula, Montana 59801.

DESCRIPTION: The VAT:ADV is a test of vocational interests and attitudes which are assessed by interpretation of fantasy information forthcoming from stimulus. There are eight cards for men and ten for women to which the subject responds by telling a story of what he or she sees in the stimulus, including what action is taking place, how things got that way, and what the outcome will be. Responses are recorded as given by the subject and are rated by general preference for the occupation, rationale for choosing that occupation, concern of the individual, and outcomes. In addition to its application in vocational guidance areas at the high school and college levels, the VAT:ADV may also be used as a general test of personality when administered by a trained examiner. Data obtained from the scoring include the subject's biographical facts, sources of conflicts, needs and pressures, identifications with peer group, solution processes, and so on.

Norms: Normative data is based on thirty-five college males and forty college females whose scores on both the 1938 edition of the Strong Vocational Interest Blanks (SVIB) for men and for women, respectively, were available. However, the nature of this instrument demands that local norms be evolved by the users of it.

Validity and Reliability: Based on the information from the normative samples, significant relationships were obtained between the VAT:ADV and the SVIB for both men and women. Further investigations resulted in findings that established the ability of the VAT:ADV to discriminate between subjects with contrasting occupational interests (Ammons, 1950).

In the same study, intrarater agreement, after a one week interval, yielded an agreement score of 86 percent. For all protocols, obviously careful training in scorer reliability is necessary.

Bibliography:

Ammons, R. B., Butler, M. N., and Herzig, S. A.: A Projective Test for Vocational Research and Guidance at the College Level. *Journal of Applied Psychology, 34, no. 3*:June, 1950.

——— , ——— , and ——— : *The Vocational Apperception Test — Advanced Form, Plates and Manual.* Missoula, Psychological Test Specialists, 1968.

Vocational Planning Inventory

Author: Science Research Associates

Variable: The Vocational Planning Inventory (VPI) is a wide-ranging assessment program yielding information for individual predictions of success in the major vocational curriculum areas.

Type of Measure: The VPI is a battery of paper and pencil tests, suitable for administration to either individuals or groups. Each subtest is individually timed, except for Survey of Values, and the entire series takes from two and one-half to three hours to complete. Scoring is done by machine at the Measurement Research Center (MRC) in Iowa.

Source from which Measure may be Obtained: Science Research Associates, 259 East Erie Street, Chicago, Illinois 60611.

Description: There are two VPI programs. The high school prediction program is used for high school students in eight major vocational curriculum areas, including pictorial reasoning, expression, assembly, memory, arithmetic, survey of values — parts I and II, verbal form, mechanics, and arithmetic index. The post high school prediction program is used during the first year of post high school training in seven major vocational areas, including pictorial reasoning, tables, scales, arithmetic, survey of values — parts I and II, verbal form, mechanics and arithmetic index. The high school program is suitable for use with students in grades 8 to 10 as an indicator of high school grade performance. Whereas, the post high school program can be effectively administered to students in grades 11 to 13 as both an indicator of grade performance and an aid in vocational selection.

Norms: The experimental test battery was administered to a nationwide sample of 7,500 ninth, twelfth and thirteenth grade vocational students between January and June of 1967. There were seventy-six separate groups involved in the testing. Distribution included criteria of sex, race and curriculum areas of study. Data are reported for general academic and vocational domains with the latter including eight specific occupational areas. Data include the predicted grade range based on VPI scores as well as percentile scores in aptitude and values areas.

Validity and Reliability: Multiple correlations between the post high school program subtest scores and the criterion of grades for varied samples of subjects ranging from 80 to 1,100 are generally in the range of .40 to .60. Cross-validation correlations are also reported to show the amount of loss in predictability. These correlation values are generally in the range of .40 to .60 also.

Test retest (time interval is not stated) yielded reliability coefficients ranging from .74 to .92 for eleven subscales. Kuder-Richardson Case IV formula yielded a reliability coefficient of .83 on verbal form B. Kuder-Richardson formula 20 yielded reliabilities of .75 for pictorial reasoning and .95 for arithmetic index. Alternate form correlations with Flanagan Industrial Tests (FIT) and Flanagan Aptitude Classification Test (FACT), two of the subtests of the VPI program, yielded coefficients ranging from .57 to .79. Overall reliability values, averaged across sample groups, yielded estimates of .93 and .90 for the high school and post high school programs, respectively.

Bibliography:

Buros, O. K.: Test number 984.

Science Research Associates: *Vocational Planning Inventory, Program Manual.* Chicago, Author, 1968.

Vocational Preference Inventory

Author: John L. Holland

Variable: The Vocational Preference Inventory (VPI) assesses certain vocational traits, specifically, interpersonal relations, interests, values, self conception, coping behavior and identifications.

Type of Measure: The VPI is a paper and pencil inventory, suitable for administration to either individuals or groups. It is untimed and typically takes fifteen to thirty minutes to complete. Scoring is done by hand.

Source from which Measure may be Obtained: Consulting Psychologists Press, 577 College Avenue, Palo Alto, California 94306.

Description: The VPI is a vocational inventory composed of 160 occupational titles. The subject responds by indicating "yes" or "no" regarding like or dislike for the particular occupations. The inventory yields eleven scores: realistic, intellectual, social, conventional, enterprising, artistic, self control, masculinity, status, infrequency and acquiescence. In addition to its use in vocational guidance and assessment, the VPI can be effectively employed as a personality inventory by measuring personality characteristics in a theory of vocational choice. Finally, it can be used as a means of increasing interest in occupational exploration at high school and college levels. Raw scores may be converted to percentile ranks with the use of the tables provided in the manual.

Norms: The standardization sample is composed of 12,433 male and female freshmen from thirty-one colleges in twenty-eight states. Eight broad-based reference groups are also available, based on samples of employed adults, salesmen, sales applicants, writers, psychologists, Veterans Administration hospital aides, Port of New York Authority supervisors and subordinates, research personnel, security salesmen, drug addicts, psychopaths, patients in Veterans Administration hospitals and others. Both male and female norms are provided for most of these groups, in addition to data for selected groups on education, age, and income.

Validity and Reliability: Numerous validity studies have been performed. Significant correlations have been established with the masculinity subscale of the VPI and sex scales in the Sixteen Personality Factor Questionnaire (16 PF), the California Psychological Inventory, and the Minnesota Multiphasic Personality Inventory, all in the desired directions. Also VPI was found to differentiate significantly between normal and psychotic patients in several studies and established strong relationship with scales from numerous well-known personality inventories. For example, a significant correlation value of .27 was obtained between supervisory ratings and the conventional scale of the VPI. Moderate predictive validity was found with VPI scores and choice of major field.

Reliability coefficients, computed by Kuder-Richardson formula 21 for males and females scored separately, ranged from .76 to .89 for all scales except infrequency, masculinity, and status which ranged from .50 to .71. The coefficients are based on administrations of the VPI — sixth revision to a normative group of college freshmen. Reliability data is also reported for employed adults and job applicants.

Bibliography:

Buros, O. K.: Test number 157.

Holland, J. L.: *Manual: Vocational Preference Inventory.* Palo Alto, Consulting Psychologists Press, 1970.

Wide Range Interest-Opinion Test

Authors: Joseph F. Jastak and Sarah R. Jastak

Variable: The Wide Range Interest-Opinion Test (WRIOT) assesses an individual's interests and attitudes as well as levels and areas of personal integration.

Type of Measure: The WRIOT is a paper and pencil inventory, suitable for administration to either individuals or groups. It is untimed and typically takes from forty to sixty minutes to administer. Scoring may be done manually with the use of a stencil or by optical scanning machine.

Source from which Measure may be Obtained: Guidance Associates of Delaware, 1526 Gilpin Avenue, Wilmington, Delaware 19806.

Description: The WRIOT includes 450 pictures arranged by triads into 150 combinations. Both males and females are given the same 450 pictures, but the results are interpreted differently. Twenty-five criterion categories, organized into separate clusters, are included in the WRIOT. Eighteen of the twenty-five clusters measure the likes and dislikes of the subject regarding art, literature, music, drama, sales, management, office work, personal service, protective service, social service, social science, biological science, physical science, number, mechanics, machine operation, outdoor, and athletics. There are seven vocational attitudes assessed, including, sedentariness, risk, ambition, chosen skill level, activity by sex, agreement, and spread. Each of the eighteen cluster scores is defined, including indication of the items pertinent to the cluster, as well as an extensive array of job titles related to the area indicated in the cluster. The vocational attitudes provide not only differentiation, but also job activities which indicate the type of occupation a subject prefers. Use of the WRIOT extends to student counseling in vocational planning, as well as personnel selection on the bases of interest and attitude.

Norms: Normative data is based on adult males and females of all educational levels and senior high school students from a suburban group. The adults ranged in age from sixteen to sixty-five, with a mean of thirty. The high school students ranged in age from fifteen to seventeen. Raw scores for the vocational and attitudinal categories are interpreted with corresponding "T" score values provided. Similar data is provided for high school students.

Validity and Reliability: Correlation coefficients between the WRIOT and the Geist Picture Interest Inventory are reported to be statistically significant. Correlation values of the WRIOT occupational clusters with the Geist subtest interest scales range from approximately .00 to .55 for the total sample of male and female subjects (N = 100).

Split-half reliability coefficients, based on 150 males and 150 females and computed by the Cureton formula, ranged from .83 to .95 for males and from .82 to .95 for females over all occupational clusters and from .84 to .95 for males and from .86 to .93 for females on the vocational attitudes scales.

Bibliography:

Jastak, J. F. and Jastak, S. R.: *Wide Range Interest-Opinion Test, Manual.* Wilmington, Guidance Associates of Delaware, 1972.

Work Values Inventory

Author: Donald E. Super

Variable: The Work Values Inventory (WVI) assesses an individual's motivation, satisfaction, and degree of success in a chosen vocation.

Type of Measure: The WVI is a paper and pencil inventory, suitable for administration to either individuals or groups. It is untimed and typically takes fifteen minutes to complete.

Scoring may be done manually with the use of a key or by machine.

Source from which Measure may be Obtained: Houghton Mifflin Company, 53 West Fifty-third Street, New York, New York 10036.

Description: The WVI assesses the goals motivating one to work, the subject's intrinsic and extrinsic values, the satisfactions sought in work, and the satisfactions obtained from work. It consists of forty-five work-related items. The subject responds by choosing one of five alternatives, from "very important" to "unimportant". The items are structured over the following dimensions: altruism, aesthetics, creativity, intellectual, stimulation, achievement, independence, prestige, management, economic returns, security, surrounding, supervisory relations, associates, way of life and variety. Uses of the WVI extend to the assessment of values in vocational guidance, as well as to the screening of applicants in business and industry. Decisions in counseling and selection can be aided by information obtained from the WVI regarding a subject's values.

Norms: The WVI was standardized by administering it in the spring of 1968 to a national sample of 10,083 students in grades 7 to 12. Subjects were about equally represented in the total sample by sex and were widely differentiated according to community type, size, and geographical region. Norms are provided separately by sex. Occupational group data is also provided in a wide variety of areas, including psychologists, engineers, CPA's, teachers, machinists, students, and others.

Validity and Reliability: Validity studies are extensive. Detailed information is shown establishing the relationship between the WVI and the Strong Vocational Interest Blank/Strong-Campbell Interest Inventory, the Kuder Preference Record — Vocational form CH, and the Allport-Vernon-Lindzey Study of Values. Further studies show significant differences in WVI scores for business school students, machinist students, Peace Corps teacher trainees and school counselors, on scales such as, altruism (counselors versus machinists) and creativity (counselors versus Peace

Corps teachers), among others.

Test retest, over a two week interval for a group of ninety-nine tenth grade students, yielded reliability coefficients ranging from .74 to .88 with a median of .83.

Bibliography:

Buros, O. K.: Test number 1042.

Super, D. E.: *Manual: Work Values Inventory.* Boston, Houghton Mifflin Company, 1970.

Chapter 7

ATTITUDE MEASURES

Academic Freedom Survey

Author: Academic Freedom Committee

Variable: The Academic Freedom Survey assesses academic freedom attitudes in colleges and universities.

Type of Measure: The survey is a paper and pencil inventory, most suitably administered to groups. It is untimed. Scoring is done by hand.

Source from which Measure may be Obtained: Psychometric Affiliates, P. O. Box 3167, Munster, Indiana 46321.

Description: The survey items, taken almost verbatim from the National Academic Freedom Committee of the American Civil Liberties Union principles, assess whether the subject feels that he or she resides within a climate of academic freedom. There are twenty-three items in the survey, broken into three categories which deal with student rights, faculty rights, and a section labeled "other rights". The subject responds by indicating the degree to which a particular right is insured, that is, "completely", "as a general rule", or "very little or none". In this way, an institution's level of academic freedom is rated by anonymous respondents, comprised of students, teachers, and administrators of that institution.

Norms: Norms were established on a sample of 144 college and university administrators, faculty members, and students.

Validity and Reliability: No validity data is stated in the manual.

The split-half method applied to the student and faculty sections separately, yielded reliability values of .87 respectively. A total scale reliability of .92 was also obtained.

Bibliography:

Academic Freedom Committee, Illinois Division: *Manual of Instructions: Academic Freedom Survey*. Compiled by P. Sherman and W. A. Kerr.

Munster, Psychometric Affiliates, 1954.

California Study Methods Survey

Author: Harold D. Carter

Variable: The California Study Methods Survey (CSMS) assesses the nature of a student's attitudes and study habits.

Type of Measure: The CSMS is a paper and pencil inventory, suitable for administration to either individuals or groups. It is untimed and typically takes thirty to thirty-five minutes to complete. Scoring may be done manually or by machine.

Source from which Measure may be Obtained: CTB/McGraw-Hill, Del Monte Research Park, Monterey, California 93940.

Description: The CSMS is designed to assess a student's attitudes, habits, and knowledge regarding school work. It is constructed on three subscales which yield information covering: attitudes toward school; mechanics of study; and planning and system. It also yields a verification score and a total. The CSMS contains 150 questions to which the subject responds by indicating "yes" or "no". The CSMS is a valuable tool in identifying the student whose intelligence level is higher than his or her performance level, as well as in discerning the reason for such a discrepancy. Its use broadens when administered in conjunction with ability or intelligence batteries, as it then serves as an indicator of academic success. Raw scores may be converted to percentile ranks or stanines.

Norms: Norms are based on 972 male and female students from grades 8 through college and from all sections of the country. Norms are presented in stanines and percentiles for combined sex groups.

Validity and Reliability: In a comparison of scores of students, identified as over- and underachievers, the overachievers scored significantly higher than the underachievers in each of the three subscores, as well as in total score. In addition, a correlation value of .57 was obtained between the CSMS total score and the grade point averages of 231 high school sophomores. Other correlation studies of the CSMS with the Henmon Nelson Tests of Mental Ability yielded a value of .36 between the CSMS total score and the Henmon Nelson scores of the same tenth grade sample.

Test retest, for 215 eighth grade students (time interval is not specified), yielded a reliability coefficient of .86. Reliability coefficients, computed by Kuder-Richardson formula 21, varied from .58 to .80 for the subscores and from .80 to .87 for the total score.

Bibliography:

Carter, H. D.: *Manual: California Study Methods Survey.* Monterey, CTB/McGraw-Hill, 1966.

Conference Meeting Rating Scale

Author: B. J. Speroff

Variable: The Conference Meeting Rating Scale assesses effectiveness of both a conference leader and the group in attendance.

Type of Measure: The rating scale is a paper and pencil inventory, most suitable for use by groups. It is untimed and typically takes ten minutes to complete. Scoring is done by hand.

Source from which Measure may be Obtained: Psychometric Affiliates, P. O. Box 3167, Munster, Indiana 46321.

Description: The rating scale is an informational source for recording the impact of a conference. Its purposes are to serve as a rating procedure for observers, for attendees and for the conference leader in assessing the group in attendance. The scale is comprised of forty items, broken into ten for each of the four dimensions: introductory outcomes, which assess the climate and rapport; procedural outcomes, which treat the methods of conference implementation; process outcomes, which emphasize the content and interaction in the conference; and summative outcomes, which define whether or not the goals of the conference were attained.

Norms: No norms are stated in the manual.

Validity and Reliability: Validity data are not stated in the manual.

Reliability, although not stated, could be established if the user employed trained observers and calculated both inter- and intrascorer reliability.

Bibliography:

Speroff, B. J.: *Manual of Instructions: Conference Meeting Rating Scale.* Munster, Psychometric Affiliates, 1959.

Inventory of Job Attitudes

Author: Life Insurance Marketing and Research Association (LIMRA)

Variable: The Inventory of Job Attitudes (IJA) intends to assist home office management in appraising the effects of its policies and actions on life and health insurance personnel.

Type of Measure: The IJA is a paper and pencil inventory, suitable for administration to either individuals or groups. It is untimed. Scoring may be done manually by the user or mechanically by LIMRA.

Source from which Measure may be Obtained: Life Insurance Marketing and Research Association, 170 Sigourney Street, Hartford, Connecticut 06105.

Description: The IJA is intended for use in life insurance companies and is available in two different forms: one for use by "combination" agents, form 2-C and one for use by "ordinary" agents, form 2-0. The items are based on material and subject matter related to management at the home office or field agency. It measures attitudes relating to satisfaction with one's job and company. Item responses intend to provide management with an index of morale rather than job satisfaction.

Norms: Normative data for the IJA are available through the voluntary cooperation of those using it. If a company desires norms, they should inquire about their availability from LIMRA. Those companies that make use of the LIMRA computer facilities automatically are given the most recent and relevant normative data.

Validity and Reliability: One validity study was applied to match groups; survivors (subjects still employed by their companies one year after administration of the IJA) versus terminators. Differences between the two groups are reported to be significant for the four part scores of the inventory as well as for the special score (Weitz and Nuckols, 1955).

Reliability data are not stated in the manual, however, it is suggested that the users contact LIMRA for this information.

Bibliography:

Life Insurance Marketing and Research Association: *Inventory of Job Attitudes, Manual.* 2nd Ed. Hartford, Author, 1956.

Weitz, J. and Nuckols, R. C.: Job Satisfaction and Job Survival. *Journal of Applied Psychology, 39, no. 4*:294-300, 1955.

Personal Development Record — Form S

Author: Richardson, Bellows, Henry and Company

Variable: The Personal Development Record assesses the perception of the content of positions held by employees, as well as their abilities to perform the functions of the positions.

Type of Measure: The record is a paper and pencil inventory, suitable for administration to either individuals or groups. It is untimed. Scoring is done by hand.

Source from which Measure may be Obtained: Richardson, Bellows, Henry and Company, 1140 Connecticut Avenue, Northwest, Washington, D. C. 20036.

Description: The record is a five part inventory. Part A includes thirty-nine functions in which the subject indicates, on a scale from one to four, the importance of his or her job and how well he or she functions in it. Part B employs forty pairs of descriptive statements in a forced choice format. The subject responds by indicating the statement which is most descriptive of his or her job performance. Part C is an evaluation by the employee of six factors which yield a subjective profile of strengths and weaknesses as seen by the employee. Part D includes twenty-six suggestions for employee improvement to which the subject responds by indicating those areas in which he or she would try to improve during the coming year. Part E asks the subject to summarize his or her personal and job objectives, areas for improvement, and so forth. The record may be used as a diagnostic or evaluative tool, because it is a source of attitudinal data as well as of information relating to the employee's job perception.

Norms: Since only parts A, B, and C are objective, norms are available only for these parts. Norms are presented in one table on over 130 males. A second table provides means and standard deviations information for six groups of managers and executives. These groups range in size from twelve to twenty subjects and are reported separately for parts A, B, and C.

Validity and Reliability: Neither validity nor reliability data are stated in the manual.

Bibliography:

Richardson, Bellows, Henry and Company: *Personal Development Record — Form S.* Washington, Author, n.d.

Purdue Instructor Performance Indicator — Form A

Authors: John H. Snedeker and H. H. Remmers

Variable: The Purdue Instructor Performance Indicator assesses a teacher's effectiveness as perceived by his or her students.

Type of Measure: The indicator is a paper and pencil inventory, most suitably administered to groups. It is untimed and typically takes twenty minutes to complete. Scoring may be done manually or by machine.

Source from which Measure may be Obtained: University Book Store, 360 State Street, West Lafayette, Indiana 47906.

Description: The indicator is available in two parallel forms, A and B. Each consists of twelve tetrads to which the subject responds by choosing one of the four alternative responses which best describes the instructor being rated. All statements are balanced for social acceptability; however two are scaled toward effective instructors, and two are scaled toward ineffective instructors. The real need for evaluation of instructor performance warrants the administration of the indicator to students who, alone, are exposed to the teaching process in the everyday situation.

Norms: Norms were derived from a sample of instructors in a large midwestern college. The sample is based on 112 college instructors, selected at random, and 16,014 students' ratings of these instructors. Norms are presented in percentiles and are available for both forms A and B.

Validity and Reliability: Content validity is inferred through the subject matter measured by the inventory. From the presence of high reliabilities, one can infer the presence of validity — as stated in the manual. No empirical validity is provided.

Internal consistency, computed by the Horst formula for 112 teachers, yielded a reliability coefficient of .96 for both forms A and B. Test retest, over a three week interval for approximately 8000 subjects, yielded a reliability of .95.

Bibliography:

Snedeker, J. H. and Remmers, H. H.: *Manual for the Purdue Instructor Performance Indicator*. West Lafayette, University Book Store, 1960.

Purdue Master Attitude Scales

Author: H. H. Remmers

Variable: The Purdue Master Attitude Scales assess individuals' attitudes in a wide variety of subject areas.

Type of Measure: The scales are a series of paper and pencil inventories, suitable for administration to either individuals or groups. They are untimed. Scoring is done by hand.

Source from which Measure may be Obtained: University Book Store, 360 State Street, West Lafayette, Indiana 47906.

Description: The scales are available for the assessment of attitudes on any of the following subjects: school subject; vocation; institution; defined group; proposed social action; practice; homemaking activity; individual or group morale; and high school. Each scale is available in two parallel forms, A and B. Use of the scales is limited only by the imagination of the user.

Norms: Norms are the group responses. No formal standardized norm group was developed for comparative purposes.

Validity and Reliability: The scales have inherent content validity. Specific validity studies are referenced in the manual or are to be developed by the user.

The original scales from which the Purdue Master Attitude Scales were developed contained more than forty items per form. Reliability values of the original scales, generated on various samples, ranged from .71 to .92.

Bibliography:

Remmers, H. H.: *Manual for the Purdue Master Attitude Scales.* West Lafayette, University Book Store, 1960.

The Purdue Rating Scale for Administrators and Executives

Authors: H. H. Remmers and R. L. Hobson

Variable: The Purdue Rating Scale for Administrators and Executives assesses administrative and executive effectiveness.

Type of Measure: The rating scale is a paper and pencil inventory, most suitably administered to groups. It is untimed. Scoring is done by hand.

Source from which Measure may be Obtained: University Book Store, 360 State Street, West Lafayette, Indiana 47906.

Description: The rating scale assesses the strengths and weaknesses of individuals in managerial positions, as well as the manner in which they perform their work. It intends to present the administrator with a behavioral view as seen by his or her subordinates. The scale consists of thirty-six multiple choice items. The subject responds by indicating the degree to which the item is descriptive of the administrator being rated. The scale may be administered in a number of ways, including: by a staff meeting method; individual completion at the subordinates' convenience; or by a personnel evaluation research service whereby Purdue University contacts the subjects individually for the purpose of rating the administrator. It is recommended that use of the rating scale be voluntary on the part of the individual being rated. In addition, anonymity of the raters is of utmost importance.

Norms: Norms are based on three groups: 54 college and university administrators, including college presidents, academic and nonacademic college administrators and department heads; 113 business and industrial executives, including subjects in banking, merchandising, chemical products and others; and 88 public school administrators, including superintendents and principals.

VALIDITY AND RELIABILITY: Validity studies are reported as reflections of the internal consistency of the rating scale, that is, the reliabilities. The consistency of measurement by raters lends credence to the validity of the rating scale. No external criterion-related validity is reported.

Average split-half reliability coefficients, for twenty raters in business and industry, ranged from .75 to .97 across the individual items. Individual item reliabilities ranged from .40 to .98 when groups of ten to twenty raters were used for other samples.

BIBLIOGRAPHY:

Remmers, H. H. and Hobson, R. L.: *Manual for The Purdue Rating Scale for Administrators and Executives.* West Lafayette, University Book Store, 1951.

The Purdue Rating Scale for Instruction

AUTHORS: H. H. Remmers and J. A. Weisbrodt

VARIABLE: The Purdue Rating Scale for Instruction assesses an instructor's performance in the classroom, as perceived by his or her students.

TYPE OF MEASURE: The rating scale is a paper and pencil inventory, most suitably administered to groups. It is untimed and typically takes twenty minutes to complete. Scoring may be done manually or by machine.

SOURCE FROM WHICH MEASURE MAY BY OBTAINED: University Book Store, 360 State Street, West Lafayette, Indiana 47906.

DESCRIPTION: The rating scale provides diagnostic direction for instructors in determining the general areas of dissatisfaction in the classroom environment. The individual ratings, provided by the scale, point out the specific aspects of an instructor's performance which fail to satisfy his or her students. The scale consists of twenty-six descriptive items. The subject responds by indicating the degree to which the statements apply to the instructor being rated. In addition to its use as an evaluative tool, the rating scale may also be applied in order to determine promotions, increased or decreased workload or responsibilities and so forth. Anonymity of the raters is essential.

Norms: Normative data is based on a group of instructors, in the state of Indiana, who volunteered to participate in a validation study. The number of cases, characteristics of the school, instructors, and students were not specified. Norms, presented in percentiles, are provided for each of the twenty-six items.

Validity and Reliability: One study (Elliott, 1950) showed a low significant relationship between the ratings students gave instructors and the students' own achievements with scholastic ability being held constant. Further studies showed no effect or difference in student collegiate status, veteran status, or sex on ratings. In addition, a comparison of students' ratings while currently engaged in a program with alumni's ratings showed no difference on the same instructors.

Split-half reliabilities on two different samples yielded correlations of .90 and .82, respectively, for overall instructor rating. Reliabilities, computed by the Horst formula, for unequal numbers of raters yielded values of .89 for the reliability by class and a .90 for the reliability by instructor for "overall rating of the instructor". Split-half reliabilities on 205 instructors ranged from .44 for "suitability of assigned textbooks" to .92 for "interest in subject", "presentation of subject matter" and "suitability of available reference material". Other reliability values are also reported for each of the items.

Bibliography:

Buros, O. K.: Test number 588.

Remmers, H. H. (editor): Studies in College and University Staff Evaluation No. XV, Studies in Higher Education LXX, Bulletin of Purdue University, March, 1950, 1-92.

_____ and Weisbrodt, J. A.: *Manual of Instructions for The Purdue Rating*

Scale for Instruction. West Lafayette, University Book Store, 1965.

The Purdue Student Teacher Opinionaire

Authors: Ralph R. Bentley and Jo-Ann Price

Variable: The Purdue Student Teacher Opinionaire (PSTO) is designed to assess student-teacher morale.

Type of Measure: The PSTO is a paper and pencil inventory, most suitably administered to groups. It is untimed and typically takes thirty minutes to complete. Scoring may be done manually or by machine.

Source from which Measure may be Obtained: University Book Store, 360 State Street, West Lafayette, Indiana 47906.

Description: PSTO includes one hundred items covering twelve factors, such as, rapport with supervising teacher, student teacher rapport with principal, teaching as a profession, professional preparation, school facilities and curriculum issues, among others. It intends to provide deans, heads of departments of education and directors of student teachers with information in order to make decisions based on objective indices of student teacher morale. A scoring and reporting service can provide item medians as well as profiles based on normative data. This service is offered by Purdue University's Measurement and Research Center, Lafayette, Indiana 47907.

Norms: Norms are based on the factor analysis of the PSTO for 4,432 student teachers enrolled in thirty-five institutions over a wide geographical area. No other information is presented.

Validity and Reliability: Construct validity studies through factor analytic procedures are reported. Fourteen factors were identified of which twelve are included in the PSTO. These included items with high factor loadings, a little overlap with other factors, as well as the logical relationship of the item to the factor and the assessment of student teacher morale.

Internal consistency reliabilities, computed by Kuder-Richardson formula, ranged from .59 to .93 for the twelve factors with an overall reliability of .96.

Bibliography:

Bentley, R. R. and Price, J.: *Preliminary Manual for The Purdue Student Teacher Opinionaire*. West Lafayette, University Book Store, 1970.

_____ and _____: *Preliminary Manual Supplement for The Purdue Student Teacher Opinionaire*. West Lafayette, University Book Store, 1970.

Buros, O. K.: Test number 589.

The Purdue Teacher Evaluation Scale

Authors: Ralph R. Bentley and Allan R. Starry

Variable: The Purdue Teacher Evaluation Scale (PTES) is designed to provide an evaluation of teachers by their students.

Type of Measure: The PTES is a paper and pencil inventory, most suitably administered to groups. It is untimed and typically takes twenty minutes to complete. Scoring may be done manually or by machine.

Source from which Measure may be Obtained: University Book Store, 360 State Street, West Lafayette, Indiana 47906.

Description: There are sixty items in the PTES which are rated by the students on a four-point scale from "very much like my teacher" to "very much unlike my teacher". Major areas of concentration within the PTES deal with student evaluations of teaching methods, assessment of learning environments in the classroom, and relationships between teachers and students. The six scales upon which the teacher is rated are: ability to motivate students, ability to control students, subject matter orientation of teacher, student-teacher communication, teaching methods and procedures and fairness of teacher. The Teacher Evaluation Scale is closely related to The Purdue Instructor Performance Indicator in that its use is most appropriate when administered to students, considering that their daily exposure to a teacher's classroom environment would elicit responses most valuable in assessing instructor performance. Anonymity of responses is essential.

Norms: Norms, based upon 5,000 students' evaluations of 198 teachers from junior and senior high schools representing the middle and upper socioeconomic classes and located in the midwestern United States, provide the basis for comparisons. Norms are presented in percentiles for each item of the scale.

Validity and Reliability: Validity may be assumed through the content judgment of experts regarding the applicability of the items to measurement of student perception of teaching behavior. No empirical validity studies are cited in the manual.

Split-half reliabilities, for 128 teachers, ranged from .83 to .91 on the six scales.

Bibliography:

Bentley, R. R. and Starry, A. R.: *Manual for The Purdue Teacher Evaluation Scale.* West Lafayette, University Book Store, 1970.
Buros, O. K.: Test number 590.

SRA Attitude Survey

Author: Science Research Associates

Variable: The SRA Attitude Survey assesses individual's attitudes in a variety of work environments.

Type of Measure: The survey is a paper and pencil inventory, most suitably administered to groups. It is untimed. Scoring is done by hand.

Source from which Measure may be Obtained: Science Research Associates, 259 East Erie Street, Chicago, Illinois 60611.

Description: The survey is designed to be a confidential assessment of a subject's perceptions of work and its environment. Anonymity of the subjects is essential, and results involve comparisons with other companies. The survey can be adapted to suit an individual company's needs. Specifically, the survey provides information regarding what job classifications exist by job categories; cause of problems regarding low morale, absenteeism, or low productivity; which problems should be attacked first, as well as the training needs of employees. There are seventy-eight items in the survey, and they represent fifteen categories of attitudes, including job demands, working conditions, pay, employee benefits, friendliness and cooperation of fellow employees, supervisor-employee interpersonal relations, confidence in management, technical competence of supervisors, effectiveness of administration, adequacy of communication, security of job and work relations, status and recognition, identification with the company, opportunity for growth and advancement and reactions to the inventory.

Norms: Norms were determined in 1970 and are available as follows: on a national basis, including a cross section of industry in the United States; on an industry basis, such as, manufacturing, retail, and others: and by occupational levels, including executive, office and clerical, supervisors, sales production and plant, and professional and technical.

Validity and Reliability: Neither of these is stated in the manual.

Bibliography:

Science Research Associates: *The SRA Attitude Survey, Guidelines.* Chicago, Author, 1970.

Study Attitudes and Methods Survey

Authors: William B. Michael, Joan J. Michael, and Wayne S. Zimmerman

Variable: The Study Attitudes and Methods Survey (SAMS) assesses the dimensions of attitude, motivation, and study habits important to academic success.

Type of Measure: The SAMS is a paper and pencil inventory, suitable for administration to either individuals or groups. It is untimed and typically takes twenty to thirty minutes to complete. Scoring may be done manually with the use of a key or by IBM machine.

Source from which Measure may be Obtained: Educational and Industrial Testing Service, P. O. Box 7234, San Diego, California 92107.

Description: The SAMS was evolved to assess factors related to success in school. Its purpose is both to identify individuals having problems in academic work, because of a lack of proper study habits or attitudes, and to provide information useful to counselors so that remedial action can be planned. Application of the SAMS extends to groups at both college and high school entry levels, whereby the information obtained can be used as a counseling foundation. The six dimensions assessed by the SAMS include: academic interest — love of learning; academic drive — conformity; study methods; study anxiety; manipulation; and alienation toward authority. There are 150 items to which the subject responds on a four point scale: from "not at all like me" to "very much like me".

Norms: Normative data is based on approximately 500 males and 450 females from a suburban junior college. The subjects ranged in age from seventeen to twenty-six, and the sample reflects ethnic group characteristics which approximate the overall population breakdown in the county of Los Angeles.

Validity and Reliability: Construct validity evidence is available through publications by the authors. Predictive validity establishing the relationship of SAMS scores to grade point averages of community college students showed that all SAMS subscores significantly related to the grade point average criterion. Further correlation evidence is presented through a comparison of SAMS scores with the Nelson-Denny Reading Test which showed that SAMS scores are independent of some cognitive measures.

Internal consistency (split-half) reliabilities range from .83 to .90. Test retest, over a four month interval for 280 community college students, yielded reliability coefficients ranging from .68 to .79 for the six SAMS scales.

Bibliography:

Michael, W. B., Michael, J. J., and Zimmerman, W. S.: *Study Attitudes and Methods Survey, Preliminary Manual of Instructions and Interpretations*. San Diego, Educational and Industrial Testing Service, 1972.

Study Habits Checklist

Authors: Ralph C. Preston and Morton Botel

Variable: The Study Habits Checklist assesses study practices typically used by high school and college students.

Type of Measure: The checklist is a paper and pencil inventory, suitable for administration to either individuals or groups. It is untimed and typically takes ten minutes to complete. Scoring may be done manually or by IBM machine.

Source from which Measure may be Obtained: Science Research Associates, 259 East Erie Street, Chicago, Illinois 60611.

Description: The checklist provides data relating to students' proficiency of study skills. It includes thirty-seven items to which the subject responds on a five point scale from "almost always" to "almost never". Instructors or counselors should interpret a student's responses in a personal conference to assist in identifying individual strengths and weaknesses.

Norms: Decile norms are provided separately by sex. Normative data is based on the results of 4,367 students in grades 9 to 12 of public and private schools and 1,630 college freshmen. The testing was done in early September 1966 with the college group and in October and November with the high school groups.

Validity and Reliability: The study by Brown (1964) established that four of the sixteen variables of the Study Habits Checklist (first edition) significantly differentiated between overachieving and underachieving college women. Also, content validity was determined through a careful development of the items in the checklist to ensure their prominence in academic study.

Reliability studies, based on separate samples of students (totaling approximately one thousand) in grades 9, 10, 11, and 12, yielded corrected split-half values of .91 in all four cases.

Bibliography:

Brown, Sara M.: Variables Associated with Overachievement and Underachievement, unpublished doctoral dissertation, University of Pennsylvania, 1964.

Buros, O. K.: Test number R.244.1.

Preston, R. C. and Botel, M.: *Administration and Interpretation of the Study Habits Checklist.* Chicago, Science Research Associates, 1967.

Tear Ballot for Industry

Author: Industrial Opinion Institute, Psychometric Affiliates

Variable: The Tear Ballot for Industry assesses individuals' job satisfaction.

Type of Measure: The Tear ballot is a "rip" method device, most suitable for use by groups. It is untimed. Scoring is done by hand.

Source from which Measure may be Obtained: Psychometric Affiliates, P. O. Box 3167, Munster, Indiana 46321.

Description: The tear ballot consists of ten items scored on a five point continuum, that is, the first alternative under each item receives a score of five points, because it is the "highest job satisfaction" response. There is also a so-called "special problems" item which treats such areas as: inconvenient or undependable transportation; unfairness in promotion policy; lack of time to take care of personal problems; lack of attention to employee recreation; among others. The subject rips the paper on which he or she has indicated responses, and anonymity is preserved. The tear ballot is recommended for remedial and diagnostic surveys of factory and business departments. Raw scores may be converted to percentile ranks with the use of the tables provided.

Norms: Norms are based on more than thirty-five surveys of various industrial and occupational groups and are presented separately for males and females. Included are sales clerks, retail supervisors, hospital nurses, carpenters, food canners, tool and die makers, and others. Also, norm tables are available for both male and female factory employees in the North and South.

Validity and Reliability: One study by Kerr (1948) showed correlation values ranging from .14 to .62 between the Tear Ballot items and tenure rate for 98 subjects in a wide variety of industries; more than one-half of the correlation values were significant. In addition, other validity studies are reported, but given the dates of these investigations, more up-to-date studies should be either identified by the reader or carried out with the use of this instrument.

Split-half reliability coefficients ranged from .65 to .88 with a mean of .83 in four separate studies.

Bibliography:

Buros, O. K.: Test number 1065.

Industrial Opinion Institute, Psychometric Affiliates: *Manual of Instructions: Tear Ballot for Industry.* Munster, Psychometric Affiliates, 1962.

Kerr, W. A.: On the validity and reliability of the job satisfaction tear ballot. *Journal of Applied Psychology, 32*:275-281, 1948.

Chapter 8

PERSONAL PERFORMANCE AND HISTORY MEASURES

Biographical and Personality Inventory

Author: Ronald C. Force

Variable: The Biographical and Personality Inventory (BPI) attempts to assess the recovery potential of delinquent youths and their readiness to respond to an opportunity for change.

Type of Measure: The BPI is a paper and pencil inventory, suitable for administration to either individuals or groups. It is untimed and typically takes sixty minutes to complete. Scoring is done with the use of a key.

Source from which Measure may be Obtained: Test Systems, Inc., P. O. Box 18432, Wichita, Kansas 67218.

Description: The BPI is available in two forms, A for males and B for females. It is intended to be administered to delinquent youths and interpreted by a trained psychologist during the decision-making process regarding remediation for those youths. The inventory consists of 200 items; 64 relate to the subject's personal history, and 136 are psychological in nature. In addition to the recovery potential score, the BPI also provides information which reveals the presence of a drug or alcohol problem. Furthermore, there are indicants of the type of treatment which would be most appropriate for the delinquent or predelinquent. Finally, a special analysis scoring yields data on items individually useful in interviews. Clinical nonnormative interpretation should be performed by a certified psychologist, in conjunction with a full battery of assessment instruments and other available social history information.

Norms: Norms are based on analyses of information from adjudged delinquents, over varying time periods. The number of cases ranged from 70 to 120 delinquents both during and after a correctional program was administered. Norms are presented in stanines.

Validity and Reliability: Validity studies indicate a correlation value of .59 for BPI scores and a criterion of delinquent coping behavior observed over a two year period. Additional studies have shown that selected items in the BPI differentiate between subjects who could adequately cope versus inadequately cope with delinquent activities in their own environment.

Reliability data are not stated in the manual.

Bibliography:

Force, R. C.: *Manual for the Biographical and Personality Inventory.* Wichita, Test Systems, Inc., 1971.

The Biographical Index

Author: Willard A. Kerr

Variable: The Biographical Index is an objective assessment of biographical information typically predictive of general success in vocations.

Type of Measure: The index is a paper and pencil inventory, suitable for administration to either individuals or groups. It is untimed and typically takes ten to twenty minutes to complete. Scoring is done by hand with the use of a key.

Source from which Measure may be Obtained: Psychometric Affiliates, P. O. Box 3167, Munster, Indiana 46321.

Description: The index consists of six pages of eighty-nine items for completion by the subject. The intention of this device is to single out individuals who are probably good job risks. Five biographical areas are assessed: Drive to excel, financial status, human relations orientation, personal adjustment, and stability. The scoring is accomplished by equating those responses of the subject which agree with background factors of successful people. The index has proven effective in the screening, selection, and placement of sales, managerial, research, and technical personnel. Raw scores may be converted to percentile ranks or standard scores with the use of the tables provided in the manual.

Norms: Norms are based on 500 subjects, including groups of key sales, managerial, and executive personnel, as well as college upperclassmen. Norms are presented in percentiles for each of the five subscales, for age groups ranging from eighteen to over fifty-nine.

Validity and Reliability: One series of validity studies showed the relationship between scores on the subscales and the criterion of monthly salary increments. For two groups of executives, the number of cases were thirty-six and twenty-six, with correlation values ranging from .00 and .60, over the five index areas.

Split-half reliability was found to be .88 for the five subscales combined, based on a normative group of 100. Split-half reliabilities ranged from .42 to .74 for the five subscales.

Bibliography:

Kerr, W. A.: *The Biographical Index, Test Administration Manual.* Chicago, William James Press, 1961.

Biographical Inventory for Students — Experimental Form

Author: Laurence Siegel

Variable: The Biographical Inventory for Students (BIS) is an experimental device to provide information in subscale form about an individual's personal history.

Type of Measure: The BIS is a paper and pencil inventory, suitable for administration to either individuals or groups. It is untimed and typically takes fifty-five to sixty minutes to complete. Scoring may be done manually or by IBM machine.

Source from which Measure may be Obtained: Educational Testing Service, Princeton, New Jersey 08540.

Description: The BIS is designed for subjects at the high school senior and college freshman level and is presently distributed for research purposes only. Uses and applications of response data are based on ten subscales, including: Action; social activities; heterosexual activities; religious activities; literature, music, and art; political activities; socioeconomic status; economic independence; dependence upon the home; and social conformity. The BIS is divided into two parts. Part I consists of forty-one multiple choice items to which the subject responds by indicating one answer only. Part II consists of fifty-two multiple choice items; however, in this case, the subject is permitted to choose as many answers as he or she wishes. The two parts of the BIS are structured in such a way as to allow individual scoring for the scales in each part. Final scores are the sum of responses to each item. Separate scoring keys are provided for males and females for each of the subscales.

Norms: Norms are based on male, tenth grade and twelfth grade high school students and college freshmen, as well as female high school seniors. The number of cases in each norm group generally exceeds five hundred. However, the user is advised to establish local norms.

Validity and Reliability: Significant correlations have been obtained for subscale scores of the BIS with scores of: The Heston Personality Inventory, the Runner Personality Analysis, the Allport-Vernon Study of Values, the Lurie Values Inventory, and the Kuder Preference Record. The significant values appear, in most cases, to be in the desired direction with those personality and interest measures mentioned. Further studies establish an interesting and valid relationship between BIS scores and achievement measures of university grades of freshmen. For example, a significant correlation is reported between the subscale of political activities and two semester grade averages, and a significant negative correlation is reported for the action and heterosexual subscales with grades. Explanation and discussion of the validity studies are included in the manual.

Split-half reliabilities, based on administration to entering freshmen at Washington State University, were found to be .65 for males and .71 for females. Test retest, over varying intervals of two to six weeks for fifty-three male high school seniors, yielded a reliability coefficient of .84 for all scales. Test retest reliability for the female form has not yet been determined.

BIBLIOGRAPHY:

Buros, O. K.: Test number 43.
Siegel, L.: *Manual, The Biographical Inventory for Students — Form K-DRD 1.* Princeton, Educational Testing Service, 1962.

Hanes Sales Selection Inventory

AUTHOR: Bernard Hanes

VARIABLE: The Hanes Sales Selection Inventory is used to assist in selecting successful salesmen.

TYPE OF MEASURE: The inventory is a paper and pencil instrument, suitable for administration to either individuals or groups. It is untimed and typically takes thirty minutes to complete. Scoring is done by hand with the use of a key.

SOURCE FROM WHICH MEASURE MAY BE OBTAINED: Psychometric Affiliates, P. O. Box 3167, Munster, Indiana 46321.

DESCRIPTION: The sales inventory is aimed at maximizing differences between the average job applicant and a potentially successful salesman. It is broken into three parts. Part I provides information about the biography of the applicant for use in an interview. Part II measures the subject's basic verbal knowledge. Part III reveals certain of the subject's personality traits; it also yields a so-called "drive score" which is considered to be a good indication of sales success. This inventory could be used in vocational guidance, as well as in the selection of sales personnel.

NORMS: Normative data is based on 140 salesmen, 70 successes and 70 failures, within a year period. Norms are presented in percentiles for Parts II and III for general applicants and successful salesmen, based on over three hundred cases.

VALIDITY AND RELIABILITY: Validity studies yielded a Rho correlation of .39 between the Hanes Sales Selection Inventory scores and the Primary Mental Abilities Test for thirty college graduates applying for sales positions.

Split-half reliability coefficients for Parts II and III are .84 and .89, respectively.

BIBLIOGRAPHY:

Hanes, B.: *Hanes Sales Selection Inventory, Interpretive Manual.* Munster, Psychometric Affiliates, 1955.

The Martin Performance Appraisal

Author: William T. Martin

Variable: The Martin Performance Appraisal is an assessment of an individual's on-the-job performance by a superior.

Type of Measure: The appraisal is a paper and pencil instrument which is typically completed by an employee's supervisor. It is untimed. The interview which normally follows after the form has been completed may be considered as the scoring process.

Source from which Measure may be Obtained: Western Psychological Services, 12031 Wilshire Boulevard, Los Angeles, California 90025.

Description: In addition to rating on-the-job performance, the appraisal assesses the employee's characteristics in relation to his or her job. It also serves as a record of employee change and growth, as well as a reference record for future promotion possibilities. The employee is rated on a three point scale: "weak" which designates unacceptable or below average performance; "acceptable", indicating the employee's performance is a little below, a little above, or just average; and "strong" which indicates good or superior job performance. The superior rates the employee on these three scales in part I, major tasks, and part II, on-the-job performance. Part III, summary and recommendations, is to be filled out after the appraisal parts I and II are complete, and the superior, using the appraisal form as a guide, interviews the employee. Part III allows for specific recommendations to be made, and there is room for comments by both supervisor and employee.

Norms: Norms are not available.

Validity and Reliability: Technical data is not available. However, the appraisal form can be considered a viable and useful tool for inquiring into employee performance and interpersonal relationships. It can provide a source of inquiry and consistency from employee to employee.

Bibliography:

Buros, O. K.: Test number 1070.

Martin, W. T.: *The Martin Performance Appraisal.* Beverly Hills, Western Psychological Services, 1966.

Personal Data Blank

Author: J. Gustav White

Variable: The Personal Data Blank (PDB) elicits personal information from an individual for use by a supervisor or counselor.

Type of Measure: The PDB is a paper and pencil inventory, suitable for administration to either individuals or groups. It is untimed and typically takes thirty to forty minutes to complete. Scoring is accomplished by the interpretation of information by a supervisor or counselor.

Source from which Measure may be Obtained: Consulting Psychologists Press, 577 College Avenue, Palo Alto, California 94306.

Description: The PDB intends to provide information ranging from a subject's personal history, such as, health, finances, problems, interests and traits, education, and occupation, to his or her preferences and attitudes. In addition, an option is provided where the subject is invited to write a short dissertation on any issue he or she wishes. Guidelines are provided for interpreting the responses to the data blank by a counselor. The counselor scores the blank without the use of an objective scoring key but, instead, uses his or her own experience and background. Uses of the PDB are varied, especially in counseling or interview situations, such as, with students, employees, patients, and others. It is interesting to note that in a case where specific information is desired other than, or in addition to, that supplied by the PDB, the user may insert a sheet containing relevant questions thereby adapting or tailoring the PDB to his or her own needs.

Norms: Norms are not provided in the manual.

Validity and Reliability: Neither of these is provided in the manual, however the interview Form can be a viable method of diagnosis and evaluation of employees.

Bibliography:

White, J. G.: *The Counselor's Data: A Manual for the Personal Data Blank.* Palo Alto, Consulting Psychologists Press, 1962.

Rutgers Social Attribute Inventory

Author: William D. Wells

Variable: The Rutgers Social Attribute Inventory is designed to record raters' impressions of persons or things.

Type of Measure: The inventory is a paper and pencil device, suitable for use by either individuals or groups. It is untimed. Scoring is done by hand.

Source from which Measure may be Obtained: Psychometric Affiliates, P. O. Box 3167, Munster, Indiana 46321.

Description: The inventory includes twenty-four descriptive words to be rated on a scale from one to eight. The words are adjectives or adverbs, and the subject responds by indicating the degree to which the descriptive word describes the person or thing being rated. For example, on a scale the word "agreeable" will appear on one end and the word "disagreeable" on the other. The rater will check off the degree to which, say, a person is "agreeable": "extremely", "very", "fairly", or "slightly". Most of the words are intended to assess personality traits, however a few, such as "short-tall" and "thin-fat", are indicative of physical characteristics. The inventory's use extends to rating of individuals, such as employees or patients, in either a one to one meeting or in the assessment of group decisions or other group confrontations. It may also be used in market research, such as in eliciting consumer responses to an ad campaign.

Norms: Distributions of responses for four of the twenty-four items, by fifty college undergraduates rating the "ideal" versus the "average" professor, are presented. One can infer that norms would be evolved depending on the environment and context in which the rating would take place.

Validity and Reliability: Neither of these is presented in the manual. The use, in which specific attention is given to subject reactions, appropriate norms, inter-rater reliability and content validity, could be determined.

Bibliography:

Wells, W. D.: *Manual of Instructions: Rutgers Social Attribute Inventory.* Munster, Psychometric Affiliates, 1959.

Chapter 9

OTHER ASSESSMENT DEVICES

GROUP 1 — CREATIVITY MEASURES

AC Test of Creative Ability

AUTHORS: Richard H. Harris and A. L. Simberg

VARIABLE: The AC Test of Creative Ability measures the quantity as well as the uniqueness of ideas which individuals can develop in a given situation.

TYPE OF MEASURE: The AC test is a paper and pencil device, suitable for administration to either individuals or groups. There are five parts of the test each of which is timed, and the entire series takes eighty minutes to complete. Scoring is done by hand.

SOURCE FROM WHICH MEASURE MAY BE OBTAINED: Industrial Relations Center, 1225 East Sixtieth Street, Chicago, Illinois 60637.

DESCRIPTION: The AC test is available in two parallel forms, revised short forms A and B. Each consists of five parts. Part I includes a twenty minute test containing five possible situations in which the subject is asked to list all possible consequences of each situation. Part II, a ten minute test of general reasoning ability, uses five unusual and not necessarily true statements, and the subject must list all the reasons he or she can think of to explain the truth of the statements. Part III, a fifteen minute test of sensitivity to problems, contains a list of five common appliances, and the subject lists any and all improvements that could be made in each. Part IV is a twenty minute test of practical judgment containing five problem situations, and the subject is asked to provide the solutions considered least expensive and time consuming. Part V, a fifteen minute test of originality, includes five common objects, and the subject lists all possible uses of each object. Parts I, II, and V are used to yield both quantity and uniqueness scores, Part II yields a uniqueness score alone, and Part IV yields a quantity score. Use of the AC test is feasible whenever an assessment of an individual's creative potential is desired, such as, in business, industry, academic institutions, and adult educational programs.

Norms: Present norms are based on 333 engineering and supervisory personnel. No other descriptive information is presented in the manual.

Validity and Reliability: One validity study determined that significant differences exist in mean performance on the AC Test of Creative Ability and judgment of high or low levels of creative ability. A similar study showed the same for a sample of engineers. Significant differences were found on most, if not all, of the part scores of the test. Other validity studies are reported, including type of engineering job and test performance and also the relationship between the test scores on the AC and mental alertness as measured by the Wonderlic.

Internal consistency reliability, computed by Kuder-Richardson, was found to be .92 for the total test. The correlation found between the scores from the parallel forms was .74.

Bibliography:

Measurement Research Division, Industrial Relations Center: *AC Test of Creative Ability, Test Administration Manual.* Chicago, Industrial Relations Center, 1959.

Biographical Inventory Creativity

Author: Charles E. Schaefer

Variable: The Biographical Inventory Creativity (BIC) identifies those personal and environmental experiences which have occurred during the formative years and purportedly foster the creativity of an individual.

Type of Measure: The BIC is a paper and pencil inventory, suitable for administration to either individuals or groups. It is untimed and typically takes twenty minutes to complete. Scoring is done by hand with the use of a key.

Source from which Measure may be Obtained: Educational and Industrial Testing Service, P. O. Box 7234, San Diego, California 92107.

Description: The BIC contains 125 multiple choice items. It is designed for subjects in the adolescent and young adult age range. The subject responds to questions typically related to past experiences covering the areas of health history, family characteristics, educational background, and work and leisure habits. In addition to assessing creativity, four subscales are structured within the test: family, education, avocational, and miscellaneous. Please note that there are separate scoring keys for males and females. Creativity of males is assessed in art-writing and math-science, whereas females are assessed only in the area of art-writing. Use of the BIC extends to guidance of students enrolled in, or considering majoring in, creative subjects, such as art or music. Potential for research also exists in academic and business environments. Raw scores may be converted to percentile ranks with the use of the table provided.

Norms: Normative data is based on a sample of male and female college students in New York City and includes means and standard deviations for each of the subscales of the BIC.

Validity and Reliability: Significant correlations were obtained for BIC scores with the Similes Test, a test of original expression; the correlation value of .32 is statistically significant. Significant correlations were also obtained for BIC scores with the Remote Associates Test. Other validity data is reported.

Test retest, over a four week interval for eighty-two college students, yielded reliability coefficients ranging from .87 to .95 for the total scale scores.

Bibliography:

Schaefer, C. E.: *Manual for the Biographical Inventory Creativity*. San Diego, Educational and Industrial Testing Service, 1970.

Cree Questionnaire

Authors: Thelma G. Thurstone and J. J. Mellinger

Variable: The Cree Questionnaire is aimed at identifying potentially creative individuals.

Type of Measure: The Cree is a paper and pencil inventory, suitable for administration to either individuals or groups. It is untimed and typically takes fifteen to twenty minutes to complete. Scoring is done by hand with the use of a key.

Source from which Measure may be Obtained: Industrial Relations Center, 1225 East Sixtieth Street, Chicago, Illinois 60637.

Description: The Cree is a partially disguised assessment device which measures creativity and inventiveness. It contains 145 personal questions to which the subject responds by indicating "yes", "no", or "undecided". It was designed to assess, specifically, engineers and engineering supervisors, research and development personnel, salesmen, craftsmen, and others where certain levels of creativity are partly essential in the work situation. In addition, the Cree may be used in the selection of personnel applying to positions which require degrees of creativity or creative potential. The research base for the Cree indicates that creative and productive people differ from less creative and less productive people in responses to the items on it. It is advisable, however, to use the Cree in conjunction with other assessments of creativity before making a final decision regarding a "hire" criterion.

Norms: Normative data is based on 496 industrial employees in four groups, including: skilled, semiskilled, and unskilled; leadmen and foremen trainees; first and second level supervisors; and engineers and executives. Norms are presented in standard scores.

Validity and Reliability: The Cree, along with other items, was given to two groups of engineers: 142 were successful creative inventors, and 141 were not. Fifty-eight of the 145 items in the Cree showed significant differences in answers between the two groups.

Reliability data is not reported in the manual.

BIBLIOGRAPHY:

Thurstone, T. G. and Mellinger, J. J.: *Cree Questionnaire, Test Administration Manual.* Chicago, Industrial Relations Center, 1959.

Purdue Creativity Test — Form G

AUTHORS: C. H. Lawshe and D. H. Harris

VARIABLE: The Purdue Creativity Test is designed specifically to measure the creative capabilities of potential engineering employees.

TYPE OF MEASURE The creativity test is a paper and pencil device, suitable for administration to either individuals or groups. It is timed for forty minutes. Scoring is done by hand.

SOURCE FROM WHICH MEASURE MAY BE OBTAINED: University Book Store, 360 State Street, West Lafayette, Indiana 47906.

DESCRIPTION: The creativity test may be employed in both the selection and placement of engineering personnel, especially in positions requiring a certain measure of creative talent, such as those which require original and creative methods in problem solving. The test is available in two forms, G and H, each consisting of twenty items. Each item appears on a separate page. Items one through eight each consist of a three dimensional drawing; the subject responds by writing down as many uses as he or she can think of for the object presented in the drawing. Items nine through twelve each consist of two 3-dimensional drawings; the subject responds by writing down as many uses as he or she can think of in which the two objects could be used together. Items thirteen through twenty each consist of a line drawing; the subject responds by writing down as many possibilities as he or she can think of that the drawing is. The test yields three subscores: flexibility, fluency, and a total. Raw scores may be converted to percentile ranks.

NORMS: Normative data is based on a sample of 106 professional working engineers in industry. However, it is advisable for the user to establish his or her own norms.

VALIDITY AND RELIABILITY: Three validity studies indicate that supervisory rating of engineers, regarding their creativity, tends to be closely aligned with scores on the Purdue Creativity Test. Probability values of superiority in creativity are presented for high and low scoring engineers. Correlation values between the Purdue Creativity Test and the Wonderlic Personnel Test are also reported. Correlation values from .15 to .16, for forty-eight subjects, tend to indicate the independence of the abilities of creativity and aptitude.

Split-half reliabilities, based on sixty-four professional engineers, were found to be .86 for flexibility, .93 for fluency, and .95 for the total score. Reliability coefficients, based on interscorer agreement, determined independently by two scorers yielded product-moment correlation values of .87 between the two sets of flexibility scores and of .97 between the two sets of total scores.

Bibliography:

Lawshe, C. H. and Harris, D. H.: *Manual of Instructions to accompany Purdue Creativity Test — Forms G and H.* West Lafayette, University Book Store, 1960.

Remote Associates Test — Forms 1 and 2

Authors: Sarnoff A. Mednick and Martha T. Mednick

Variable: The Remote Associates Test (RAT) assesses an individual's capability to think creatively.

Type of Measure: The RAT is a paper and pencil test, suitable for administration to either individuals or groups. It is timed for forty minutes. Scoring is done by hand with the use of a key.

Source from which Measure may be Obtained: Houghton Mifflin Company, 53 West Forty-third Street, New York, New York 10036.

Description: The RAT is designed to assess the creative thinking process. This is accomplished by the presentation of thirty items, each consisting of three words selected from remote associative clusters. The items are presented on the basis that they appear to be remotely related. The subject responds by writing a word which he or she considers to be the "link" to the three stimulus words, that is, a connective word which would cause the three stimulus words to become associated. The RAT is available in two forms, I and II, for use at the college and professional levels. Application of the RAT extends to student counseling regarding the selection of careers in the creative fields, such as music and art, or employee selection, such as for placement in a position requiring a certain degree of creative talent.

NORMS: Normative data is based on male and female college students majoring in such areas as: liberal arts, engineering, architecture and design, and nursing. Professional groups included in the norm sample included research scientists, IBM systems research institute trainees, IBM scholarship and fellowship applicants, IBM engineers, and IBM suggestion winners (technicians). The number of subjects in the college sample exceeded five thousand and in the professional group exceeded five hundred. Norms are reported in percentiles, with means and standard deviations for each group.

VALIDITY AND RELIABILITY: In one criterion validity study, correlation between RAT scores obtained by twenty students in a college of architecture, and faculty ratings of the students' creativity was .70. A second study administered the RAT to graduate students in Psychology one to two years later, and correlation between the students' research creativity and their RAT scores yielded a value of .55 which is statistically significant. In an industry study, the number of proposals written by scientists was significantly related to RAT scores showing a correlation of .29. Other industry validity studies are reported.

Odd-even reliability coefficients were found to range from .86 to .92 on three of the college norm groups; total number of cases was 500. Test retest, using forms 1 and 2 on a group of seventy-one undergraduates, over an unspecified time interval, yielded a correlation value of .81.

BIBLIOGRAPHY:

Buros, O. K.: Test number 445.

Mednick, S. A. and Mednick, M. T.: *Examiner's Manual: Remote Associates Test.* Boston, Houghton Mifflin Company, 1967.

Torrance Tests of Creative Thinking

Author: E. Paul Torrance

Variable: The Torrance Tests of Creative Thinking assess individual thinking along four dimensions associated with creativity: fluency, flexibility, originality, and elaboration.

Type of Measure: The Torrance Tests are paper and pencil instruments, suitable for administration to either individuals or groups. The tests are timed. Scoring is done by hand using a guide provided in the manual.

Source from which Measure may be Obtained: Personnel Press, Education Center, P. O. Box 2649, Columbus, Ohio 43216.

Description: The Torrance tests include a figural test and a verbal test; each is available in two parallel forms, A and B. The verbal test forms are suited for use with individuals in elementary school and up into the adult range, and the figural test may be used with subjects from childhood through the adult range. The underpining concepts of creative thinking and its assessment are explained in the test manual which includes an extensive bibliography. Some of the items in the verbal subtest include activities on cause-effect relationships, production of different approaches in using ideas, and determining consequences of different conditions or situations, among others. The figural tasks include activities, such as, creative forming of pictures, completion of partial figures, and others. The tests are available in foreign languages, including, but not limited to, German, Japanese, Norwegian, and Italian. Torrance's suggested uses for the tests of creative thinking include: as a tool which yields data regarding the functions and development of the human mind; as an assessment of student's needs; and as an indicator of performance or potential difficulty in school students, such as, in identifying the potential dropout or delinquent.

Norms: Normative data is extensive at all age levels. For the adult, norms are based on male and/or female college students, nursing students, graduate students, geographically spread across the United States. Norms are available for subscale scores and are presented by the standard "T" score.

Validity and Reliability: Content validity apparently exists in the sense that the tasks and activities of the tests include those to be found in the universe of creativity. Validity data is so extensive that only selected studies on adults are presented here for the area of concurrent validity. In one study, Wallace (1961) showed that saleswomen in highly creative sales positions outscored their counterparts in noncreative sales positions on tasks in the creativity tests. Predictive validity of the Torrance tests and academic criteria are also cited as being able to add to the predictive validity of intelligence scores of male and female high school students.

Reliability of the Torrance tests is based partly on inter- and intrascorer consistency, because the nature of the test elements demands expertise in the scoring of responses. Studies with trained test scorers yielded correlation coefficients in the .95 and over range for consistency of scoring on each of the four forms. Test retest, over varying intervals from one week to eight months for different samples, yielded reliability coefficients ranging from .60 to .90 for forms A and B.

Bibliography:

Buros, O. K.: Test number 448.

Torrance, E. P.: *Torrance Tests of Creative Thinking, Norms-Technical Manual.* Research edition. Columbus, Personnel Press, 1966.

Wallace, H. R.: Creative Thinking: A Factor in Sales Productivity. *Vocational Guidance Quarterly,* 223-226, Summer, 1961.

GROUP 2 — MANAGERIAL MEASURES

The Leadership Ability Evaluation

Authors: Russell N. Cassel and Edward J. Stancik

Variable: The Leadership Ability Evaluation (LAE) assesses both the decision-making process and the working environment developed by an individual functioning in a leadership role.

Type of Measure: The LAE is a paper and pencil inventory, suitable for administration to either individuals or groups. It is untimed and typically takes forty-five minutes to complete. Scoring is done by hand.

Source from which Measure may be Obtained: Western Psychological Services, Box 775, Beverly Hills, California 90213.

Description: The LAE addresses itself to the individual performing in a leadership role and assesses that person's methods of influencing other individuals or groups to move toward his or her objectives. In this case, leadership refers to methods employed to direct the behavior of others. There are fifty multiple choice problems in the LAE which attempt to present plausible life situations as encountered by an individual in western culture. These problems are constructed equally over five categories: home and family life, work and vocational pursuits, play and advocational pursuits, school and educational pursuits, and community life. The subject responds by choosing the one of four alternatives which he or she feels is the course of action indicative of a leader. Each of the four choices reflects a distinct decision-making pattern or social leaning: laissez faire (LF), democratic-cooperative (DC), autocratic-submissive (AS), and autocratic-aggressive (AA). The subject's pattern is determined by using weighted scores for the individual scores of LF, DC, and AS, and an unweighted score for AA. The score provides for discriminations among groups of outstanding leaders versus typical individuals when intelligence and maturity factors are held constant. Suggested uses for the LAE include the screening of employees to be considered for leadership positions, as well as assessments of current leadership styles being utilized by persons presently in leadership rolls.

Norms: Normative data is available on 2,000 individuals, 400 outstanding leaders, and 100 United States Air Force full colonels chosen from "general officer potentials". Further descriptive information is also available on eight other groups of men, or men and women, including guidance counselors, chaplains, "gifted" ninth and eleventh graders, in-prison adults, delinquents, above and below average "typical" youth.

Validity and Reliability: Validity is established first through content inspection of the items. The problems are typically of life activities of an individual. Status validity, or the ability of the test to discriminate, is shown by comparisons of scores of outstanding leaders and "typical" individuals. Data indicates that, with age and intelligence held constant, significant discriminations were found.

Corrected split-half reliability coefficients ranged from .73 to .91. The more experienced, more intelligent, and high social status groups have higher reliability coefficients.

Bibliography:

Cassel, R. N. and Stancik, E. J.: *Manual: The Leadership Ability Evaluation.* Beverly Hills, Western Psychological Services, 1961.

______ : *Manual, Tables Supplement: The Leadership Ability Evaluation.* Beverly Hills, Western Psychological Services, 1961.

Leadership Evaluation and Development Scale

Author: Harley W. Mowry

Variable: The Leadership Evaluation and Development Scale (LEADS) identifies individuals with leadership potential.

Type of Measure: The LEADS is a paper and pencil inventory, suitable for administration to either individuals or groups. It is untimed. Scoring may be done manually with the use of a key or by machine.

Source from which Measure may be Obtained: Psychological Services, Inc., 1800 Wilshire Boulevard, Los Angeles, California 90057.

Description: The LEADS is comprised of eight simulated, work-related situations. The subject responds by answering several multiple choice questions about each case. The scoring intends to provide the user with information which identifies a subject's potential leadership capabilities. Please note that the LEADS is intended for use as a supplement to information, already known about an employee, on which promotions to leadership positions are based. The items in the LEADS are based on case studies from the Armstrong

Cork Company and were tried out on supervisors in twelve industrial firms.

Norms: The results of only one study for the final form are available. The group upon which the data was collected consisted of 113 manufacturing supervisors in a rocket engine development and manufacturing firm.

Validity and Reliability: Three validity studies with a prototype device yielded biserial correlation values ranging from .53 to .74 for LEADS scores with superiors' rating of supervisors' ability to handle people and their overall success in so doing. The number of subjects varied from ten to forty in the three validity studies. Further studies yielded significant correlation of the LEADS inventory with Fleishman's Leadership Opinion Questionnaire subtests, structure and consideration. Also, significant correlation of the LEADS score with a criterion of salary, corrected for age and seniority, was also established.

One study yielded a corrected split-half correlation value of .81, while another study, using a prototype of the LEADS on 146 supervisors from thirty-eight companies, yielded an odd-even reliability of .79.

Bibliography:

Buros, O. K.: Test number 1148.

Mowry, H. W.: *Preliminary Manual for the Leadership Evaluation and Development Scale.* Los Angeles, Psychological Services, Inc., 1965.

The Leadership Q-Sort Test

Author: Russell N. Cassel

Variable: The Leadership Q-Sort Test (LQT) assesses an individual's values with respect to leadership.

Type of Measure: The LQT is a paper and pencil and card sort inventory, suitable for administration to either individuals or groups. It is untimed and typically takes forty-five minutes to complete. Scoring is done by hand and is very involved.

Source from which Measure may be Obtained: Psychometric Affiliates, P. O. Box 3167, Munster, Indiana 46321.

Description: The LQT measures the degree of importance that a subject places upon those factors considered to be indicative of effective leadership and in so doing, identifies those qualities in the subject. This is accomplished by comparing the subject's test score with appropriate norms which have been obtained from the ratings of multiple groups of leaders. The LQT is comprised of sixty items in a forced choice format. Included in the material required for administration are: test booklet; a Q-sort deck of cards upon each of which is printed a statement which corresponds in item number to a statement in the test booklet; and a Q-sort board consisting of eleven squares upon which the subject must place, by degree of importance to effective or good leadership, the cards. The subject is required to rate the items, beginning with square number eleven and (with the decreased feeling of the item's importance to effective or good leadership) ending with square number one, by placing the cards on the board as follows: one card on the number eleven square and one on the number one square, three cards each on the numbers ten and two squares, five cards each on the numbers nine and three squares, seven cards each on the numbers eight and four squares, nine cards each on the numbers seven and five squares, and ten cards on the number six square. Application of the LQT extends to the screening of employees regarding their leadership potential. It is especially useful for subjects with limited reading skills or in situations in which the nature of the test is to be disguised.

Norms: Normative data is based on adults of both sexes. Different scoring keys are provided for secondary school youth, United States Air Force colonels, chaplains, research psychologists, federal reformatory prisoners. Also provided is a key based on all groups' combined data, except for the last group. Although different scoring keys exist, the norms are based on an averaged score key.

Validity and Reliability: Validity data is extensive. Face or content validity was reported through examination of test materials by advanced psychology students. Criterion-related validity was established using institution ratings; results indicated that LQT scores are significantly related to both peer status and instructor ratings for a group of United States Air Force preflight cadets' scores on the LQT. Although no descriptive data, such as age or academic grades, is provided, significant relationships were established with the subtests of the Group Personality Projective Test. Finally, predictive validity studies are also presented showing that the LQT can be used for discriminating among individuals with varied levels of leadership competency.

Corrected split-half reliabilities, based on two different samples of U.S.A.F. preflight cadets, were found to range from .83 to .84. Subscore reliabilities are also reported.

Bibliography:

Cassel, R. N.: *Manual: The Leadership Q-Sort Test.* Munster, Psychometric Affiliates, 1958.

Management Aptitude Inventory

Author: Psychological Business Research

Variable: The Management Aptitude Inventory (MAI) assesses those characteristics considered to be indicative of successful individuals in managerial positions.

Type of Measure: The MAI is a paper and pencil inventory, suitable for administration to either individuals or groups. It is untimed and typically takes fifteen to twenty minutes to complete. Scoring is done by hand.

Source from which Measure may be Obtained: Psychological Business Resarch, 11000 Cedar Avenue, Cleveland, Ohio 44106.

Description: The MAI is a self-descriptive inventory presented in a forced choice format. It is divided into three parts. Section I consists of fifty pairs of phrases to which the subject responds by indicating the one of each pair that is more descriptive of himself or herself. Section II consists of another twenty-five pairs of phrases to which the subject responds by indicating the one of each pair that appeals to him or her more. Section III includes twenty-three phrases to which the subject responds by indicating whether or not the phrase describes him or her. There are four subscales structured in the MAI, including: intelligent job performance; leadership qualities, proper job attitude; and relations with others. Application of the MAI extends to assessing how well an individual will work with a particular supervisor, how well the individual will perform the job, whether he or she is suited to a job in relation to sense of values, and how a certain individual will perform in a managerial position, among others.

Norms: The normative sample consisted of 500 male job applicants to positions, including industrial salesman, engineer, production supervisor, accountant, and administrator. Norm tables are reported in percentiles for each of the form characteristics or traits. In a supplement (March, 1975) to the MAI manual, evidence, in the form of means and standard deviations, indicates the nondiscriminatory content of this inventory. Data is based on studies of six groups, including: an entire group of Negro high school students; employed production workers in a meat packing plant; all of the minority applicants to the aforementioned plant; sheet metal apprentices with one to four years experience, all of whom were high school graduates age eighteen to twenty-four; applicants, referred by company clients, to professional or managerial positions at Psychological Business Research (PBR); and a norm group reported in the MAI manual, similar in age, experience, and recruiting source of the PBR group.

Validity and Reliability: Content, construct, and concurrent validity studies are presented. Content validity was determined through the development of items from a universe of material used by management personnel. Concurrent validity studies have yielded significant multiple correlations predicting such criteria as sales (in industrial selling positions) and overall job performance measures from the four scales of the MAI. Other external validity studies report significant multiple correlations with job ratings from factory foremen. (Interrater reliability for job ratings was found to be .62.) In addition, correlation values are reported for the MAI with the Otis Mental Ability Test and the Survey of Interpersonal

Values.

Test retest, over a two week interval for a group of 113 college students, yielded reliability coefficients ranging from .61 to .66 for the four subscales. Odd-even reliabilities ranged from .83 to .92.

BIBLIOGRAPHY:

Psychological Business Research: *The Management Aptitude Inventory.* Cleveland, Author, 1967.

______ : *Supplement: The Management Aptitude Inventory.* Cleveland, Author, 1975.

OTL Managerial Tests

AUTHOR: Organizational Tests Limited

VARIABLE: The OTL Managerial Tests are a broad and encompassing battery for assessing management knowledge and skills.

TYPE OF MEASURE: The OTL is a battery of paper and pencil tests, suitable for administration to either individuals or groups. The tests are untimed, and each typically takes thirty minutes to complete. Scoring is done by hand with the use of a key.

SOURCE FROM WHICH MEASURE MAY BE OBTAINED: Organizational Tests Limited, Box 324, Fredericton, New Brunswick, Canada.

DESCRIPTION: There are seven OTL Managerial Tests, whose use is indicated by the nature of the instrument, including: Management Change Inventory, Management Coaching Relations, Management Communication Relations, Management Control Inventory, Management Disciplinary Inventory, Management Human Relations, and Union Management Relations. Each of the inventories consists of eighty true-and-false statements. Management Change Inventory assesses one's knowledge of methods of introducing change at both worker and supervisory levels. Management Coaching Relations assesses one's knowledge of methods of coaching subordinates. Management Communication Relations assesses a manager's knowledge of communication methods for use with other managers. Management Control Inventory assesses one's sound management, job control techniques. Management Disciplinary Inventory assesses one's knowledge of accepted disciplinary techniques for use by managers of supervisors only. The Management Human Relations Inventory assesses one's attitudes toward workers, supervisors, or subordinate managers. Finally, Union Management Relations assesses managers' attitudes toward unions.

Norms: The OTL tests have a conversion scale which converts raw scores to percentile ranks. The number of subjects expressed in the norm table is 1,895; no other data is provided.

Validity and Reliability: "All of the tests were constructed by skilled trainers and all tests were inspected by from ten to over a hundred judges." (p. 7, Test Administration Guide)

No reliability data is provided.

Bibliography:

Organizational Tests, Ltd.: *Test Administration Guide for the Seven OTL Managerial Tests.* Fredericton, N.B., Canada, Author, 1972.

Response to Power Measure — Form A

Author: Authur B. Sweney

Variable: The Response to Power Measure (RPM) assesses an individual's preferences in relation to superior and subordinate roles.

Type of Measure: The RPM is a paper and pencil inventory, suitable for administration to either individuals or groups. It is untimed and typically takes ten to fifteen minutes to complete. Scoring is done by hand.

Source from which Measure may be Obtained: Test Systems, Inc., Box 18432, Wichita, Kansas 67218.

Description: The RPM includes ninety-six short items to which the subject responds by indicating agreement, disagreement, or uncertainty. The roles distinguishable in the RPM include superior or leadership roles, subordinate roles, and individual roles which include authoritarian, permissive, participative, submissive, rebel, cooperator, and confrontive roles. Roles can also be assessed in relation to interactions, such as, authoritarian-pleaser, rebel-permissive, participator-cooperator. The six subscales of the RPM are: authoritarian, equalitarian, permissive, critic, ingratiator, and rebel. Uses of the RPM extend to: assessment of individuals regarding preferences of superior and subordinate roles; assessment of superior-subordinate relations; as well as selection of styles regarding effective placement of superiors and subordinates within the structure of a company or department.

Norms: Norm samples include college students totalling 374 and general population totalling 1,417. The general population includes middle management, students, and Air Force personnel. No other demographic information is provided. Norms are presented in standard scores.

Validity and Reliability: Numerous content, construct, and predictive validity studies have been carried out. The predictive validity studies include correlations of the Sixteen Personality Factor Questionnaire (16 PF) subscales with the six scales of the RPM yielding from negative values to +.39 for 115 subjects. For example, a value of +.27 was found between the dominance scale of the 16 PF and the authoritarian scale of the RPM.

Corrected split-half reliability coefficients were found to range from .43 to .78 for all subscales. Estimated reliabilities, computed by Kuder-Richardson formula 20, ranged from .65 to .78.

Bibliography:

Sweney, A. B.: *Response to Power Measure Handbook: A Test of Superior and Subordinate Role Preference.* Wichita, Test Systems, Inc., 1972.

Responsibility Index

Authors: Nancee S. Elsass and Arthur B. Sweney

Variable: The Responsibility Index (RI) assesses the role styles of subordinates in a business environment.

Type of Measure: The RI is a paper and pencil inventory, suitable for administration to either individuals or groups. It is untimed and typically takes ten to twenty minutes to complete. Scoring is done by hand.

Source from which Measure may be Obtained: Test Systems, Inc., P. O. Box 18432, Wichita, Kansas 67218.

Description: The RI includes thirty-four, three alternative items. The manager or supervisor is asked to rank alternative roles of subordinates in terms of the items in the inventory. The results from the RI are the identifications of ingratiator, cooperator, and rebel roles of subordinates as perceived by their manager. Briefly, the cooperator is the more objective role of a subordinate; this role is indicative of the problem-oriented, confident, and objective individual. The ingratiator or "yes man" is oriented toward pleasing others, while the rebel is concerned with rule abiding through confrontation and power seeking. The RI is basically intended to be administered to a manager or supervisor who responds by indicating how he or she feels subordinates should behave. Raw scores may be converted to standard scores with the use of the tables provided. The RI also provides a profile sheet.

Norms: Norms are based on both middle management and military and are also provided for employees at entry level position. The norm table states that the number of cases is 267 and does not specify any other biographical, demographic information. The Supervise Ability Scale manual (Sweney and Elsass, 1970) provides additional norms on 157 military personnel.

Validity and Reliability: Validity studies establish a correlation value in the .40 to .60 range for the RI with the Response to Power Measure (RPM) based on a sample of 208 subjects. Further studies establish correlation values in the .20 to .40 range for the three RI subscores of rebel, critic (cooperator), and ingratiator, with average ratings of the superordinates themselves and subordinates' ratings of these superordinates (Sweney and Weber).

Internal consistency reliability coefficients ranged from .74 to .90 as determined by Elsass (1971) and from .81 to .92 in a study by Weber and Marsteller. Equivalency reliability, corrected for attenuation between forms B and C, ranged from .89 to .92 for the three scales.

Bibliography:

Elsass, N. S.: Development of two instruments for measuring superior-subordinate role perceptions. Unpublished thesis. Wichita State University, 1971.

——— and Sweney, A. B.: *Responsibility Index, Manual.* Wichita, Test Systems, Inc., 1972.

——— and Weber, M.: A study: Rating bias in supervisor role. Wichita State University, 1971.

Sweney, A. B.: *Response to Power Measure Handbook: A Test of Superior and Subordinate Roles.* Wichita, Test Systems, Inc., 1972.

——— and Elsass, N. S.: *Supervise Ability Scale — Form A.* Wichita, Test Systems, Inc., 1970.

——— and Marsteller, S.: Harmony Index. Unpublished report. Wichita State University, 1971.

(Please note that Weber et al. is not referenced in the manual.)

Supervise Ability Scale

Authors: Nancee S. Elsass and Arthur B. Sweney

Variable: The Supervise Ability Scale (SAS) assesses management role styles which an individual perceives to be appropriate and important.

Type of Measure: The SAS is a paper and pencil inventory, suitable for administration to either individuals or groups. It is untimed and typically takes ten to twenty minutes to complete. Scoring is done by hand.

Source from which Measure may be Obtained: Test Systems, Inc., P. O. Box 18432, Wichita, Kansas 67218.

Description: The SAS consists of thirty items in a forced choice format. Each item involves three possible responses from which the subordinate selects his or her strongest and least strong preference in terms of appropriateness. The scales identified in the SAS are authoritarian, equalitarian, and permissive. The authoritarian role tends to generate conflicts, is task oriented, and is usually fault finding. The equalitarian is a balance between task and people orientation, is not overconfident but works well with people. The permissive style is overreactive to situations, will tend to please people and, in so doing, may be seen as apathetic. Application of the SAS extends to: selection of management personnel: assessment of individuals to be promoted into managerial positions; as well as assessment of current managers or assessment by subordinates of their managers.

NORMS: Normative data is based on a sample of 157 military personnel, 115 business personnel, and 147 in a general adult sample. No other descriptive information is presented.

VALIDITY AND RELIABILITY: Validity studies (Weber), establishing the relationship between the SAS and the Response to Power Measure (Sweney, 1970), showed correlation values of .17 for equalitarian, .20 for permissive, and .78 for authoritarian scales, which are common dimensions to both instruments. Another study (Weber) showed correlation values ranging from .25 to .49 for the three SAS scale scores, achieved by subordinates, with supervisors' self ratings.

Internal consistency reliability coefficients, computed by a split-half method, ranged from .51 to .66 in a study by Elsass (1971) and from .73 to .80 in a study by Weber and Marsteller over the three scales of the SAS for two sample sizes of 40 and 130 cases. Equivalency reliability between forms A and B yielded correlation values ranging from .81 to .83 in a study by Sweney (1970) and from .68 to .88 in a study by Elsass (1971).

BIBLIOGRAPHY:

Elsass, N. S.: Development of two instruments for measuring superior-subordinate role perceptions. Unpublished thesis. Wichita State University, 1971.

——— and Sweney, A. B.: *Supervise Ability Scale, Manual.* Wichita, Test Systems, Inc., 1972.

Sweney, A. B.: Organizational power roles. *Professional Management Bulletin, 10*:5-13, June, 1970.

——— : *Response to Power Measure Handbook: A Test of Superior and Subordinate Role Preference.* Wichita, Test Systems, Inc., 1972.

(Please note that neither Weber nor Weber and Marsteller are referenced in the manual.)

Part Three
RESOURCES FOR THE READER

EDUCATIONAI RESOURCE INFORMATION CENTER CLEARINGHOUSES

Career Education
Northern Illinois University
204 Gabel Hall
DeKalb, Illinois 60115

Counseling and Personnel Services
University of Michigan
School of Education Building, Room 2108
East University and South University Streets
Ann Arbor, Michigan 48104

Disadvantaged
Teachers College
Columbia University
Box 40
New York, New York 10027

Early Childhood Education
University of Illinois
805 West Pennsylvania Avenue
Urbana, Illinois 61801

Educational Management
University of Oregon
Eugene, Oregon 97403

Handicapped and Gifted Children
The Council for Exceptional Children
1920 Association Drive
Reston, Virginia 22091

Higher Education
George Washington University
One DuPont Circle, Northwest, Suite 630
Washington, D. C. 20006

Information Resources
Stanford Center for Research and Development in Teaching
Stanford, California 94305

Junior Colleges
University of California at Los Angeles
Powell Library, Room 96
405 Hilgard Avenue
Los Angeles, California 90024

Languages and Linguistics
Center for Applied Linguistics
1611 North Kent Street
Arlington, Virginia 22209

Reading and Communication Skills
National Council of Teachers of English
1111 Kenyon Road
Urbana, Illinois 61801

Rural Education and Small Schools
New Mexico State University
Box 3 AP
Las Cruces, New Mexico 88001

Science, Mathematics, and Environmental Education
Ohio State University
400 Lincoln Tower
Columbus, Ohio 43221

Social Studies and Social Science Education
Social Science Education Consortium, Inc.
855 Broadway
Boulder, Colorado 80302

Teacher Education
American Association of Colleges for Teacher Education
One DuPont Circle, Northwest, Suite 616
Washington, D. C. 20006

Tests, Measurement, and Evaluation
Educational Testing Service
Princeton, New Jersey 08540

RESEARCH AND DEVELOPMENT CENTERS AND REGIONAL LABORATORIES

Appalachia Educational Laboratory, Inc.
P. O. Box 1348
Charleston, West Virginia 25325

CEMREL, Inc.
3120 59th Street
St. Louis, Missouri 63139

Far West Laboratory for Educational Research and Development
1855 Folsom Street
San Francisco, California 94103

Learning Research and Development Center
University of Pittsburgh
3935 O'Hara Street
Pittsburgh, Pennsylvania 15260

Mid-continent Regional Educational Laboratory
104 East Independence Avenue
Kansas City, Missouri 64106

National Laboratory for Higher Education
Mutual Plaza
Durham, North Carolina 27701

Northwest Regional Educational Laboratory
700 Lindsay Building
710 Southwest Second Avenue
Portland, Oregon 97204

Research for Better Schools, Inc.
Suite 1700
1700 Market Street
Philadelphia, Pennsylvania 19103

Center for Educational Policy and Management
University of Oregon
1472 Kincaid
Eugene, Oregon 97401

Center for Occupational Education
North Carolina State University
P. O. Box 5096
Raleigh, North Carolina 27607

Center for Research and Development in Higher Education
University of California, Berkeley
2150 Shattuck Avenue, Fifth Floor
Berkeley, California 94704

Center for Social Organization of Schools
The Johns Hopkins University
3505 North Charles Street
Baltimore, Maryland 21218

Center for the Study of Evaluation
University of California at Los Angeles
UCLA Graduate School of Education
145 Moore Hall
Los Angeles, California 90024

Center for Vocational and Technical Education
The Ohio State University
1960 Kenny Road
Columbus, Ohio 43210

Research and Development Center for Teacher Education
University of Texas, Austin
Education Annex 3.203
Austin, Texas 78712

Southwest Educational Development Laboratory
800 Brazos Street
Austin, Texas 78701

Southwestern Cooperative Educational Laboratory, Inc.
229 Truman, Northeast
Albuquerque, New Mexico 87108

Wisconsin Research and Development Center for Cognitive Learning
University of Wisconsin, Madison
1025 West Johnson Street
Madison, Wisconsin 53706

OTHER INSTITUTIONS

American College Testing Program
P. O. Box 168
Iowa City, Iowa 52240

American Dental Association
211 E. Chicago Avenue
Chicago, Illinois 60611

Educational Records Bureau
116 Maple Avenue
Greenwich, Connecticut 06830

Educational Testing Service
Princeton, New Jersey 08540

Martinus Nijhoff
P. O. Box 269
The Hague, Holland

National Board of Medical Examiners
3930 Chestnut Street
Philadelphia, Pennsylvania 19104

National Foundation for Educational Research in England and Wales
The Mere, Upton Park Slogh
Bucks, England

National League for Nursing
10 Columbus Circle
New York, New York 10019

United States Employment Service
(check for your local listing)

PUBLISHERS AND SOURCES OF MEASURES

American Guidance Service, Inc.
Circle Pines, Minnesota

Martin M. Bruce
New Rochelle, New York

Center for Psychological Service
Washington, D. C.

Consulting Psychologists Press, Inc.
Palo Alto, California

Counselor Recordings and Tests
Nashville, Tennesse

CTB/McGraw-Hill
Monterey, California

Education-Industry Service
Chicago, Illinois

Educational and Industrial Testing Service
San Diego, California

Educational Testing Service
Princeton, New Jersey

Guidance Associates
Wilmington, Delaware

Harcourt Brace Jovanovich
New York, New York

Houghton Mifflin Company
New York, New York

Industrial Relations Center
University of Chicago, Illinois

Institute for Personality and Ability Testing
Champaign, Illinois

Institute of Administrative Research
Columbia University, New York

Institute of Living
Hartford, Connecticut

International Tests, Inc.
Stevens Point, Wisconsin

Life Insurance Marketing and Research Association
Hartford, Connecticut

James H. Morrison
Overland Park, Kansas

National Computer Systems
Minneapolis, Minnesota

National Institute for Personnel Research
Johannesburg, South Africa

Organizational Tests, Ltd.
Fredricton, N. B., Canada

Personnel Press, Inc.
Princeton, New Jersey

Psychological Business Research
Cleveland, Ohio

Psychological Corporation, The
New York, New York

Psychological Services, Inc.
Los Angeles, California

Psychological Test Specialists
Missoula, Montana

Psychometric Affiliates
Munster, Indiana

John E. Reid and Assoc.
Chicago, Illinois

Richardson, Bellows, Henry & Co.
Washington, D. C.

Science Research Associates, Inc.
Chicago, Illinois

Stanford University Press
Stanford, California

W. Clement & Jessie V. Stone Foundation
Chicago, Illinois

Teachers College Press
New York, New York

Test Systems, Inc.
Wichita, Kansas

University Book Store
West Lafayette, Indiana

Western Psychological Services
Beverly Hills, California

William Lynde & Williams
Painesville, Ohio

William James Press
Brookport, Illinois

SPECIAL DOCUMENT

United States of America v. Georgia Power Company et al, No. 71-3447.

Charles King et al, and Willie Moreman v. Georgia Power Company et al, No. 71-3229.

On Appeal from the United States District Court for the Northern District of Georgia, Atlanta Division. U.S. Court of Appeals, Fifth Circuit. Filed: July 26, 1972.

Brief for the Executive Committee of the Division of Industrial and Organizational Psychology (Division 14), American Psychological Association, as *Amicus Curiae.*

TEXTBOOKS AND JOURNALS

American Psychological Association: *Standards for Educational and Psychological Tests and Manuals*. Washington, D. C., Author, 1974.

Anastasi, A.: *Differential Psychology*. New York, MacMillan, 1958.

______ : *Psychological Testing*. 2nd ed. New York, MacMillan, 1961.

______ : *Psychological Testing*. 3rd ed. New York, MacMillan, 1968.

Buros, O. K.: *Tests in Print II*. Highland Park, The Gryphon Press, 1974.

______ : *The Seventh Mental Measurements Yearbook*. 2 vols. Highland Park, The Gryphon Press, 1972.

Cattell, R. B. and Cattell, A. K. S.: *Handbook for the Culture Fair Intelligence Test*. Champaign, Institute for Personality and Ability Testing, 1959.

Cronbach, L. J.: *Essentials of Psychological Testing*. 3rd ed. New York, Harper, 1970.

______ and Gleser, G. C.: *Psychological Tests and Personnel Decisions*. 2nd ed. Urbana, University of Illinois Press, 1965.

Davis, F. B.: *Educational Measurements and Their Interpretation*. Belmont, Wadsworth, 1964.

Freeman, F. S.: *Theory and Practice of Psychological Testing*, 3rd ed. New York, Holt, 1962.

Ghiselli, E. E.: *Theory of Psychological Measurement*. New York, McGraw-Hill, 1964.

______ : *The Validity of Occupational Aptitude Tests*. New York, Wiley, 1966.

Guilford, J. P.: *The Nature of Human Intelligence*. New York, McGraw-Hill, 1967.

Goldman, L.: *Using Tests in Counseling*. 2nd ed. New York, Appleton-Century-Crofts, 1971.

Kamin, L. J.: *The Science and Politics of I.Q.* Potomac, Lawrence Erlbaum Associates, 1974.

Nunnally, J. C.: *Tests and Measurements: Assessment and Prediction*. New York, McGraw-Hill, 1959.

Thorndike, R. L. and Hagen, E.: *Measurement and Evaluation in Psychology Education*. 3rd ed. New York, Wiley, 1969.

Appendix I

FAMILY EDUCATIONAL RIGHTS AND PRIVACY ACT 08, 1974

"Protection of the Rights and Privacy of Parents and Students"

"Sec. 438. (a)(1) No funds shall be made available under any applicable program to any State or local educational agency, any institution of higher education, any community college, any school, agency offering a preschool program, or any other educational institution which has a policy of denying, or which effectively prevents, the parents of students attending any school of such agency, or attending such institutions of higher education, community college, school, preschool, or other educational institution, the right to inspect and review any and all official records, files, and data directly related to their children, including all material that is incorporated into each student's cumulative record folder, and intended for school use or to be available to parties outside the school or school system, and specifically including, but not necessarily limited, to, identifying data, academic work completed, level of achievement (grades, standardized achievement test scores), attendance data, scores on standardized intelligence, aptitude, and psychological tests, interest inventory results, health data, family background information, teacher or counselor ratings and observations, and verified reports of serious or recurrent behavior patterns. Where such records or data include information on more than one student, the parents of any student shall be entitled to receive, or be informed of, that part of such record or data as pertains to their child. Each recipient shall establish appropriate procedures for the granting of a request by parents for access to their child's school records within a reasonable period of time, but in no case more than forty-five days after the request has been made.

"(2) Parents shall have an opportunity for a hearing to challenge the content of their child's school records, to insure that the records are not inaccurate, misleading, or otherwise in violation of the privacy or other rights of students, and to provide an opportunity for the correction or deletion of any such inaccurate, misleading, or otherwise inappropriate data contained therein.

"(b) (1) No funds shall be made available under any applicable program to any State or local educational agency, any institution of higher education, any community college, any school, agency offering a preschool program, or any other educational institution which has a policy of permitting the release of personally identifiable records or files (or personal information contained therein) of students without the written consent of their parents to any individual, agency, or organization, other than to the following —

"(A) other school officials, including teachers within the educational institution or local educational agency who have legitimate educational interests;

"(B) officials of other schools or school systems in which the student intends to enroll, upon condition that the student's parents be notified of the transfer, receive a copy of the record if desired, and have an opportunity for a hearing to challenge the content of the record;

"(C) authorized representatives of (i) the Comptroller General of the United States, (ii) the Secretary, (iii) an administrative head of an education agency (as defined in section 409 of this Act), or (iv) State educational authorities, under the conditions set forth in paragraph (3) of this subsection; and

"(D) in connection with a student's application for, or receipt of, financial aid.

"(2) No funds shall be made available under any applicable program to any State or local educational agency, any institution of higher education, any community college, any school, agency offering a preschool program, or any other educational institution which has a policy or practice of furnishing, in any form, any personally identifiable information contained in personal school records, to any persons other than those listed in subsection (b)(1) unless —

"(A) there is written consent from the student's parents specifying records to be released, the reasons for such release, and to whom, and with a copy of the records to be released to the student's parents and the student if desired by the parents, or

"(B) such information is furnished in compliance with judicial order, or pursuant to any lawfully issued subpoena, upon condition that parents and students are notified of all such orders or subpoenas in advance of the compliance therewith by the educational institution or agency.

"(3) Nothing contained in this section shall preclude authorized representatives of (A) the Comptroller General of the United States, (B) the Secretary, (C) an administrative head of an education agency or (D) State educational authorities from having access to student or other records which may be necessary in connection with the audit and evaluation of Federally-supported education program, or in connection with the enforcement of the Federal legal requirements which relate to such programs: *Procided.* That except when collection of personally identifiable data is specifically authorized by Federal law, any data collected by such officials with respect to individual students shall not include information (including social security numbers) which would permit the personal indentification of such students or their parents after the data so obtained has been collected.

"(4)(A) With respect to subsections (c)(1) and (c)(2) and (c)(3), all persons, agencies, or organizations desiring access to the records of a student shall be required to sign a written form which shall be kept permanently with the file of the student, but only for inspection by the parents or student, indicating specifically the legitimate educational or other interest that each person, agency, or organization has in seeking this information. Such form shall be available to parents and to the school official responsible for record maintenance as a means of auditing the operation of the system.

"(B) With respect to this subsection, personal information

shall only be transferred to a third party on the condition that such part will not permit any other party to have access to such information without the written consent of the parents of the student.

"(c) The Secretary shall adopt appropriate regulations to protect the rights of privacy of students and their families in connection with any surveys of data-gathering activities conducted, assisted, or authorized by the Secretary or an administrative head of an education agency. Regulations established under this subsection shall include provisions controlling the use, dissemination, and protection of such data. No survey or data-gathering activities shall be conducted by the Secretary, or an administrative head of an education agency under an applicable program, unless such activities are authorized by law.

(d) For the purposes of this section, whenever a student has attained eighteen years of age, or is attending an institution of post secondary education, the permission or consent required of and the rights accorded to the parents of the student shall thereafter only be required of and accorded to the student.

"(e) No funds shall be made available under any applicable program unless the recipient of such funds informs the parents of students, or the students, if they are eighteen years of age or older, or are attending an institution of post secondary education, of the rights accorded them by this section.

"(f) The Secretary, or an administrative head of an education agency, shall take appropriate actions to enforce provisions of this section and to deal with violations of this section, according to the provisions of this Act, except that action to terminate assistance may be taken only if the Secretary finds there has been a failure to comply with the provisions of this section, and he has determined that compliance cannot be secured by voluntary means.

"(g) The Secretary shall establish or designate an office and review board within the Department of Health, Education, and Welfare for the purpose of investigating, processing, reviewing, and adjudicating violations of the provisions of this section, according to the procedures contained in sections 434 and 437 of this Act."

(b)(1)(i) The provisions of this section shall become effective ninety days after the date of enactment of section 438 of the General Education Provisions Act.

(2)(i) This section may be cited as the "Family Educational Rights and Privacy Act of 1974".

Appendix II

GUIDELINES FOR THE ASSESSMENT OF SEX BIAS AND SEX FAIRNESS IN CAREER INTEREST INVENTORIES*

THESE guidelines have been developed as part of the National Institute of Education (NIE) Career Education Program's study of sex bias and sex fairness in career interest inventories. They were developed by the NIE Career Education Staff and a senior consultant and nine-member planning group of experts in the fields of measurement and guidance, appointed by NIE. The draft guidelines were discussed in a broadly representative three-day workshop sponsored by NIE in Washington, D. C., in March 1974. Through successive revised drafts, culminating in this edition of the guidelines, the diverse concerns of inventory users, respondents, authors, and publishers were taken in consideration and resolved as far as possible.

During the development of the guidelines, the following working definition of sex bias was used:

Within the context of career guidance, sex bias is defined as any factor that might influence a person to limit — or might cause others to limit — his or her considerations of a career solely on the basis of gender.[1]

The working definition expresses the primary concern that career alternatives not be limited by bias or stereotyped sex roles in the world of work.[2] The guidelines represent a more specific

---

*From *Measurement and Evaluation in Guidance*, *8*(1):7-11, Copyright 1975, American Personnel and Guidance Association. Reprinted with permission.

[1]For a comprehensive analysis of the many forms in which sex bias appears in written materials, the reader is referred to the guidelines of Scott, Foresman and Company (1972).

[2]An alternative interpretation of sex bias has been suggested by Dale Prediger and Gary Hanson. They define sex restrictiveness in interest inventory reporting procedures and indicate under what conditions sex restrictiveness is evidence of sex bias. This

definition of the many aspects of sex fairness in interest inventories and related interpretive, technical, and promotional materials than was previously available. The issues identified in the course of guideline development are dealt with in commissioned papers published by the U.S. Government Printing Office as a book, *Issues of Sex Bias and Sex Fairness in Career Interest Measurement* (1975).

The term "career interest inventory," as used in these guidelines, refers to various formal procedures for assessing educational and vocational interests. The term includes, but is not limited to, nationally published inventories. The interest assessment procedures may have been developed for a variety of purposes and for use in a variety of settings. The settings include educational and employment-related settings among others, and the uses include career counseling, career exploration, and employee selection (although the latter may also involve other issues of sex bias in addition to those discussed here).

The guidelines do not represent legal requirements. They are intended as standards (a) to which we believe developers and publishers should adhere in their inventories and in the technical and interpretive materials that the American Psychological Association (APA) *Standards for Educational and Psychological Tests* (1974) requires them to produce and (b) by which users should evaluate the sex fairness of available inventories.

---

interpretation can be stated as follows: An interest inventory is sex restrictive to the degree that the distribution of career options suggested to males and females as a result of the application of scoring or interpretation procedures used or advocated by the publisher is not equivalent for the two sexes. Conversely, an interest inventory is *not* sex restrictive if *each* career option covered by the inventory is suggested to similar proportions of males and females. A sex-restrictive inventory can be considered to be sex biased unless the publisher demonstrates that sex restrictiveness is a necessary concomitant of validity.

Still another interpretation has been suggested by John L. Holland: An inventory is unbiased when its experimental effects on female and male respondents are similar and of about the same magnitude — that is, when a person acquires more vocational options, becomes more certain, or learns more about himself (herself) and the world of work ... The principles can be extended to any area of bias by asking what differences proposed revisions of inventories, books, teacher and counselor training would make.

There are many essential guidelines for interest inventories in addition to those relating to sex fairness. The guidelines presented here do not replace concerns for fairness with regard to various ethnic or socioeconomic subgroups. They are not a substitute for statutes or federal regulations such as the Equal Employment Opportunity Commission (EEOC) selection guidelines (1970) and Title IX of the Education Amendments of 1972 or for other technical requirements for tests and inventories such as those found in the APA *Standards*. The guidelines thus represent standards with respect to sex fairness which supplement these other standards.

The guidelines address interest inventories and related services and materials. However, sex bias can enter the career exploration or decision process in many ways other than through interest inventory materials. Several of the guidelines have clear implications for other materials and processes related to career counseling, career exploration, and career decision-making. The spirit of the guidelines should be applied to all parts of these processes.

GUIDELINES

I. The Inventory Itself

A. The same inventory form should be used for both males and females unless it is shown empirically that separate forms are more effective in minimizing sex bias.

B. Scores on all occupations and interest areas covered by the inventory should be given for both males and females, with the sex composition of norms — i.e. whether male, female, or combined sex norms — for each scale clearly indicated.

C. Insofar as possible, item pools should reflect experiences and activities equally familiar to both females and males. In instances where this is not currently possible, a minimum requirement is that the number of items generally favored by each sex be balanced. Further, it is desirable that the balance of items favored by each sex be achieved within individual scales, within the limitations imposed by validity considerations.

D. Occupational titles used in the inventory should be presented in gender-neutral terms (e.g. letter carrier instead of mailman) or both male and female titles should be presented (e.g. actor/actress).

E. Use of the generic "he" or "she" should be eliminated throughout the inventory.

II. Technical Information

A. Technical materials provided by the publisher should describe how and to what extent these guidelines have been met in the inventory and supporting materials.

B. Technical information should provide the rationale for either separate scales by sex or combined-sex scales (e.g. critical differences in male-female response rates that affect the validity of the scales vs. similarity of response rates that justify combining data from males and females into a single scale).

C. Even if it is empirically demonstrated that separate inventory forms are more effective in minimizing sex bias, thus justifying their use, the same vocational areas should be indicated for each sex.

D. Sex composition of the criterion and norm groups should be included in descriptions of these groups. Furthermore, reporting of scores for one sex on scales normed or constructed on the basis of data from the other sex should be supported by evidence of validity — if not for each scale, then by a pattern of evidence of validity established for males and females scored on pairs of similar scales (male-normed and female-normed for the same occupation).

E. Criterion groups, norms, and other relevant data (e.g. validity, reliability, item response rates) should be examined at least every five years to determine the need for updating. New data may be required as occupations change or as sex and other characteristics of persons entering occupations change. Test manuals should clearly label the date of data collection for criterion or norm groups for each occupation.

F. Technical materials should include information about how suggested or implied career options (e.g. options suggested by the highest scores on the inventory) are distributed for samples of typical respondents of each sex.

G. Steps should be taken to investigate the validity of interest inventories for minority groups (differentiated by sex). Publishers should describe comparative studies and should clearly indicate whether differences were found between groups.

III. Interpretative Information

A. The user's manual provided by the publisher should describe how and to what extent these guidelines have been met in the inventory and the supporting materials.

B. Interpretive materials for test users and respondents (manuals, profiles, leaflets, etc.) should explain how to interpret scores resulting from separate or combined male and female norms or criterion groups.

C. Interpretive materials for interest inventory scores should point out that the vocational interests and choices of men and women are influenced by many environmental and cultural factors, including early socialization, traditional sex-role expectations of society, home-versus-career conflict, and the experiences typical of women and men as members of various ethnic and social class groups.

D. Manuals should recommend that the inventory be accompanied by orientation dealing with possible influences of factors in C above on men's and women's scores. Such orientation should encourage respondents to examine stereotypic "sets" toward activities and occupations and should help respondents to see that there is virtually no activity or occupation that is exclusively male or female.

E. Interpretive materials for inventories that use homogeneous scales, such as health and mechanical [scales], should encourage both sexes to look at *all* career and educational options, not just those traditionally associated with their sex group, within the broad areas in which their highest scores fall.

F. Occupational titles used in the interpretive materials and in the interpretation session should be stated in gender-neutral terms (e.g. letter carrier instead of mailman) or both male and female titles should be presented (e.g. actor/actress).

G. The written discussions in the interpretive materials (as well as all inventory text) should be stated in a way which overcomes the impression presently embedded in the English language that (a) people in general are of the male gender and (b) certain social roles are automatically sex-linked.

H. The user's manual (a) should state clearly that all jobs are appropriate for qualified persons of either sex and (b) should attempt to dispel myths about women and men in the world of work based on sex-role stereotypes. Furthermore, ethnic occupational stereotypes should not be reinforced.

I. The user's manual should address possible user biases in regard to sex roles and to their possible interaction with age, ethnic group, and social class and should caution against transmitting these biases to the respondent or reinforcing the respondent's own biases.

J. Where differences in validity have been found between dominant and minority groups (differentiated by sex), separate interpretive procedures and materials should be provided that take these differences into account.

K. Interpretive materials for respondent and user should encourage exploratory experiences in areas where interests have not had a chance to develop.

L. Interpretive materials for persons re-entering paid employment or education and persons changing careers or entering post-retirement careers should give special attention to score interpretation in terms of the effects of stereotyping and home-career conflict, the norms on which the scores are based, and the options such individuals might explore on the basis of current goals and past experiences and activities.

M. Case studies and examples presented in the interpretive materials should represent men and women equally and should include, but not be limited to, examples of each in a variety of nonstereotypic roles. Case studies and examples of mature men and women and of men and women in different social class and ethnic groups should also be included where applicable.

N. Both user's manuals and respondent's materials should make it clear that interest inventory scores provide only one kind of helpful information, and that this information should always be considered together with other relevant information — skills, accomplishments, favored activities, experiences, hobbies, influences, other tests scores, and the like — in making any career decision. However, the possible biases of these variables should also be taken into consideration.

REFERENCES

American Psychological Association: *Standards for Educational and Psychological Tests.* Washington, D. C., Author, 1974.

Equal Employment Opportunity Commission: Guidelines on Employee Selection Procedures. *Federal Register, 35*:149, 1970.

Diamond, E. E. (Ed.): *Issues of Sex Bias and Sex Fairness in Career Interest Inventories.* Washington, D. C., U. S. Government Printing Office, 1975.

Scott, Foresman and Company: *Guidelines for Improving the Image of Women in Textbooks.* Glenview, Author, 1972.

AUTHORS OF MEASURES INDEX

J

K

L

M

O

P

R

S

INDEX OF MEASURES

G

H

I

J

K

L

M

N

O

P

PUBLISHERS OF MEASURES INDEX

GENERAL SUBJECT INDEX

U

V

W